GOLD FUTURES

facts
&
figures

trading
strategies
&
tactics

KEVIN • COMMINS

PROBUS PUBLISHING COMPANY
Chicago, Illinois

© 1990, Kevin Commins

Library of Congress Cataloging-in-Publication Data Available

ISBN 1-55738-108-9

Printed in the United States of America

1   2   3   4   5   6   7   8   9   0

Contents

CHAPTER 1

Gold Futures Basics

On December 31, 1974, the gold market entered a new phase as gold futures contracts were introduced on the New York Commodity Exchange (COMEX), the Chicago Mercantile Exchange (CME), and the Chicago Board of Trade (CBOT). Although the contracts got off to a slow start, they came of age during the spectacular increase in gold prices in the late 1970s and early 1980s. In the next few years, a number of overseas exchanges followed the U.S. lead and introduced gold futures contracts of their own. Trading volume continued to grow, until, by the mid-1980s, gold had become one of the commodity industry's most widely traded contracts.

By virtue of the many strategies they make possible, gold futures have significantly altered the gold market. Gold futures can be used to speculate, to hedge, or to engage in esoteric strategies involving commodity spreads and interest rates. Every gold market participant—from mining companies to retail investors—has occasion to use gold futures. Indeed, any serious gold market participant who ignores gold futures does himself a disservice.

The first part of this chapter serves as an introduction to gold futures contracts, briefly describing what they are, how they're used, and why they're important. The second part of the chapter presents a short history of gold futures trading, focusing on trading volume growth and competition between the various exchanges. The Chapter 1 appendix in the back of the book includes the contract specifications and trading rules for all gold futures contracts in the world.

ELEMENTS OF GOLD FUTURES

A futures contract is a standardized contract that provides a means for buyers and sellers to exchange a fixed amount of a commodity at a specific date in the future. Futures contracts have been traded around the world since the 1600s. In the U.S., futures contracts were introduced in the 1860s, however, for many years they were limited to agricultural and industrial commodities. In the past two decades, futures contracts were introduced on precious metals and financial instruments. Despite the wide variety of futures contracts now in existence, all futures contracts are structured in a similar fashion.

Futures contracts are called futures contracts because all contracts are for future delivery. A buyer of a futures contract agrees to purchase a fixed amount of a commodity at a specific price and date. A seller agrees to sell a fixed amount of a commodity at a specific price and date. When a trader buys a contract, he is said to have entered into a long position. When a trader sells a contract, he has entered into a short position.

Since contracts are for future delivery, a trader can sell, or short, a futures contract without owning the underlying commodity. For example, if a trader sells a December gold contract, he has, in effect, entered into a transaction that obligates him to deliver 100 ounces of gold at a specified price, on a specific day in December. However, to enter into the contract, the trader need not own any gold, nor need he have any intention of obtaining any gold. In a similar fashion, a trader can buy a commodity futures contract without ever taking delivery of the commodity or having any intention of taking delivery.

Futures can be traded without any regard to delivering or receiving the underlying commodity because positions can be readily liquidated. The seller of the December gold contract, for example, can buy a December gold contract, and thereby eliminate his futures market position. Similarly, a trader who has bought a contract can sell a contract prior to expiration to liquidate his position. Of course, if a trader holds onto his initial position, he will be obligated to deliver or receive the underlying commodity upon expiration of the contract. In actual fact, however, relatively few contracts are held until expiration.

Although on the surface, futures contracts might appear to be similar to forward contracts, they are quite different. A forward contract, whether for gold, currencies or any other commodity, represents an agreement between two parties to execute a transaction at a future date. Unlike in the futures market, the parties in a forward contract cannot cancel their obligations by making an offsetting trade with another party. An offsetting trade would allow them to neutralize their exposure, however, they would still be obligated to fulfill the terms of the original contract. In the futures market, in contrast, any position can be completely eliminated by executing an equal and opposite trade.

Forward contracts, unlike futures contracts, are only as good as the creditworthiness of the two parties involved. If one party reneges on his obligation, the counterparty suffers. In the futures industry, the counterparty to all trades is the clearing house. In effect, the clearing house guarantees all trades. (The role of the clearing house is discussed in detail in Chapter 2.)

In order to facilitate trade, futures contracts are standardized in terms of size, minimum price fluctuation, delivery months, trading hours, and product quality. This standardization allows the contracts to be traded interchangeably. A buyer of a gold contract, for example, can turn around and sell the same contract at the same exchange without worrying about the grade of gold or the size of the transaction. Each contract is exactly alike. Without that benchmark, price negotiation would become more complex as traders would have to consider different grades of gold and different size transactions. The variances in the underlying commodity being traded undoubtedly would sap the liquidity of the market.

Table 1.1 lists key specifications for the major gold futures contracts. A complete description of all gold futures contracts is contained in the appendix.

Before elucidating on the purpose and uses of gold futures, let's first define the various components of a gold futures contract.

Contract Size

The contract size specifies the amount of gold represented by one contract. As inferred in the earlier examples, most gold contracts are 100 ounces, although the MidAmerica Commodity Exchange and the Chicago Board of Trade have smaller contracts. Whatever the size, trades can only be made in full contracts; there's no such thing as a half-contract or a quarter-contract.

Awareness of contract size is vital in determining the value of a price movement. Gold futures prices are always quoted in dollars per ounce,

Table 1.1   Contract Specifications

Exchange	Contract Size	Minimum Price Change	Delivery
New York Commodity Exchange *Trading hours: 8:20–2:30*	100 oz.	10 cents/oz. $10/contract	Current calendar month and following two months. Also Feb., April, June, Aug., Oct., Dec.
Chicago Board of Trade *Trading hours: 7:20–1:40 5:00–8:30 PM*	100 oz.	10 cents/oz. $10/contract	Current calendar month and following two months. Also Feb., April, June.
Chicago Board of Trade *Trading hours: 7:20–1:40*	1 kilogram (32.15 oz.)	10 cent/oz. $3.22/contract	Feb., April, Aug., Oct., Dec.
MidAmerica Commodity Exchange *Trading hours: 7:20–1:40*	33.2/oz.	10 cents/oz. $3.32/contract	All months
Chicago Mercantile Exchange* *Trading hours: 7:20–3:00*	100 oz.	10 cents/oz. $10/contract	All months

*Although the CME's gold contract is still listed, the exchange has no plans to revive the contract in the foreseeable future, according to a spokesman.

Exchange	Contract Size	Minimum Price Change	Delivery
Singapore International Monetary Exchange	100 oz.	10 cent/oz. $10/contract	Feb., March, April, June, Aug., Sept., Oct., Dec.
Trading hours:	Singapore, 9:30–5:15 Chicago, 7:30 PM–3:15 AM		
Sydney Futures Exchange *Trading hours:* 8:30–4:00	100 oz.	10 cent/oz. $10/contract	Same as New York Commodity Exchange
Hong Kong Futures Exchange *Trading hours:* 9:00–12:00, 2:00–5:30	100 oz.	10 cent/oz. $10/contract	Even months, spot, and following two months
Tokyo Commodity Exchange	1 kilo	1 yen yen/kilo	Spot month, plus next six months
Bolsa Mercantil & de Futuros *Trading hours:* 10:00–4:30	250 gm.	Cz$0.10/gm	Even months

not in dollars per contract. To determine the change in value in a futures contract position, a trader that has bought one contract must multiply the price move per ounce by 100. If a trader bought one contract at $400 and the price moved to $405, he would have a $500 profit on his contract. If he had bought five contracts at $400, he would have a $2500 profit.

Buy one contract at $400/oz.	Sell the contract later at $405/oz.

Profit per ounce: $5/oz.

Profit per contract: $500

Over the years, in an attempt to compete with the Comex, other exchanges have offered gold contracts of differing sizes. Traders that are interested in using non-Comex contracts should double-check the contract sizes, since competing exchanges have altered the sizes more than once. Because the Comex contract is the most widely used gold futures contract, all examples in this book will be based on 100-ounce contracts.

Minimum Price Fluctuation

The minimum price fluctuation for all gold contracts currently traded is 10 cents per ounce. That means prices move in 10-cent intervals, for example, $400, $400.10, $400.20, $400.30 and so on. In the vernacular of the futures industry, each 10 cent interval is known as a tick. Frequently, in rapidly moving markets, the price may jump more than one tick. However, the price can never move less than one tick, that is less than 10 cents. Thus, there could never be a gold futures price of, say, $432.37; the price will always be a multiple of 10 cents.

Minimum Grade Requirement

Critical to the success of any futures contract is an assurance of the quality of the underlying commodity. In the case of gold, most futures contracts call for delivery of a grade of at least 995 fineness, in bar form. The bars must be stamped by refiners approved by the particular exchange. A list of the approved refiners for each exchange is provided in the appendix.

Trading Hours

Trading hours simply refers to the hours in which gold contracts are open for trading at the respective exchanges. All futures trades must be consummated on the floor of the exchange; thus, it is impossible to trade before or after official trading hours.

The trading hour limitations can present a problem for traders because the cash market in gold trades before and after U.S. gold futures trading hours. If a major event transpires after futures trading hours, the futures trader must wait until the following morning to react, whereas the cash market trader has access to global markets on a nearly 24-hour basis.

This problem may be overcome soon. At the time this chapter was written, U.S. exchanges were exploring computerized trading, a development that would create nearly 24-hour futures trading. Under proposed systems offered by the Chicago Mercantile Exchange and the Chicago Board of Trade, floor trading would continue during normal, daytime hours. However, after the floor closes, trading would commence on computerized networks. The CBOT and the CME both hope to entice other exchanges, including New York's Commodity Exchange, to join their respective systems.

Computerized trading is the third approach tried by exchanges to extend trading hours. Previously, U.S. exchanges attempted to extend trading by forging links with exchanges in different time zones and by extending their own trading hours into the night and early morning. The latter two approaches have proved disappointing, and there's no guarantee that computerized trading will be any more successful. Nonetheless, it appears that the futures industry is moving inexorably to 24-hour trading.

Delivery Month

The delivery month refers to the month in which the contract will expire. Each delivery month is a separate contract. The contract that is closest to expiration is known as the nearby contract. Contracts that expire after the nearby are known as deferred contracts. For example, in the month of April, the contract for April delivery would be the nearby. The May, June, August, October, and December contracts would be deferred contracts.

The delivery process is one of the most important components to a futures contract. As pointed out earlier, most futures market participants do not hold their position through expiration. Nonetheless, some strategies call for receiving or delivering gold through the futures market. Precise knowledge of the delivery process is vital for traders engaged in these strategies. Moreover, a smoothly working delivery process is a prerequisite to the success of any futures contract.

In general terms, the delivery process works in the following manner. Traders who wish to deliver or receive gold in fulfillment of their contract obligations must notify the exchange clearing house of their intent prior to a specified date. The clearing house then matches the buyers and sellers and thereupon notifies the participants of the matches. On a specified date, the sellers transfer a certificate of ownership for the gold to the buyer and the buyer pays the seller for the gold.

Details of how the delivery process works vary between exchanges. Generally, the exchanges have a number of approved gold depositories or banks through which physical deliveries are transacted. At the Comex, six banks are licensed to function as gold depositories: Chase Manhattan Bank, Citibank, Iron Mountain Depository Corp., Irving Trust Co., Republic National Bank of New York, and Swiss Bank Corp. Deliveries of gold in fulfillment of Comex gold contracts can only be accomplished through these licensed depositories.

A seller of a gold futures contract who wishes to fulfill his contract by delivering gold must have gold on deposit at one of the licensed depositories. Once the gold is in place at the depository, the seller notifies the exchange clearing house that he intends to deliver gold. Generally, the exchanges set a date for notification of delivery and a later date for actual delivery.

At the Comex, the notice of intent to deliver must contain the name of the refiner of the physical gold, the warehouse receipt number for the gold, the weight and fineness of the gold, and the name of the depository bank.

According to the Comex rules, the delivery notice must be in the form shown in Figure 1.1.

The trader who wants to take delivery of gold in fulfillment of a long futures position must present a similar notification to the exchange clearing house by the last notice day. Upon receipt of the gold from the seller, the buyer is required to immediately pay the seller with a certified check drawn from a New York City bank, according to Comex rules.

Although relatively few futures traders get involved in the delivery process, an efficient delivery mechanism must be in place to establish confidence in the contract. If commercial users are frustrated in their efforts to deliver or take delivery of the commodity, the price relationship between the cash and futures market may flounder. When that happens, the futures contract loses its economic utility.

GOLD FUTURES USES AND USERS

The purpose of all futures contracts is to provide a means to transfer price risk from one party to another. Frequently, parties involved in the production or consumption of a commodity—whether it be oil, wheat, or gold—want to reduce their exposure to changing prices. An oil refiner may want to eliminate the possibility that crude oil prices will increase in the next six months. A gold mining company might want to ensure that it will be able to command a minimum price, say $400 an ounce, for the gold it produces in the coming year. Both these objectives can be accomplished with futures contracts. In the vernacular of the futures

---

Figure 1.1   Comex Gold Delivery Notice

Commodity Exchange Inc.

Notice of Intention to Deliver Gold

Clearing member ID   Clearing member name

House Customer

Total number of notices   Issuance date

To Clearing Association Inc.

Take notice that on _____, 19__ for each delivery notice record attached, we shall deliver to the clearing member to which you allocate this notice 100 troy ounces (5% more or less) of bar gold assaying not less than 995 fineness of the brand or marking and from the licensed warehouse or vault indicated on each record in accordance with the terms of our contract sale to said clearing member at the delivery notice price established by the Clearing Association.

Signed

---

industry, commercial parties that reduce their exposure to price risk through the use of futures are called hedgers.

Hedgers, of course, need someone to trade with and absorb the price risk that they're attempting to defray. That purpose is fulfilled by speculators. Speculators, quite simply, hope to profit from the rise and fall in prices. Unlike hedgers, who usually have a position in both the cash and futures market, speculators usually limit themselves to the futures market. Thus, while hedges are designed so that the losses in one market are offset by gains in another market, speculative positions are designed to produce profits when the market moves in the anticipated direction.

Although commodity speculators do not enjoy the best of reputations, they're indispensable to the futures industry. Speculators create the trading volume which is necessary to make contracts useful to hedgers. For example, a refiner who wants to protect against rising crude oil prices might need to buy 100 futures contracts to cover an anticipated purchase of 100,000 barrels of crude oil. If the futures market is relatively illiquid due to a lack of speculative trading, the refiner may be unable to execute the 100 contract order. And even if he could execute the order, in an illiquid market he probably would have to pay a premium.

Frequently, the speculator's role is misunderstood. Many outsiders believe speculators distort the supply, demand, and pricing mechanism of markets. Allegedly, they create excessive volatility, or, even worse, manipulate markets for their own ends. Although such charges rarely have had any basis in fact, they crop up repeatedly, particularly when markets fall abruptly.

In defense of commodity speculators, it should be acknowledged that futures markets are, in fact, designed to encourage speculation and that the ultimate success of any futures contract requires a balance between speculative and hedge-related trading. Partially because of the large amount of speculative trading, futures markets tend to respond faster to outside events. Some people view that phenomenon as symptomatic of an undesirable volatility. Others say that futures markets are simply more efficient. In either case, it's clear that the futures markets, in some respects, behave differently than cash markets. For traders, that means the futures markets possess different opportunities and risks.

In the gold futures market, the most obvious speculative strategy is also the most common—buying in anticipation of higher prices and selling in expectation of lower prices. However, gold futures can be used to pursue other speculative strategies as well, particularly strategies designed to take advantage of the relationship of gold to the broader economic environment.

Many of these strategies involve the use of spreads. Spreads are trades in which one futures contract is traded against another in the expectation that the price difference will either increase or decrease. Through the use of spreads, gold futures can be traded against other precious metals and interest rate contracts. In addition, spreads can be constructed between gold futures with different delivery dates.

In the gold market, the most widely used spreads involve the other precious metals: silver and platinum. Generally, the precious metals move in the same direction, however, the pace of movement between them often differs. In a typical spread, a trader might buy gold and sell platinum in anticipation that the price difference will narrow. More complicated gold spreads can be devised using currencies or interest rate instruments.

The point is, gold futures are an extremely flexible tool for both speculators and hedgers. They can be used a variety of ways to accomplish a multitude of purposes.

THE HISTORY OF GOLD FUTURES TRADING

The history of gold is a history of the world economy. Discovered in Egypt around 3000 B.C., gold developed into a medium of exchange and later became the standard by which international currency values were fixed. In the process, a host of extraordinary events occurred around gold: mad rushes to exploit discoveries in California and Alaska, William Jennings Bryan's famous "Cross of Gold Speech" to win the Democratic presidential nomination, and a legion of international economic conferences dealing with gold's role in the world economy.

But while the history of gold, the metal, is extraordinarily rich and varied, the history of gold futures is somewhat less dramatic. The first gold futures contract was introduced at the Winnipeg Exchange in Canada in 1972. Throughout the 1970s, Winnipeg traded a 100-ounce and a 400-ounce contract. Although the contracts enjoyed a modest degree of success, volume began to diminish as the U.S. markets matured. In 1981, in hopes of carving out a new niche, Winnipeg shifted to a

20-ounce contract. However, the smaller contract failed to attract interest and Winnipeg discontinued all gold futures trading in April 1988.

Gold futures trading began in earnest in 1975, when the U.S. exchanges entered the market. In the forty years previous, U.S. citizens were prohibited from buying, selling, or holding gold except if the gold was in the form of jewelry or numismatic coins. Enacted by President Franklin Roosevelt, this prohibition was designed to alleviate the banking panic brought on by the depression. The restrictions stayed in force until 1974, when they were abolished by President Gerald Ford, a development that paved the way for U.S. gold futures contracts.

On December 31, 1974, the Commodity Exchange, the Chicago Board of Trade (CBOT), the Chicago Mercantile Exchange, and the Mid-America Commodity Exchange (MidAm) introduced gold futures contracts. Early on, the Comex and CME contracts attracted the greatest participation, while the CBOT and MidAm contracts lagged considerably. Eventually, the Comex contract emerged as the preferred futures contract for the professional gold trading community, a development that came about largely because of its location in New York. Over time, professional gold traders with major banks and bullion houses in New York opted for the local contract because it was easier and less expensive for them to set up support operations in New York than in Chicago.

However, Comex's reign as the dominant exchange in futures trading has been far from smooth. On a handful of occasions, trading and clearing difficulties at the Comex have raised questions about the exchange's ability to maintain an open, and smoothly functioning marketplace. Each time there's been a problem at the Comex, the Chicago exchanges experience an upsurge in volume, however, they have been unable to permanently capture business from the Comex. Comex officials insist that all past problems have been corrected.

The success of gold futures trading in the U.S. has led a number of foreign exchanges to introduce gold futures contracts of their own, or in affiliation with a U.S. exchange: the Singapore International Monetary Exchange, the Hong Kong Futures Exchange, the Sydney Futures Exchange, the Tokyo Gold Exchange and the London Gold Futures Exchange. With the exception of the Tokyo contract, none of the non-U.S. contracts had developed significant volume by 1990. Indeed, London discontinued gold futures trading due to a paucity of volume.

Since gold is traded 24 hours a day, it's not surprising that it has been at the forefront of efforts to develop futures trading capabilities beyond U.S. trading hours. Gold was part of the first international exchange link between the Chicago Mercantile Exchange and the Singapore International Monetary Exchange (Simex). Under the accord, selected contracts on both exchanges could be traded interchangeably. A trader who purchased a gold contract on the CME in the morning could liquidate the contract that evening on the Simex. For a U.S. trader, that meant the market was open 7:20 AM to 2:00 PM (at the CME) and then from 7:30 PM to 3:15 AM (Chicago time) at the Simex. For all the publicity surrounding the link, it has generated little volume, at least by U.S. standards.

The Comex developed a similar arrangement with the Sydney Futures Exchange. Under that accord, the normal Comex hours of 8:20 AM to 2:30 PM were extended to include a 4:00 PM to midnight session via the Sydney link. Although the Comex-Sydney link perhaps had a better chance of success than the CME-Simex link, due to the preeminent position of the Comex gold contract, it too has proved to be a disappointment. Now, with the arrival of computerized trading, most exchanges appear to be abandoning the linkage concept.

Just as computerized trading may make exchange links obsolete, it could do the same for the Chicago Board of Trade's experiment with an evening session from 5 PM to 8:30 PM. Designed primarily for its Treasury bond contract, the CBOT added gold to the session in hopes of attracting trade from the Far East. So far, however, the evening gold session has attracted little interest.

During this time that the exchanges were struggling to institute some form of 24-hour trading, the volume of gold futures trading continued to decline from its 1982 peak. The decline was largely attributable to the drop in inflation and the relative stability in the international economic and political scene. In addition, the stock market crash of 1987 dampened interest in gold in the months that followed.

The subdued condition of the gold market in the late 1980s was in marked contrast to the late 1970s and early 1980s, when inflation and skyrocketing oil prices drove gold prices to their historic highs (as high as $850 an ounce in 1980). The surge in gold prices helped to build trading volume in gold futures and contributed mightily to the contracts' creditability. Indeed, the introduction of gold futures in the U.S. was perfectly timed to coincide with what turned out to be a modern-day gold rush.

In the early years of gold futures, a great deal of the trading volume emanated from retail speculators. They correctly realized that futures offered several advantages over physical gold for purposes of speculation. On the other hand, commercial gold users—particularly mining companies—were slow to utilize futures. By the 1980s, however, that began to change. Now, virtually all major players in the gold cash market—mining companies, jewelry manufacturers, and bullion houses—use gold futures in some fashion.

CHAPTER 2

Mechanics of Gold Futures Trading

In Chapter 1, we defined the elements of a gold futures contract. However, the contract itself is part of a larger marketplace that includes exchanges, clearing houses, local floor traders, brokers, and regulators. In this chapter, we will describe how these bodies work together to form the structure of the marketplace.

EXCHANGES

A commodity futures exchange provides the environment where futures contracts are bought and sold. The function of the exchange, in essence, is to encourage trade. To fulfill that function, exchanges set up and enforce rules to ensure that trading is carried out in an equitable manner and that disputes are fairly resolved. Moreover, the exchanges provide price, volume, open interest, and other types of information to the public so that investors and hedgers have the tools to make informed trading decisions.

Exchange trading floors are near-perfect examples of free market capitalism. Everyone, regardless of size or background, is on an equal footing in the trading pit. No one has an advantage. No one has the ability to obstruct trade. Buyers and sellers compete with one another for the best price in an environment that provides equal access to the latest market information. In so doing, price responds almost instantaneously to the slightest shifts in market sentiment.

The foundation of a futures exchange is its membership. To become a member, one simply buys a seat. Seat prices fluctuate with supply and demand. Normally, in periods of market volatility and high trading volume, seat prices rise. During lackluster trading periods, seat prices normally decline.

The individual or firm applying for membership must also pass exchange-set standards for character and financial responsibility. These tests are not particularly stringent. Most anybody with a net worth greater than the cost of the seat can become a member. Membership in and of itself, however, does not allow the member to begin trading. The member still must set up an account with an exchange clearing firm.

For individuals, membership confers the right to trade directly on the floor without going through an intermediary. Besides reducing trading costs, floor trading presents the individual trader with an opportunity to take advantage of the bid/ask spread, a practice known as scalping. Generally, there will be at least a one-tick difference between the bid and ask prices in a futures market. A nonmember trader usually is forced to buy at the ask, the higher price, and to sell at the bid, the lower price. The floor trader, however, is positioned to buy at the bid and sell at the offer, a strategy that enables him to eke out a small profit. Multiplied many times over, scalping can provide a floor member with a fairly substantial income.

Trading firms, of course, receive the same benefits as individuals through exchange membership. For such firms, membership is almost a prerequisite if they want to develop a high volume brokerage business. Just as with individuals, membership allows the firm to trade without going through another broker. In addition, by being directly on the floor, the firm is positioned to provide better price execution services for its customers.

Exchanges are controlled by their members. The members appoint a board of directors, which usually includes both members and nonmembers. The nonmember directors generally are associated with the commodity industry in some capacity. As with any corporation, the board of directors establishes the overall direction and the operating procedures for the exchange. However, major exchange decisions usually require ratification by the membership.

The board normally appoints a president to run the exchange's day-to-day operations. The president appoints a staff to fulfill a variety of necessary functions, including monitoring the conduct and operations of exchange members, collecting and disseminating statistics about the markets, developing new contracts and new business approaches, marketing the exchange, and providing the news media and other interested parties with information about the exchange and the markets.

Exchange members strongly influence exchanges through member-run committees. Separate committees are set up to oversee every aspect of the exchange's operations, from floor trading rules to marketing to developing new contracts. In addition, at most exchanges, every major product category—such as precious metals, currencies, or meats—has a corresponding committee.

CLEARING HOUSE

Without question, the clearing house is the most important component of a commodity exchange. It guarantees the financial integrity of the exchange and of each individual trade, it serves as the conduit through which flows all money associated with trading, and it oversees the delivery process. Without the clearing house, futures trading could not exist.

The most important function of the clearing house is to guarantee the opposite side of all open positions entered into by traders. When a trade is made in the pit that leaves one trader short and the other long, the two traders are unconcerned about the ability of their counterpart to make good on the trade. That's because both traders are not short and long against each other—as would be the case in a conventional business transaction; instead, they are short and long against the clearing house. If the long side of the trade proves profitable, the trader will collect his winnings from the clearing house. Similarly, the clearing house will debit the trader that was short.

The clearing house guarantee, in effect, removes the credit risk associated with trading with individuals or firms. If one party to a transaction can't meet his obligation, the counterparty is still guaranteed that he will be able to collect his profits. His exposure is to the clearing house, not to any individual trader. This guarantee is vital to attracting participation in the commodity markets.

Moreover, in a technical sense, the clearing house guarantee is the mechanism that allows a trader to offset his original trade with any other trader. Without the clearing house guarantee, a trader would have to renegotiate his trading commitment to his original counterparty. With the clearing house guarantee, the trader is free to offset his original commitment with any other trader.

The clearing house of an exchange consists of a number of separate clearing members. Generally, membership in the clearing house is restricted to exchange members, however, not all exchange members are clearing members. Those exchange members who are not clearing members—for example, individual speculators—must have their trades cleared by a clearing member. Clearing members, on the other hand, can clear their own trades, a capability that provides an advantage in developing brokerage businesses. Ultimately, everyone who trades futures is connected with a clearing member, either directly or through a broker.

The clearing member is the first party that guarantees the integrity of any futures transaction: supplying profits to winning trades and debiting losses for losing trades. However, if an individual clearing member experiences financial difficulties, the contract guarantee becomes the responsibility of the clearing house. In such situations, the other clearing members are required to pay an assessment to cover the losses of the insolvent member. In that manner, the integrity of the clearing house is maintained, even if an individual clearing member cannot meet his obligations.

MARGIN

A distinguishing feature of the futures markets is the degree of margin, or good faith deposit, required to enter into a transaction. In most instances, a trader need only post 5 percent to 15 percent of the total value of the contract in order to trade. In the securities market, in contrast, a trader must post at least 40 percent of the value of the stocks. The low margin requirement on futures is the primary reason that futures are often considered a very risky market for a retail investor.

The low margins on futures are designed to encourage trade, particularly from speculators. Remember, in order for a futures contract to be useful to hedgers, trading volume must be of a sufficient size to handle the needs of hedgers on a regular basis. Low margins—because they make it easier for speculators to participate in the markets—play a major role in accomplishing that purpose.

Consider the financial requirements of trading futures if there were no margins. If a Comex gold contract was priced at $400, the total value of the contract would be $40,000 ($400 X 100 ounces). With no margin, the trader would have to post the full $40,000 to buy the contract. If the trader wanted to buy 10 contracts, he would have to post $400,000. In contrast, with the current margin of $2500 per contract (margins are adjusted periodically; so margins may be different at the time of reading), the trader need only post $2500 to buy one contract and only $25,000 to buy 10 contracts. If the $25,000 sounds steep, remember it controls $400,000 worth of gold.

Margins are set by the futures exchanges. The level of the margin deposit is supposed to account for the maximum daily price swing in the commodity. Therefore, in periods of extended volatility, exchanges frequently raise margins to cover the potential of larger daily price swings. In periods of low volatility, exchanges may reduce margins.

It should be noted that margins on futures are quite different than margins on stocks. When an investor buys a stock on margin, he has, in effect, purchased a stock with a down payment and debt financing. In contrast, an investor who buys or sells a futures contract has not purchased or sold anything; he has simply committed himself to buy or sell at a later date. Thus, the futures margin really represents a performance bond providing some guarantee that the trader can make good on his commitment. Unlike margin in the stock market, no debt financing is involved.

Every futures trader must deposit margin. Margins are collected by clearing members and deposited in the exchange clearing house. Although margins are set by the exchanges, clearing members and brokers may require their customers to post higher margins than those set by the exchanges. However, brokers and clearing members cannot allow their customers to maintain margins below the exchange requirements.

MARK TO MARKET

Every day, the profits or losses on every futures position are accounted for by the exchange clearing house, a process known as mark-to-market accounting. If a trader's position shows a profit, cash from the clearing house is credited to the trader's account. Similarly, if a trader's position shows a loss, cash from his account is transferred into the clearinghouse.

At the end of the day, the clearing house itself should be flat, since for every profitable trade in which money is paid out there is an equal losing trade in which money is received.

Mark-to-market accounting gives rise to the two words most dreaded by all futures traders: margin calls. Very simply, when the money in a margin account drops below a specified amount, the trader must deposit additional funds into the account to bring it back up to the current margin requirement. If the trader does not deposit the additional funds, the clearing member or broker has the right to liquidate the position.

The combination of low margins and mark-to-market accounting serves to create an impression that futures trading is a fraught with peril. In actual fact, futures prices themselves generally are no more volatile than the prices of most stocks, bonds, or currencies. However, since a small cash deposit can control a large amount of an underlying commodity, a futures position can show large gains or losses in a short time, relative to the initial margin deposit.

FLOOR TRADERS

All commodity trades, irrespective of where they originate, must be consummated by floor traders in the trading pit through a process called open outcry. When a trader receives an order from a customer or when he decides to trade for his account, he communicates to the rest of the trading pit the price and quantity that he wants to buy or sell. This communication is accomplished by shouting and by hand signals. If another trader accepts the terms that are offered, he communicates his acceptance through the same methods.

All floor traders are either members of the exchange, representatives of a firm that is a member, or are lessees of a seat from another member. Some floor traders, particularly those representing a brokerage firm, are limited to executing customer orders. Other floor traders, mainly those who trade for themselves, make most of their profits from scalping, the activity described earlier in this chapter. Still other floor traders are position traders—that is, they attempt to profit from price swings in the commodity.

OFF-EXCHANGE PARTICIPANTS

Futures Commission Merchants and Introducing Brokers

Futures commission merchants (FCMs) and introducing brokers (IBs) are firms or individuals who act as intermediaries between outside traders and the trading floor. They differ in that FCMs can accept funds from customers for the purposes of trading, whereas IBs can take customer orders, but they cannot handle customer money. In most other respects, however, IBs and FCMs are similar. The FCM can be, but need not be, a clearing member of the exchange.

FCMs come in all shapes and sizes, from the large international firms like Refco to individual floor traders. FCMs vary according to the services they offer and the exchanges where they can execute trades.

Probably the biggest difference amongst FCMs is the amount of research and trading advice they offer customers. So-called discount brokers, for example, eschew research and advice and simply function as order takers for their customers. Full-service brokers, on the other hand, provide extensive research and advice to their customers. Consequently, full service brokers usually charge higher commissions than discount brokers.

Commodity Trading Advisor

Commodity trading advisors (CTAs) are individuals or firms that have been accredited by the Commodity Futures Trading Commission to advise others in the trading of futures. Newsletter writers, for example, must receive regulatory sanction before they can offer their advice to the public.

Commodity Pool Operators

Commodity pool operators are firms or individuals that accept funds from investors for the purpose of trading in the commodity markets. Unlike FCMs or IBs, commodity pool operators make their own trading decisions regarding their customers' funds. Like CTAs, commodity pool operators must receive regulatory approval to operate and they must disclose to potential customers relevant information about their trading history and business experience.

Regulators

The primary regulator of the futures industry is the Commodity Futures Trading Commission (CFTC), a federal agency established in 1975 under the Commodity Exchange Act (CEA). The CEA gives the CFTC exclusive jurisdiction over every aspect of the industry. In general terms, the CFTC is responsible for ensuring the financial integrity of the industry and preventing fraud.

Although the CFTC is the sole regulator of the industry, the agency has delegated a great deal of power to the exchanges and to an industry self-regulatory organization, the National Futures Association (NFA). For the most part, the exchanges and the NFA deal directly with market professionals and trading firms, with the CFTC acting as the overseer.

More specifically, the NFA has been empowered by the CFTC to establish training and accreditation standards for individuals and firms involved in a sales or advisory role, such as FCMs, IBs, CTAs and CPOs; establish minimum financial and capital requirements on industry participants; and establish rules and penalties governing sales practices. Moreover, the NFA has the power to audit a firm's or individual's records to ensure that all standards are being met.

CHAPTER 3

Gold Futures Pit Trading

Futures trading pits are fascinating economic arenas. In these small, octagonally shaped structures, enormous amounts of money change hands daily as traders battle each other and the vagaries of the market. For every winning trade, there is a losing trade. For every fortune made, a fortune is lost. There is no safety net, no assurance of security. Every trader, every day, must rise or fall on the basis of his own skill and resources.

To the outside observer, however, the romance of the pits is belied by the chaos and the decidedly unglamorous nature of pit activity. The noise and the physical pushing and shoving typical of a busy trading pit resembles nothing as much as the New York City subway system during rush hour, except the strangers on the subway generally are more polite. In tightly packed pits, traders frequently poke each other with pencils, step on each others toes, and push each other out of the way to get into better position to trade. Not surprisingly, arguments between traders often break out, and every once in a while, punches are thrown.

Beneath the apparent chaos, however, there is an order. Everyone in the pit is fulfilling a function, and those functions, in aggregate, are geared to a single end: to execute trades at the best possible price and in the quickest manner possible. Indeed, this competition between orders is the driving force behind the pandemonium of the pits.

The best way to understand the pit is to understand the functions of the various players: the clerks and runners, the brokers, the speculators, and the exchange floor personnel.

THE PLAYERS

Brokers

Many of the traders on the floor are brokers. Their mission is to execute trades for customers at the best possible price. Most brokers represent trading firms, although many individual members also broker trades. Under the rules in effect when this book was written, brokers could also trade for their own account, an activity known as dual trading. Because of the possible conflict of interest inherent in dual trading, there is a move underway to ban the practice.

The largest brokers generally stand on the top steps of the pit so that they can readily communicate with the phone clerks and runners who carry the trading instructions from customers. In many cases, orders are transmitted by hand signal to the broker. In other cases, particularly on complex orders, the order is written out on paper and brought into the pit by a runner. Since customers use limit orders frequently, it's not unusual for a broker to carry a deck of trading cards into the pit, each one of which instructs the broker to execute a transaction once certain price parameters are met.

The income of brokers is derived from the commissions they receive on their customer trades. The more trades brokers execute, the more money they make. This incentive system provides brokers with an inducement to procure optimum trade executions for their customers. After all, to attract customers over the long run, the broker must consistently execute at the best possible prices. Anything less, and customers might be tempted to try another broker.

One of the arguments for retaining dual trading is that brokers who trade for their own account frequently can procure better prices for their customers than brokers who limit themselves to brokering. This argument is based on the empirical conclusion that dual traders usually are more skillful traders than full-time brokers. Accordingly, if dual trading is banned and dual traders are forced to choose between brokerage and personal trading, the better traders will choose to speculate for themselves while the less skilled traders will opt for full-time brokerage. In the end, customers will be left with the worst traders in the pit.

Speculators

Speculators provide the pits with much of their color and appeal. Unlike brokers, speculators trade purely for their own account. Based on their talent and their financial resources, speculators hope to make a living by beating the market. Some succeed and become fabulously wealthy, while others fail and quickly go broke. A handful endure and learn how to earn a steady income by limiting risk and exploiting the advantages of the pit.

This latter group of speculators, those geared to taking advantage of their position in the pit, function as market makers or scalpers. Market makers do precisely what their name implies: they provide continuous bids and offers so that anyone can come to them and make a trade. Their profits derive from the small difference between the price they buy at and the price they sell at, a technique known as scalping.

Although market making generally is less risky than outright speculation, traders that function in this manner must be careful not to develop an unbalanced position, because at any time the market might move away from them. For example, a market maker that goes long 100 contracts at the bid price normally would hope to turn around and sell the 100 contracts at the offer price, which normally would be a tick or two higher than the bid. However, if the market drops before the trader can sell at the previous offer, he will be forced to take a loss on the trade or gamble that the market will rally.

Market makers do best when the order flow coming into the pit is well-balanced between buys and sells, because that allows them to move in and out of positions quickly. Conversely, they are most exposed to danger in one-sided, trending markets. The goal of the market maker, therefore, is to earn sufficient profits from scalping the bid/offer spread in stable markets so that they can more than offset the inevitable losses that occur in trending markets.

Although market making might appear to be a rather prosaic activity, it is essential to the functioning of the markets. By continually providing a bid/offer spread, market makers assure public customers—be they hedgers or speculators—that their trades will be executed. Indeed, without market makers, there is no market.

Market makers are distinguished from other speculators by the short time they hold onto their positions. This short time horizon limits their risks and maximizes the advantage of being located in the trading pit. In contrast, other floor speculators hold onto trades for longer periods of time, ranging from a few minutes to days and weeks. These individuals are known as position traders.

Position traders are looking to make larger profits than market makers. Consequently, they expose themselves to more risk. The key to their success is their ability to forecast the market. Some position traders use technical trading systems such as Elliott Wave or the Market Profiles®. Others rely on intuition and experience. Still others trade off the rumors and gossip that constantly filter through the pit. Interestingly, few position traders rely exclusively on fundamental analysis.

In the gold pits, some of the traders might best be described as spreaders. They take advantage of the mispricings that periodically develop between various contract months. For example, when an onslaught of public buy orders in the most active contract month drives that contract to a premium to other less-active months, the spreader will step in and buy the less-active contracts and sell the most-active month in anticipation that the spread will narrow.

Clerks and Runners

The function of clerks and runners, in essence, is to facilitate public participation in the markets by reporting pit prices and by rapidly getting public orders into the hands of brokers in the pits. They must perform quickly and accurately. Clerks and runners generally are very young and are paid very little; many of them are aspiring traders.

Brokerage firms generally place clerks around the periphery of the pits and in telephone stations adjacent to the pits. The clerks near the pits communicate through hand signals the best bids and offers to the clerks manning the telephones. In turn, the phone clerks communicate that information to other members of the firm or to the firm's customers.

At the same time the clerks are relaying price information, they are also responsible for getting customer orders into the pits. Usually, the orders are transmitted from the telephone area to the pit through either hand signals or written order slips. When the trade is completed, the clerks then relay that information back to the telephone station so that the customer can be informed of the trade.

Floor Personnel

An exchange employee, usually called a pit observer, is assigned to each pit to report on prices. As trades are executed, the employee notes the price and within seconds the price is being disseminated by various news agencies and data services. In large, active pits, it's sometimes difficult for the exchange representative to get a handle on where the market is trading. Frequently, the quotes that are disseminated to the public do not precisely reflect what's happening in the pit.

DYNAMICS OF THE PIT

There is a tremendous amount of game playing and interaction between brokers, market makers, and speculators. To a large extent, market makers make their living off of the public orders that are brought into the pit by brokers. Consequently, the market makers crowd around the brokers, hoping to be the first to get a crack at the public business.

Typically, a floor broker might receive an order to buy 50 contracts at the market. Instead of simply announcing the order to the pit, the broker might ask for a bid/offer spread in the relevant contract month. Presumably, market makers will respond, indicating, perhaps, that they will buy at $380.10 and sell at $380.30, a two-tick spread. The broker, in hopes of helping his customer, might bid at $380.20, one tick below the market maker's offer. If the market maker relents and lowers his bid, the broker may consummate the trade. If not, the broker may solicit other market makers for quotes or he may decide to accept the higher offer.

Of course, there's no rule that brokers must trade with market makers. When the broker calls for the market, other brokers or speculators can just as easily quote a spread as the market makers. In that manner, everyone in the pit gets a sense of where the market is and those traders who find their prices to be noncompetitive are forced to adjust their quotes or to refrain from trading. The overall process provides a rapid and efficient means of price discovery.

Generally, the trader who responds first at the price the floor broker wants will get the order. The necessity of being first accounts for much of the shouting and frantic waving that is common to the pits. Traders must be recognized by brokers in order to get the customer business that the broker is bringing into the pit. If two traders make the same quotes, the one who is loudest and most aggressive usually will get the order.

Given the dynamics of the pit, it's easy to understand why stop orders often are activated just prior to the market moving in the opposite direction. The market makers recognize they can make a handsome profit by taking short positions as the market moves down and then bidding on the brokers' sell-stop orders once they're activated. When the strategy is successfully completed, the market makers have no more incentive to encourage the market down because they have already taken out the stop orders and thus have no assurance of being able to unload further short positions. As a result, the market begins to rally, much to the dismay of the public customer who has been stopped out.

Obviously, brokers attempt to conceal from market markers the location of their customers' stop orders. Nonetheless, by a feel for the market, by rumors, and by observation, market makers often have a reasonably good idea of the location of stops. And invariably, market makers will help move the market in the direction of the stops in the belief that they will be able to liquidate their positions at a profit once the stops are hit. Of course, this strategy can backfire if the market fails to reach the stop levels or if the market maker is unable to execute with the broker holding the stops. Despite the risks, however, market makers pursue this strategy every day on the floor of most futures exchanges.

Not surprisingly, the rapid-fire buying and selling in the trading pits frequently leads to errors and misunderstandings between traders, occurrences known as outtrades. Outtrades are uncovered by clerks in the clearing house when they attempt to match the transactions from the previous session. In many cases, the discrepancies reflect an error in the inputting of trades. In other cases, however, the discrepancies reflect real disagreements between traders as to what actually happened on the trading floor. The disagreements can revolve around a host of variables: price, the number of contracts traded, the contract month, who was the buyer and who was the seller, and even if a trade was executed at all. Regardless of the nature of the disagreement, all outtrades must be reconciled before the next trading session.

If what happened on the trading floor can be re-constructed sufficiently to determine which trader was in error, then that trader is held responsible. If no determination of fault can be made, then the traders negotiate a settlement. In most cases, if the dispute involves a trade between two floor brokers or between two market makers, the traders will split the difference. However, in a dispute involving a floor broker executing for a customer and a market maker, the market maker usually will bear the whole cost of the outtrade.

The nature of the trading pits provides a self-policing mechanism that penalizes traders that renege on their trades. If a trader repeatedly denies making trades that later turn out to be unprofitable, he is quickly ostracized in the pit—no one else will trade with him. As a result, virtually all pit traders stand by their trades—both winners and losers.

THE PUBLIC ORDER

What happens to an order from a public customer? Since a public customer has an account open with a brokerage firm, the first step in the process entails the customer calling his broker with trading instructions. As soon as the broker receives the order, he stamps it with the time at which it was received.

The broker then calls the order to the desk on the floor. Again, the clerk on the desk places a time stamp on the order. At that stage, the order is conveyed to a broker in the pit either by a runner carrying an order slip or by hand signals.

Once the pit broker receives and executes the order, he signals back to the runner or to the desk that the order has been consummated. That information is then conveyed back to the customer contact who then informs the customer of the trade.

Depending on the particular brokerage firm and customer involved, the process may be a bit more streamlined. For example, many customers call their orders directly into the trading desk, bypassing the upstairs broker. And some customers have their contingency orders in the hands of pit brokers, allowing them to bypass both the upstairs broker and the trading desk.

As exchanges become more automated and as computerized trading develops, the order process will become even more streamlined. For example, exchanges are developing systems which would allow an upstairs broker to type in customer orders on a computer and then have the order quickly printed out at a station adjacent to the pit. The order would be taken from the printer to the floor broker by a runner. Once the order was filled, the process would be reversed via a computer on the exchange floor.

Computerized trading would be even more direct. Under systems contemplated by the Chicago Mercantile Exchange and the Chicago Board of Trade, an exchange member would enter a customer order into the system and the trade would be matched with another order. The number of human hands involved in the trade, and hence, the chances for error, would be substantially reduced.

CHAPTER 4

Trading Gold Futures

Gold futures can be used four basic ways: to speculate by buying and selling contracts; to speculate or to engage in arbitrage by trading one gold contract against another or by trading gold contracts against other commodities such as silver; to hedge gold price risk; and to deliver or take delivery of physical gold. This chapter will deal with gold futures as tools to speculate and to deliver or take delivery of gold. Spread trading and hedging will be explored in subsequent chapters.

For those wishing to speculate in the gold market, futures offer the maximum reward and the maximum risk. With a margin deposit of $3000, a trader can control one contract consisting of 100 ounces of gold. If an ounce of gold is trading at $400, that means the trader is controlling $40,000 worth of gold with his $3000 margin deposit. A $10 rise or fall in the price of gold translates into a $1000 profit or loss for the trader, a substantial sum when considered against the $3000 margin requirement. Remember, of course, that margin requirements can be changed at any time by the exchange.

The simplest and most common strategy using gold futures is to buy in anticipation of higher prices and to sell in anticipation of lower prices. Of course, the same strategy can be used with physical gold, with gold options, or even, to a certain extent, with gold company stocks. Depending on one's investment goals and financial situation, any of these instruments may be appropriate since each offers different risk/reward profiles.

Gold futures are distinct from other gold instruments in that they generally offer a much higher degree of leverage. As noted above, by using all the available leverage, a trader is positioned to add or lose a high

31

proportion of his margin deposit in response to a relatively minor movement in gold prices. The risks and rewards are huge. If a trader is right, he can double his money in a matter of days. If he's wrong, he can be wiped out just as quickly. Thus, if one wants to make the maximum use of one's capital in the gold market—while at the same time one is prepared to take on a great deal of risk—gold futures are the instrument of choice.

It should be remembered, however, that although the risk associated with trading gold futures is commensurate with leverage, a trader need not utilize all the available leverage. A trader, if he desires, can post a margin deposit in any amount greater than that required by the clearing house. Indeed, a trader can post a margin covering the entire price of the contract, thereby creating a position analogous to buying or selling physical gold for future delivery. In so doing, the trader removes the possibility of a large percentage of principal loss or gain resulting from a small movement in the price of gold. The advantages of this kind of strategy will be explained later in the chapter.

It should also be pointed out that options can be used to construct risk/reward ratios very similar to futures positions. For example, a long futures position can be devised synthetically by buying a call and selling a put at the same strike price. A short futures position can be devised by buying a put and selling a call at the same strike price. Options are extremely flexible; they can be used to create virtually any position that a trader desires. In some instances, options may be the preferred instrument. For readers wishing to learn more about options, there is a list of recommended books in the appendix.

If one is going to use futures to speculate, several things should be kept in mind. First, by their very nature, gold futures require precise market timing skills and an ability to monitor the market on a regular basis. A speculator cannot afford to allow the price to move against him very long in the belief that eventually the market will move in his direction. Consequently, anyone trading gold futures should have access to a real-time quotation service. If that's impossible, the trader should at least choose a broker that's willing to alert the trader to changes in market activity. Without regular access to price information, the trader is virtually guaranteed that his decisions to buy or sell will lag the market. Trading is difficult enough without adding a time-lag burden.

More specifically, a trader should not enter the gold futures market armed only with fundamental knowledge. Over the long term, there's no question that fundamentals determine the price of gold, but over the short term, the market vaults up and down in a seemingly chaotic fashion. Technical trading systems can help a trader cope with this volatility by signaling the optimum time to enter and exit the market. In later chapters, we examine two very popular technical trading systems: Elliot Wave and the Market Profile®), however, there are dozens of other systems for a trader to choose from.

When evaluating technical systems, a trader should keep in mind that most systems work well in certain types of markets, but do poorly in other kinds of markets. Many systems, for example, are excellent at identifying and following a trend, however, they give false signals in a trading range type of market. Similarly, Elliot Wave Theory is better at identifying so-called impulse waves but is less successful at identifying corrective waves. Before adopting a system, a trader should assess the system's strengths and limitations and determine whether the system is consistent with other tools that he uses and with his overall trading objectives.

TRADING RULES

Hundreds of books have been written on how to trade futures. Although many of the books offer distinctly different advice, there is also a great deal of agreement among them. The following is a summary of the rules that most successful futures traders follow.

Have A Trading Plan

Before ever placing an order, a prospective trader should explicitly define the amount of money he's prepared to risk, the types of situations that he hopes to trade, and the criteria by which he will exit a losing position or take profits in a winning position.

Moreover, a trader should rehearse in his mind how he will respond to different types of adversity and prosperity in the market. This type of preparation helps a trader develop a rational approach to what can often seem to be an irrational marketplace. In so doing, the preparation lays the groundwork for self-discipline, a quality that's absolutely essential to success in the futures market.

Cut Losses Short and Let Your Profits Ride

This is perhaps the most important rule in trading, yet one that virtually all traders violate at one time or another. The problem here, as with most trading rules, is that application of the rule frequently runs counter to human nature. Traders may refuse to cut losses short because they feel strongly that their market analysis is correct. On the other hand, some traders may take profits too quickly because they lack sufficient conviction in their analysis and want to be sure to at least capture some profit.

Many successful commodity traders are right only about half the time. They tend to accumulate a number of small losses, along with a handful of highly profitable trades. Frequently the bulk of their income derives from less than five percent of their trades. The secret of their success is to cut short the losing positions quickly and stay with the major trends for the duration of the move.

Never add to a losing position.

When the market moves against a position, some futures traders are tempted to engage in a technique known as averaging a loss. When the market moves down against a long position, a trader will buy more contracts. When the market rises against a short position, a trader will sell more contracts. Obviously, if the market comes back to the trader, this technique can limit losses. The danger lies in those few occasions when the market doesn't come back at all. When that happens, a trader will suffer enormous, possibly catastrophic losses. Generally speaking, this is a technique that works most of the time. However, when it doesn't work, the losses can be so severe that it can force the trader out of the market permanently.

Don't Focus on Profits and Losses

At first glance, this might seem contradictory to previous rules, which obviously call for awareness of profits and losses; however, it's really a necessary complement. Because money can be made or lost very quickly in the futures market, there's a natural tendency to focus on the bottom line. Unfortunately, this tendency can be overdone and can cloud decision making.

A trader who has had some recent success may begin thinking about how much money he'll make for the entire year if he continues at his present pace. As a result, the next time the trader enters the market, he may have profit expectations that weren't in his mind when he began his hot streak. Although his next trade may prove to be profitable initially, the trader may stick with the position too long because he wants to duplicate his recent success. Eventually, the market moves against him and he ends up losing money on the trade.

Instead of constantly adding up profits and losses on an existing position, traders should strive to monitor market activity in an objective fashion and adjust the position in line with any changes in that activity. The goal is to make trading decisions in a logical, consistent manner. Focusing too much on money can corrupt the decision making process.

When You Don't Understand, Stand Aside

One of the persistent problems in bank trading rooms is the inclination of traders to trade even when the particular market they're responsible for is relatively inactive. Understandably, traders find it difficult to do nothing all day, so, they take positions out of boredom, or perhaps out of a sense of responsibility that they should be doing something.

Similarly, traders may feel obliged to take positions when they don't quite understand what's going on in the market. At the Chicago Board of Trade in the mid-1980s, a number of veteran grain traders moved over to the new financial pits because the grain markets had become relatively dull. Some of the grain traders attempted to apply the principles they learned in trading the grains to the new financial instruments. Unfortunately, the financial instruments had very different trading characteristics. As a result, a few of veteran grain traders suffered huge losses. On the other hand, a few of the grain traders recognized early on that their grain trading skills couldn't be immediately transferred to the financial pits. Instead of jumping into a market they didn't understand, they simply stood in the pits and observed. Only when they felt comfortable with the new markets did they begin to trade.

MARKET ORDERS

One of the most overlooked aspects of commodity trading by novices is how to place an order. There are a number of different types of orders that a trader can send into the pit. Familiarity with orders and knowing which type of order is most appropriate in a given circumstance can have a substantial impact on a trader's results.

Briefly, there are several points of information that a trader must impart when he decides to enter an order: whether to buy or sell; the number of contracts; the contract delivery month; the commodity; the price at which the order is to be executed; the exchange at which the order is to be executed; and the time limit of the order. Every order, regardless of how simple or complicated, must impart this basic information.

When calling a broker to make an order, a trader should slowly and clearly enunciate each aspect of the order. If there's anything particularly unusual about the order, the trader should repeat it. For example, if a trader normally uses the Comex, but for this particular order he is using the MidAm, he should repeat MidAm twice. Then, after giving the broker the instructions, the trader should ask the broker to repeat the order back to him. If there are any errors, the whole order process should be repeated.

Market Order

The most frequently used and abused order is what is called a market order. A market order instructs the broker to buy or sell at whatever price is available in the market. The market order is commonly used when a trader believes gold prices will soon rise or fall and the trader wants to establish a position as quickly as possible.

The problem with market orders is that the execution of the trade often works to the disadvantage of the trader. All too frequently, a market order to buy results in a fill at a price that is rather high considering the trading range during the time of execution. Similarly, a market order to sell often results in a fill at a lower price than the trader might have otherwise have hoped. In both cases, the trader is exposed to less-than-desirous trade locations.

There are a number of reasons why trade execution on market orders is frequently poor. In many instances, an individual trader's order may be one of dozens of orders to hit the pit simultaneously. The influx of orders causes prices to rise or fall rapidly. However, the individual trader's order may have been entered a few seconds after a number of similar orders. Thus, by the time the trader's order is executed, the market has moved substantially in the anticipated direction and the trader is filled at a price that puts him in the middle, rather than toward the beginning, of a major rally or break.

Execution of market orders can also be handicapped by the activity of locals. As a new market trend emerges, locals customarily will test the strength of the trend by aggressively pushing prices in one direction. In that environment, a market order is likely to get executed at the worse possible price. For example, if a market order to buy comes into the pit as the market is rising, the locals in the pit may raise their offer price by a tick or two in reaction to the new order. Since the market order contains no price parameters, that will be the level at which the order will be executed.

Even if the market is not trending when the market order enters the pit, the order will always receive the worst side of the bid/offer spread. Remember, in any futures market, pit traders are willing to buy at one price and to sell at a slightly higher price. A market order to buy will always be executed at the high price of the bid/offer spread and a market order to sell will always be executed at the low price of the spread.

Despite the drawbacks, market orders do have advantages. Most other types of orders create conditions that have to be met before the order is activated. When those conditions are not met, no trade is executed. That can be a particularly frustrating experience for a trader when he is correct in his market assessment. Market orders, because they call for execution at whatever price is available, are always executed. Thus, if a trader is certain about the direction the market will move, and he wants to be absolutely sure to get into the market, a market order is the best avenue.

Limit Order

A variation of the market order is the limit order. A limit order states that a trade is to be executed at a certain price or at a more favorable price. For example, a trader might issue a limit order to buy at $502. That means the trade is to be executed at $502, or at any price below $502. In no case, can the trade be executed above $502.

Limit orders give the trader some measure of control over trade execution. In essence, a limit order says to a broker, if you can't do it at this price or better, don't do it at all. Limit orders protect the trader from the very poor executions that sometimes occur with market orders. On the other hand, limit orders may prevent a trader from getting into a market because his price limit is not hit or it is hit so briefly that the broker can't execute the trade.

Stop Order

The second most widely used orders are stop orders. Stop orders are most frequently used to limit losses on an existing position, but they can also be used to take profits or even to initiate a new position. Stops are distinct from market orders in that they specify a price level that must be reached before the trade is executed. However, once the stop price is reached by the market, the stop then becomes a market order to buy or sell. Consequently, placing a stop order at a particular price is no guarantee that the trade will be executed at that price.

Typically, stop orders are used to limit losses on an existing position. For example a trader might buy a gold contract at $405 an ounce and place a sell stop at $398 an ounce. If the market touches $398, the stop is activated and the position is liquidated. However, depending on where the market goes after it hits $398, the trade could be executed either above or below the $398 level. Nonetheless, since the stop order is in place on the trading floor, execution on stops is generally better than execution of a new market order that's entered at the same time that the price hits the stop-loss level.

A trader who is long gold will obviously place a protective sell stop order below the current market level and a trader who is short gold will place a buy stop order above the current market level. The problem confronting the trader is where to place the stop. On the one hand, if he places it to close to the current market price or to the price at which his position was entered, he runs the risk of taking a small loss even though the market eventually may move in his direction after hitting the stop. On the other hand, if he places the stop too far away from his position, he stands to suffer a large loss before the stop is hit.

The biggest drawback to stop orders, in the opinion of many traders, is the propensity of the market to take out stops in one direction before commencing a large move in the opposite direction. Some traders believe this tendency reflects corruption in pit trading practices. As they see it, pit traders know where the stop orders are and they intentionally push the market to take out the stops so that they can position themselves for what they know will be a major move in the opposite direction. In this regard, one often hear traders complain that the pit "was gunning" for their particular stop order.

In reality, the tendency of the market to take out stops is probably more a reflection of the intrinsic price discovery processes of the market than the nefarious motivations of floor traders. Over the course of a trading day, commodity markets usually test both buying and selling strength. On many days, a market moves in one direction, finds little activity, and then moves in the opposite direction for the rest of the day. Markets constantly explore the limits of price acceptance on both the downside and the upside.

When the market moves to take out sell stops, the market is simply testing to see the strength of selling activity. If, after taking out the sell stops, there's still a good deal of selling hitting the floor, the market will continue to move down. On the other hand, if the selling activity is exhausted after taking out the stops, the market is then poised to rally in the opposite direction. In a sense, the market indeed does gun for stops, particularly those stops that are near the current price. However, more fundamentally, the market is testing buying and selling strength.

In addition to protecting against large losses, stops are also useful in locking in profits on an existing position. A trader who sold gold at $405 may want to place a buy stop at $395 after the market fails to penetrate $390 on the downside. The inability of the market to break the $390 support may be an early signal that the price decline is over. If the market now rallies to $395, the trader may surmise that the decline is definitely over. Therefore, he places the stop at what he perceives to be the next crucial resistance point, a move that will ensure around a $1000 per contract profit depending on execution.

Stops, of course, can be adjusted as the market changes. In the example above, the trader might lower the stop to $390 if the market fails to reach $395 and then quickly drops to $380. With the new stop, the trader would be assured of a profit of around $1500 per contract depending on execution. By adjusting the stop in this manner, the trader is able to stay with the trend and, at the same time, he is assured of quickly getting out of the market should the trend change.

Stops can also be used to initiate positions. With the market at $465, a trader might put a buy stop in at $471 and a sell stop at $449. The first stop to be hit is activated. Again, once the stop price is hit, the order becomes a market order, which means, of course, that the actual execution may be at a price quite different from the stop price.

Many traders believe they receive better executions with stop orders than market orders. With a stop order, the trade is already in the pit when the price is hit. At that point, the trader's stop order puts him on virtually equal footing with other pit traders. Depending on the skill of the floor broker, there's an excellent chance that the stop order will be executed on the favorable side of the bid/offer spread. That rarely happens with market orders.

By combining elements of the market, limit, and stop orders, traders have devised a number of more complicated orders. In most cases, these orders have developed in response to trading strategies used in different types of markets.

Market-on-Close Order

A market-on-close order instructs the trader to buy or sell during the close of the market. The close is not one particular price, but rather is a range of prices traded at the end of the day. Market activity generally picks up at the close as many traders seek to exit their positions. Frequently, prices move abruptly during the close. As a result, execution on market-on-close orders can be inconsistent.

The opposite of the market-on-close is the *market-on-open order*. Again, the opening price is really a range of prices and the trader executing the order is only obliged to make the trade within that range. Market-on-open orders are frequently combined with a specific price order. For example, a trader might send in an order to buy gold at $395 or less (in effect, a limit order) during the opening. If the trade can't be executed during the opening, it is then canceled unless the trader instructs otherwise.

Fill or Kill Order

A fill or kill order must be executed immediately at a specific price or it is canceled. For example, a trader may send in a fill or kill order for 20 Comex gold contracts at $510. The pit trader is obliged to fill any or all of the order immediately at the specified price. If he can't execute the order, either in whole or in part, then all or the remaining part of the order is canceled.

Contingent Order

Contingent orders are popular among traders who focus on the relationships between different futures contracts. For example, a trader may place an order that calls for a market order purchase of 10 gold contracts if the price of the Swiss franc breaks .6400. Don't expect very good execution on conventional contingent orders, because they're really only a form of a market order. Of course, a trader conceivably could place a limit order on the tail end of a contingent order in the hope of receiving better execution. However, there comes a point at which the possibility of better execution is outweighed by the possibility of an error due to the complexity of the order.

One-Cancels-the-Other Order

In this type of order, a trader lays out two trades, usually at specific price levels. Whichever trade is hit first is executed, and the other trade is thereupon canceled. For example, a trader might send in an order to buy 10 contracts of gold at $476 or to sell 10 contracts at $469. If gold hits $476, then the sell order is canceled. This kind of order is particularly useful when the market is poised to break out of a trading range.

Spread Trade Order

Spread trades are very popular among gold traders. As described in Chapter 8, spreads involve buying one contract and selling another in the belief that the price difference between the two contracts is likely to narrow or widen. Spreads can be executed between two different contract months of the same commodity, two different commodities, or the same commodity that's traded on different exchanges.

A spread order can be executed like a market order. For example, a trader can simply instruct his broker to buy the nearby gold contract and sell the six-month contract. Frequently, however, spreads are put on and taken off on the basis of the price differential between the two contracts. For example, a trader can instruct his broker to buy the nearby and sell the deferred when the price differential rises to $20. Similarly, he can take profits in the spreads (in effect a stop order) by telling his broker to sell the nearby and buy the deferred when the price differential comes back down to $15.

Switch Order

Switch orders are used to move from one contract month to another. For example, a trader who has an existing long position would liquidate that position in one contract month and would immediately reopen the position in another contract month.

Although probably 98 percent of gold trades are made using the orders described here, there are, in fact, several other more detailed kinds of orders. Some of these involve adding to or reducing a position as the market changes. Others involve giving the floor broker a certain amount of discretion in attempting to transact at the most favorable price. The variety of orders is only limited by your imagination, exchange rules, and the forbearance of your broker.

MARKET ORDERS AND STRATEGY

Familiarity with market orders can be helpful when formulating a trade. In many cases, market orders can be constructed to precisely conform to a particular market outlook and strategy.

For example, a trader may decide that the behavior of the dollar is the critical short-term determinant of gold prices. Thus, if the dollar strengthens, the trader is prepared to short the gold market. If the trader hasn't thought much about orders, he may decide to simply call his broker with a market order when the dollar begins to move. Unfortunately, by the time the order reaches the pit, it will probably be behind a number of similar orders from other traders watching the same relationship. Consequently, the execution is likely to be poor.

Instead of a market order, the trader in this example would probably be better served by a contingent order. He could instruct his broker to sell 10 gold contracts if the dollar touches 0.55 deutsche marks in the futures market. Since the order is already on the floor, or at least in a broker's hand, the chances are better that the order will be executed at a favorable price. It should be noted, however, that many brokers will not accept this type of order.

If a trader wants to enter the market after a particular support or resistance point is broken, he should consider using a buy stop or a sell stop order, rather than chasing the market with a market order. For example, if $437 is a key resistance point, the trader might want to place a buy stop at $437.10. Thus, as soon as the resistance is broken, the trader is positioned to bid at the next offer.

As mentioned earlier, a "one-cancels-the-other" order can be an effective order in a market that's poised to move strongly in one direction or the other, a condition that arises quite frequently. For example, after a market has rallied for a week or two, the buying activity may slow and the market may enter something of a test period. Buyers are reluctant to bid the market higher, while sellers are afraid to be aggressive because they believe the rally may soon resume. At some point, the situation will come to a climax, and the rally will continue or the market will break. A one-cancels-the-other order that places buy and sell orders at key resistance and support points can be an effective way to deal with this type of market.

Orders can be constructed to deal with a trader's personal situation as well as a particular trading strategy. If a trader wants to exit a position on a Friday, but hopes to execute at a certain price, he can combine a limit order with a market-on-close order. The order might call for a limit order to sell at a price of $512. However, if the market fails to reach $512, the position will be closed at the end of the trading day via a market-on-close order. With a position like that in place, the trader can leave work and start the weekend early.

FUTURES AS A DELIVERY MECHANISM

Although gold futures most commonly are used to speculate or to hedge, they are also used to deliver and take delivery of gold. Depending on the objectives of the investors, gold futures can be a less costly alternative to buying and selling physical gold in the cash market.

The problem with buying and holding physical gold, is that gold doesn't pay interest. That's the major reason why gold prices tend to weaken when real interest rates are high. It's very difficult for any investor to hold a nonpaying asset when he can realize a five percent real return in short-term interest rate instruments. In most instances, the possibility of gold price appreciation cannot justify forfeiting the risk-free rate of return represented by short-term government securities.

Gold futures, however, provide an opportunity to participate in gold price movements without giving up money-market style returns. Suppose, for example, an investor buys 100 ounces of gold at a price of $500 per ounce—that represents a $50,000 investment. Unfortunately, the $50,000 is tied up in physical gold and doesn't pay any interest or dividends. Indeed, if the gold is held at a bank, the investor has to pay a fee for storage and insurance. In contrast, if the investor posted a $3000 margin deposit and purchased one gold contract, he would have an equal exposure to gold price movements, but he would have $47,000 left over to invest with as he pleases.

Of course, if the price of gold declines substantially, the trader would have to post additional margin. However, since margin can be placed in the form of interest-bearing Treasury bills, the trader can earn a return on both the margin deposit and the cash that otherwise would have been used to purchase physical gold. To avoid any margin payments at all, the trader could post Treasury bills for the full value of contract as margin.

If the trader decides to take delivery of the gold by allowing the long futures contract to expire, he will receive a warehouse receipt from the exchange. Unfortunately for the buyer, under exchange rules, the seller has the option of choosing the particular exchange-approved depository to consummate the delivery.

If the trader wishes to take possession of the physical gold and move it to another location, this will present an added cost burden. However, if the trader maintains the gold in the same depository, he will only be obliged to take over the insurance and storage fees. In addition, by keeping the gold in the exchange-approved depository, the trader is positioned to sell the gold through the futures market should the occasion warrant.

Besides freeing up capital to use for other purposes, taking delivery of gold through the futures markets saves money through reduced commissions and fees. A retail gold broker may charge a commission ranging from 0.5 percent to 8 percent of the total value of the purchase. In addition, brokers charge fees for insurance, storage, shipping, and possibly a sales tax, depending on the state. Assuming a trader buys 100 ounces of gold at $500 an ounce, that means a brokerage fee of more than $250 at a minimum. When the trader wants to sell the gold, he has to pay another $250. In addition, if the trader has taken delivery of the gold himself, when he wishes to sell he probably will have to have the gold authenticated by an assayer, a service that will add to the transaction costs.

In contrast, if a trader takes delivery of gold through the futures market, he only has to pay the commission cost, which ranges from $30 to $75.

Once he owns the gold, of course, he's subject to insurance and storage fees, however, the only cost upfront is the trading commission. In addition, if the trader keeps the gold in an exchange-approved depository, he can resell the gold without having to have it assayed for purity.

While the foregoing may make the reader wonder why anybody would want to take delivery of gold through the cash market, there is one important caveat: the future price of gold generally discounts the interest rate component. For example, if spot gold is $500 and one-year deposits are paying 10 percent, the future contract for delivery in one year will be around $550. In that case, which is typical of the gold market, there would be little advantage to buying gold futures on margin and investing the balance in interest-bearing instruments. The interest income would not compensate for the fact that the futures price was higher than the spot price. Thus, there would be no apparent advantage to the investor in taking delivery through the futures market; he might as well buy gold on the spot market and hold onto it.

On the other hand, the future price of gold is calculated on the basis of overnight interest rates to brokers. It assumes that the investor in gold futures will invest his remaining capital in some sort of short-term interest rate instrument. However, if the trader wants to invest in other instruments, such as the stock market or junk bonds, then there may be an advantage to utilizing futures to create an exposure to the gold market. By using futures, the trader can maximize the amount of money available to devote to other instruments.

Moreover, a trader can retain an exposure to the gold market through futures without ever taking delivery. When his contract approaches expiration, the trader can "roll it over," by selling the contract and recreating the long position in another expiration month. Theoretically, this can be carried on indefinitely.

CHAPTER 5

Gold Supply

Like any commodity, the price of gold is determined by supply and demand. In the next two chapters, we will examine supply and demand separately, with the goal of providing insight into how these two fundamental forces affect and are affected by the price of gold.

There are three sources of gold supply: mining, recycling gold scrap, and government and central bank sales. Each of these sources of supply respond to and impact gold prices differently, so each must be broken down and analyzed on its own.

The most important source of gold supply is mining, which has accounted for roughly 70 percent of new gold supply in recent years. Generally speaking, mining production is inelastic, that is, it responds slowly to changes in price. When gold prices jumped sharply in 1979 and 1980, worldwide mining production remained unchanged until 1981 and didn't rise appreciably until 1983.

Gold is mined from two sources: lodes and placers. Lode deposits are mined through underground tunnels or shallow surface mines. Placers—which are found in river beds in the form of gold flakes, nuggets, or dust—are mined by dredging, panning, and washing.

A great deal of the world's production originates from deep, narrow veins known as reefs, some of which run 10,000 feet into the earth. The mining process involves drilling into the vein, blasting the rock, and then hoisting the broken material to the surface. Once on the surface, the rocks are crushed and pulverized, and finally are shipped to a mill where the gold is separated from the rock.

Known world reserves of gold are estimated at 1.1 billion ounces. Total world reserves may be two to three times as high. About 50 percent of the world's reserves are in South Africa and 20 percent are in the Soviet Union.

Since the sharp price rise in gold in 1979, recycling of gold scrap has become an important contributor to supply, accounting for between 10 percent to 20 percent of annual supply in recent years. Scrap originates from jewelry, coins, and industry. The material is melted down and reshaped into gold bars and bullion.

Production of scrap appears closely related to changes in the price of gold. In 1980, for example, 482 tons of gold were recycled, the largest amount of recycling ever recorded. As gold prices backed down from their 1980 peak, the amount of recycling diminished.

By far the most volatile component of supply is government sales. Government sales include those of centrally planned economies (mainly the Soviet Union); central banks, which customarily maintain a sizable amount of gold as a monetary reserve; and international economic organizations, such as the International Monetary Fund.

The needs and motivations of these various government bodies are varied and changeable, which makes it very difficult to forecast their behavior in the gold market. Unlike mining companies or producers of scrap, government activity in the gold market over the long term appears to bear little relation to price. Moreover, the governments do not simply act on the supply side of equation; in some years, they end up as net buyers, a tendency which further complicates the analysis.

Before embarking on a detailed analysis of gold supply, it should be noted that gold is a unique commodity and frequently doesn't behave in accordance with conventional supply/demand principles. Remember, unlike commodities such as oil or wheat, gold has relatively little intrinsic value and its monetary value is determined largely by psychological factors. Thus, there have been occasions when in response to higher prices, demand actually increased, contrary to conventional economic behavior. Or, there have been occasions when the gold supply rose in a given year, despite the fact that prices were depressed.

Also, unlike most other commodities, gold isn't consumed. Over the centuries, it's estimated that over 3 billion ounces of gold have been mined and perhaps 80 percent, or around 2.5 billion ounces, can be accounted for today. With that tremendous overhang of accumulated supplies, yearly additions to supply usually amount to less than 2 percent of total supply. Given that perspective, it's not particularly surprising that year-to-year fluctuations in new supply frequently bear little relation to price.

MINING

Mining production is by far the single largest source of gold supply, however, its contribution to total supply has varied considerably in recent years. Throughout the 1950s and in several years in the 1960s and 1970s, mining accounted for 100 percent of the years' gold supply. By the mid-1970s and into the 1980s, however, the proportion of gold supply accounted for by mining fell consistently below 100 percent, reaching a low of 56 percent in 1979.

One of the problems with calculating the contribution of mining production to total supply on a historical basis is the lack of reliable figures on recycling prior to 1980. Consolidated Gold Fields PLC, the preeminent statistical authority on the gold market, only began estimating recycling activity in 1980. As a result, pre-1980 supply figures only include mining production and government sales, while post-1980 figures include mining, production, and recycling. Obviously, the inclusion of recycling activity as a component of gold supply after 1980 tends to reduce the proportionate amount of supply accounted for by mining.

Nevertheless, an examination of gold supply figures since 1950 makes clear that mining production accounted for a smaller proportion of total supply in the 1970s and 1980s than it did in the 1950s and 1960s, even if one discounts recycling in the 1980s. Broadly speaking, this trend is a result of the fact that governments around the world tended to be net buyers of gold in the 1950s and 1960s—thereby, reducing gold supply—and net sellers in the 1970s and 1980s—a move which increased supplies and reduced the proportional contribution of mining to supply. (Please note in table 5.1, however, that these are general trends only; several years turned out to be exceptions, particularly in the late 1980s.)

But while mining accounted for a smaller portion of total worldwide gold supply in the 1970s and 1980s, actual mine production began to increase in the early 1980s, after declining throughout the late 1970s. Much of the increase in production came from secondary producing countries such the United States, Canada, and Australia. In contrast, production from South Africa, the world's primary producer, remained relatively stable during this period.

SOUTH AFRICA

Although South Africa remains the world's largest producer of gold, its level of dominance has been declining in recent years. Total production peaked in 1970 at 1000 metric tons, and has dropped gradually ever since. Similarly, the proportion of world mining output accounted for by South Africa fell to under 50 percent in the late 1980s, after hitting a peak of 83 percent in 1980.

The drop in South African production is a result of declining ore-grades and rising production costs. At the extreme, these forces have led to large production cutbacks at several high-cost, low-grade mines. More typically, however, these forces have simply kept a large number of mines at stagnant or slightly declining production levels for a number of years.

The rise in gold production costs in South Africa can be traced to two sources: the working cost of mining and treating a ton of ore and the amount of gold extracted from each ton. Since 1980, the working cost of mining and treating a ton of ore increased from 137 Rand (R137) to R585 in 1988, an increase of 327 percent. Although at first glance this appears to be a huge increase, in fact, it is commensurate with South Africa's inflation rate over this period.

A more telling factor contributing to the decline in South African gold production has been the reduction in the quality of ore mined since the early 1980s. In 1980, each ton of ore treated yielded 7.73 grams of gold. By 1987, that figure had declined to 5.13 grams of gold per ton. Thus, while the costs of mining and treating ore basically tracked domestic inflation since 1980, the amount of gold produced per unit of labor dropped.

The decline in the quality of ore mined in South Africa primarily reflects the maturation of many working mines. Generally, when a new mine opens, the higher grade gold deposits are mined first. Over the years, unless new high-grade veins are found, the producers exploit most of the high-grade ores and eventually are left mainly with lower quality ores. The producers then decide whether to continue to mine the lower grade ores, cease production in hopes of higher prices, or close the mine and devote its resources elsewhere. In the case of South Africa in recent years, many producers have opted for the later two options.

In addition to the maturation of many mines, mining regulations have also contributed to the reduction in the quality of ore mined in South

Africa. Under these regulations, South African mining companies are obligated to exploit lower grade ores when the Rand price of gold is high enough to cover the cost of mining, processing, and marketing the lower quality ores.

The minimum value at which ore can be mined and treated in order to break even is known as the pay limit. Since 1970, the pay limit has decreased from five grams per ton of ore to 3.2 grams per ton in 1987. As a result, recovery grades in the industry have fallen from an average of 13.3 grams per ton in 1970 to an average of 5.1 grams per ton in 1987.

Thus, as a result of the combination of the maturation of many South African mines and government policies geared to exploiting lesser-quality ores, the South African mining industry has been producing less gold per ton of ore mined throughout the 1980s. Since the tonnage of ore mined has stayed relatively steady, this has led to a decline in overall South African production.

Rising production costs have been exacerbated in recent years by the growing aggressiveness of South African unions representing gold mine workers. South African miners, particularly black miners, are paid substantially less than their counterparts in other producing countries and substantially less than industrial workers in South Africa. However, the unions have been able to negotiate large wage raises in recent years, a development that has increased the cost of South African production. Since South African gold production is more labor-intensive than other countries, labor wage increases have a particularly significant impact.

Despite the rather bleak recent history of South African gold production, it should be noted that new mines and production areas continue to be opened. Although the new areas are not expected to substantially boost South African production, they should ensure that South Africa remains the world's largest producer for some time to come.

On the other hand, it's possible that the South African government, in an attempt to reduce inflation, will adopt policies that force marginal producers out of business. Throughout the 1980s, the South African government allowed the Rand to depreciate in order to bolster the domestic price of gold. If the government decides to allow the Rand price of gold to fall well below 1000R, it's estimated that some 25 tons of production could be imperiled.

AUSTRALIA

While South African production has been declining in recent years, Australia has been in the midst of a mining boom. Since 1980, Australia's production has risen from 17 tons to 157 tons in 1988, to become the third largest producer in the Western World.

The boom is really something of a modern-day gold rush as mining companies hurry to exploit newly discovered gold deposits in Western Australia. At the end of 1987, the Australian government estimated that the country contained 1274 tons of gold that could be profitably mined at the then current price. That estimate reflected a three-fold rise from 1983.

The Australian gold boom was reflected as well in the number of new mines opened in recent years. In 1986 and 1987 alone, some 30 mines were opened in Western Australia and a handful of additional mines were opened in the north country and in Queensland. Although, as *Consolidated Gold Field* reports, most of the mines were small, the cumulative impact has been tremendous.

The only cloud on the horizon for the Australian gold industry is the planned imposition of a 39 percent gold production tax on January 1, 1991. For years, the gold industry was exempted from the 49 percent corporate tax rate in Australia. However, as part of a reduction in the corporate tax from 49 percent to 39 percent, the gold industry lost its exemption.

Although it's possible a new government could restore the gold industry's exemption, if it is implemented as planned, there's little question that it will raise production costs and discourage more marginal mining operations. In 1988, Australia's operating costs per ounce rose to $238, $24 and $9 more than operating costs in Canada and the U.S. respectively. The operating cost-jump was the result of a higher Australian dollar, increased domestic inflation, and the opening of several relatively high-cost mines. The imposition of the corporate tax on top of these other cost factors undoubtedly will further erode Australia's international cost position.

The biggest question mark as a result of the new tax is whether it will discourage producers from expanding shallow open-pit mines into underground operations. Most of the new mines have been of the open-pit variety, and at some point, many producers will have to decide whether to invest the money required to develop underground mining capabilities.

In that regard, though, the impact of the new tax will be mitigated somewhat because the producers will be able to deduct capital expenditures, a substantial cost in mining operations, from their taxable income. Moreover, producers will be able to deduct capital expenses incurred before 1991 on their post-1991 taxes.

Despite the imposition of the new tax on the gold mining industry, the Australian government appears to be committed to supporting the industry in other ways, probably because gold has become Australia's third leading export behind wool and coal. A new government body has been formed, GoldCorp Australia, which is charged with the promotion of Australia as an international gold producer and with the development of new markets for Australian gold. It has already introduced a gold coin called the Nugget and it has several other products on the drawing board.

UNITED STATES

Gold production in the U.S. also has risen dramatically in recent years, from 30 metric tons in 1980 to 205 metric tons in 1988, making it the second largest producer in the Western World. In a broad sense, the increase in gold production in the U.S. reflects a long-term, somewhat delayed reaction to the rise in gold prices in the beginning of the 1980s and the concomitant revitalization of the U.S. gold mining industry after a long period of dormancy.

The history of gold mining in the U.S. is particularly colorful. In the 1800s, the settlement of the farther reaches of the continent ignited three gold rushes: California in 1849, Comstock Lode in 1860, and Alaska in the 1870s. However, the periodic gold frenzies of the 19th century gave way to a vastly more subdued market in the 20th century after President Franklin Roosevelt decided to outlaw private ownership of gold by U.S. citizens in 1933.

By outlawing private ownership of gold, Roosevelt aimed to increase U.S. government supplies of gold and thereby provide the basis for a vast expansion in government credit, which he hoped would pull the country out of the Depression. Prior to his order, there had been something of a run on government gold supplies as more and more people elected to buy

gold rather than hold onto dollars. Understandably, Roosevelt felt com-
pelled to reassert confidence in the U.S. dollar.

Roosevelt's first move to forestall the flight from dollars to gold was
to declare a three-day bank holiday, an action which temporarily pre-
vented people from withdrawing money and purchasing gold. A few
weeks later, he ordered that all gold in private hands—save numismatic
coins and gold used for industrial purposes—be turned over to the Federal
Reserve at the fixed rate of $20.67. Then, in the following year, he
devalued the dollar to a fixed rate of $35 per ounce, a price that stayed
in effect until 1971.

The increase in the price of gold to $35 an ounce stimulated a doubling
of U.S. gold production from the 1930s to the 1940s. During World War
II, however, the government discouraged gold mining and production
dropped sharply. Following the war, the $35 per ounce price was no
longer sufficient to encourage production. As a result, the U.S. gold
mining industry went into a long period of dormancy which it's only truly
revived from in the 1980s.

In the late 1960s, foreign investors and central banks recognized that
the official U.S. exchange rate of $35 an ounce represented an excellent
bargain in a world economy that was on the verge of an inflationary price
spiral. Consequently, U.S. gold stocks came under pressure again, similar
to the 1930s; this time, however, the gold buyers were foreigners. U.S.
citizens were still barred from owning gold.

The situation, which was a long time in the making, was closely
intertwined with the breakdown of the 1944 Bretton Woods agreement.
Under Bretton Woods, the world's major democracies adopted the dollar
as the official reserve currency, established fixed currency-rates (within
narrow bands) and agreed to exchange dollars at a rate of $35 per ounce
of gold. The agreement worked well through the 1950s. However, by the
1960s, the U.S. had begun to run a large balance of payments deficit and
inflation began to creep upward, developments which put downward
pressure on the dollar within the prescribed Bretton Woods ranges. In
line with the agreement, foreign central banks were obliged to purchase
dollars, an action which forced them to print more of their own currency
to exchange for dollars. In effect, by supporting the weak dollar in line
with Bretton Woods, foreign central banks were importing inflation from
the U.S.

The situation grew increasing intolerable throughout the 1960s. Instead of holding onto U.S. dollars, foreigners (including central banks) began cashing in their dollars for gold at $35 an ounce. Since the amount of dollars held overseas was more than the amount of gold held by the U.S. Treasury, the U.S. pledge to sell gold at $35 an ounce was threatened. Something had to give.

In 1971, President Richard Nixon finally closed the U.S. Treasury gold window. The move effectively decoupled the U.S. dollar and gold, allowing both commodities to float freely in price. Not surprisingly, the value of the U.S. dollar plummeted and the price of gold began what would become an historic rally.

But while the price of gold was allowed to float, U.S. citizens were still prohibited from buying or selling the metal. This didn't change until, December 31, 1974, the same time in which gold futures contracts were introduced.

Although the price of gold jumped following the abolition of the gold standard, the gold mining industry was slow to respond to the higher prices, in part because there wasn't much U.S. gold mining industry left. Also, the price of gold didn't vault straight up; after rising to almost $200 in the early 1970s, it dropped to close to $100 in the summer of 1976. Naturally, the price decline caused some companies to have second thoughts about increasing production.

In fact, in the late 1970s, U.S. gold production dropped to its lowest levels since World War II. It wasn't until after gold hit a peak of $850 an ounce in 1980 that U.S. gold production really began to increase.

Much of the increased gold production in the U.S. in the late 1980s came out of Nevada, particularly an area known as the Carlin Trend, which is possibly the most promising gold production site outside of South Africa and the Soviet Union. Analysts believe production from this area will continue at high levels well into the next century, a development which bodes well for the U.S. gold mining industry.

CANADA

Like the other major secondary producing countries, Canada's gold production has more than doubled in the 1980s, reaching 128.5 million tons in 1988. Indeed, so intense has the Canadian mining industry's focus been on gold exploration and production, the country's reserves of copper and zinc have fallen markedly, while gold reserves have jumped 94 percent since 1981.

Gold production is dispersed throughout Canada. Quebec and Ontario account for about 70 percent of the production, however, gold is now produced in every province except for Prince Edward Island. In 1987, a mine was even opened in Newfoundland.

In the late 1980s, several new Canadian mines failed to fulfill deposit expectations and, as a result, a few projects were closed. The problem appeared to stem from the over-optimism that gripped the industry a few years earlier when investment funds for new mines were plentiful. Apparently, in their haste to get mines into production, companies overestimated the amount of gold that could be profitably mined.

Since 1983, financing of Canadian production has been encouraged by the government through the Canadian Exploration Incentive Program. The program allows individuals to write off 100 percent of their investment in mineral exploration against their personal income. From 1983 to 1988, the program raised about $3 billion for exploration, with $1 billion alone raised in 1987.

In recent years, the Canadian gold mining industry (and, to a lesser extent, the U.S. industry) has been going through a period of consolidation and restructuring. In the late 1980s, as a result of weak equity markets and a bearish gold market, many small and medium-sized Canadian companies had difficulty raising money. Consequently, many of these companies forged links with larger producers that had better access to the capital markets. Observers in Canada expect this trend will continue.

OTHER PRODUCERS

Sizable quantities of gold are produced in other parts of the world as well, particularly from the Latin American countries of Brazil, Colombia, Chile, and Venezuela, the Philippines, and Papua New Guinea. Excluding the communist bloc, production from these other regions generally accounts for 15-20 percent of the world total on an annual basis.

In Latin America, economic problems have substantially altered the gold market in recent years. Generally, governments have been encouraging gold production as a means to build their foreign exchange reserves and to ease foreign debt service burdens. At the same time hyper-inflation and repeated currency devaluations have led companies and individuals in Latin America to increase their gold holdings at the expense of the local currency. The end result is that production is increasing, but the amount of gold leaving the region is not keeping pace.

In Brazil and Colombia, the two largest Latin American producers, about 80 percent of the gold is produced by individual miners known as garimpeiros. In 1988, it's estimated there were 800,000 garimpeiros working in the Amazon Basin in Brazil, a phenomenon driven by an economy devastated by high inflation and weak growth. Indeed, there's an inverse relationship between the state of the economy and garimpeiro mining: as the economy worsens, the number of garimpeiros mining for gold increases.

There are problems with the garimpeiros on the horizon. In a short while, many of the ore bodies that they mine are likely to be depleted. Moreover, environmental regulations restricting the ability of garimpeiros to mine gold could be enacted. As a result, Latin American production, particularly in Brazil, could level off in the 1990s.

Despite the possibility that Latin American production could slow, production from secondary producing countries around the world should be watched closely in the years ahead because of heightened exploration activity now under way. Just as production in the U.S., Canada, and Australia soared in the 1980s, production from these other countries could become a much more important factor in the gold market in the 1990s.

THE COMMUNIST BLOC

The Soviet Union is the world's second largest gold producer and together with other communist countries probably accounts for roughly 20 percent of annual world production. Since 1933, under orders from Josef Stalin, the Soviet Union has refused to disclose its gold production. Consequently, Western analysts try to estimate Soviet production based on information from articles in Soviet technical journals and from unofficial sources.

According to these estimates, Soviet production increased perhaps by as much as 50 percent during the 1970s, before stabilizing in the 1980s at around 300 tons a year. In the mid-1980s, apparently, Soviet production was insufficient to meet its export and internal needs, a development that forced the country to dip into its accumulated stocks. It's unclear whether the need to sell accumulated stocks will lead Soviet authorities to press for higher production levels or reduced sales in the years ahead.

Of all the governments involved in the gold market, the Soviet Union is clearly the most important. Not only is the Soviet Union the second leading producer in the world, it also holds a substantial amount of accumulated stocks. When it decides to sell those stocks, it has the power to rock the market.

It's generally believed that Soviet gold sales are motivated primarily by the need for foreign exchange rather than by the price of gold. In 1980, when the average price of gold was over $600, gold sales from the Communist bloc totaled 2.9 million ounces. In contrast, in 1985, when the average gold price was below $325, Communist bloc sales reached 10 million ounces. Obviously, at least in those two years, factors other than price were at work.

In support of the idea that Soviet gold sales are motivated by foreign exchange needs, many analysts have noted a correlation between Soviet grain purchases and Soviet gold sales. Very simply, in years of high Soviet grain imports, it tends to sell a large amount of gold in order to generate the currency needed to purchase the grain. Conversely, when Soviet grain imports are down, gold sales also fall off, presumably because the Soviet Union's need for foreign currency is less pressing. In 1982, for example, when the Soviet Union imported $2.32 billion of grain (the highest amount over the 1980-85 period), it exported 6.5 million ounces of gold. In 1983, however, when grain imports hit a five-year low of $983 million, gold sales dropped to 3 million ounces.

Although the link between Soviet grain imports and gold sales holds up in most years, it is imperfect because the Soviet Union's foreign exchange needs reflect a number of other factors, such as oil and natural gas exports. If oil and gas prices are weak, then the Soviets may be forced to sell more gold to compensate for the lost hydrocarbon revenue. Many analysts believe that was a major factor in the upsurge in Soviet gold sales in 1985.

The relationship between grain imports and gold sales may become further skewed as a result of the vast changes taking place in the Soviet economy. On the one hand, the goal of importing more consumer and industrial goods from the West will place strains on the Soviet Union's foreign currency reserves, a development that presumably could motivate increased gold sales. On the other hand, if Western credits are more readily available, as it appears will be the case, the foreign-exchange burden on gold may be reduced. Indeed, instead of selling gold to get hard currency, the Soviets may increasingly use gold as collateral to obtain hard-currency denominated credits.

China is gradually becoming a significant gold producer. Annual production in the 1980s doubled, and the government announced in 1988 that it intends to double output again by 1993. As in Latin America, a number of Chinese individuals have rushed to the gold producing regions in hopes of striking it rich. And, as in Latin America, a great deal of China's production is smuggled out of the country and sold for dollars in order to avoid selling to the government at well below the free-market price. In 1989, the government raised its purchase price to a level commensurate with free-market prices, however, since black-market dollars command a premium to the official exchange rate, the temptation to smuggle will continue.

THE OFFICIAL SECTOR

As we mentioned earlier, no other component of gold supply is more important to the price of gold than government sales. All told, government bodies—mainly central banks and quasi-governmental agencies like the International Monetary Fund (IMF)—own about one-third of the world's total gold supply, around 1.5 billion ounces. Since those holdings dwarf yearly production by such a large amount, it's clear why government activity in the gold market is so important.

Historically, central bank sales have been the most volatile component of gold supply. Changes in mining production tend to occur slowly and over a long period of time. Sales from the Soviet Union and other centrally planned economies, although more volatile than mining production, at least always add to total yearly supply. In contrast, central bank activity vacillates between net buying and net selling, and frequently exhibits huge year-to-year changes.

Between 1979 and 1980, for example, central banks went from net sellers of 544 tons of gold to net buyers of 276 tons. The abrupt change reduced the 1980 gold supply by about 50 percent, creating the backdrop for a doubling in gold prices.

In recent years (1985-1988), central banks have been net purchasers of gold, a development that has been partially driven by the weak U.S.

dollar. On the one hand, the weak dollar means that most foreign currencies are highly valued and thus, in foreign currency terms, gold is relatively inexpensive. Moreover, as a result of efforts to support the dollar as part of international monetary agreements, many foreign central banks found themselves flush with dollars in the late 1980s. Rather than hold dollars, many central banks, most notably in Japan and Taiwan, elected to convert a portion of the dollars to gold.

Another noteworthy development in recent years has been the growing practice of gold-producing countries in the developing world to purchase large amounts of their domestic production. Such purchases allow the countries to replenish their official reserves without any foreign exchange cost since they pay for the gold in their local currencies. Brazil, the Philippines, Colombia, Peru, and Ecuador have all adopted this strategy.

Since a large number of central banks are active in the gold market, it's difficult to get a handle on what the banks in aggregate are doing. Each country has its particular economic goals and policies; rarely do they act in concert when it comes to gold. Indeed, in certain countries in the 1980s, central bank buying of domestic gold production in order to bolster official reserves was quickly followed by open market sales which were needed to avoid a foreign exchange crisis. This type of volatility makes forecasting central bank activity exceedingly difficult.

The best way to keep abreast of central bank activity is through the International Monetary Fund, which gathers and publishes data on the gold holdings of the world's central banks. The IMF data, unfortunately, does not distinguish between gold sales and gold loans or swaps, which can make the numbers misleading. Nonetheless, it's the best that's available.

RECYCLING GOLD SCRAP

Recycled gold scrap refers to the sale and recycling of gold from jewelry, industrial equipment, and even dental fillings. The gold content from these products is recovered, formed into new products, and brought back onto the market. By far the single most important component of gold scrap is jewelry.

For the most part, year-to-year changes in gold scrap production are driven by changes in gold prices. Indeed, scrap production is by far the most price elastic of the three gold supply components. When prices rise, people tend to sell their jewelry for a profit. When prices fall, they tend to hold onto their jewelry.

In 1980, the year gold reached $850 per ounce, 482 tons of gold were recycled, the highest amount of recycling ever. The following year, as gold prices dropped sharply, the amount of recycling declined to 232 tons.

But, while scrap supplies tend to closely follow gold price movements, it should be noted that there can be instances when supply lags price movement. Frequently, when gold prices rally, some people intend to sell their gold; however, they hold onto their gold too long in hopes of still higher prices. Eventually, after the rally peaks and prices have declined for some time, these people sell their gold at the lower prices. Essentially, this is what happened in 1982 when the amount of gold recycled increased by five tons from the previous year, despite significantly lower prices. Most of these people probably held onto their gold through the 1980 rally and weathered the decline of 1981 thinking the rally would soon resume. When prices continued to fall in 1982, they finally decided it was time to sell.

The supply of scrap onto the market is governed, not just by the dollar price of gold, but by the price of gold in local currency terms as well. This is particularly important because gold recycling is much more widespread in the Middle East, the Far East, and the Indian subcontinent than in North America or Europe. In many of these countries, buying and selling gold jewelry is a long-standing tradition.

In the final analysis, the flow of gold scrap onto the market can presage the end of a price trend. When the amount of recycled gold jumps, it could indicate that a price rally may be losing momentum. Similarly, when the supply of scrap coming onto the market dwindles, a price decline may be coming to an end.

GOLD LOANS

In recent years, gold supplies have been profoundly affected by gold loans, particularly after the October 1987 stock market crash, which made raising money in the equity market more difficult. In 1988, for example, it's estimated that banks lent out 150 tons of gold. Although some analysts suggest the level of loans may stabilize or decline, there's little doubt that gold loans have become a permanent part of the gold industry.

In the typical gold loan, a commercial bank lends gold at an interest rate of one to three percent to a gold producer. The producer then sells the gold on the market and uses the proceeds of the sale to finance production or for other purposes. When the loan comes due, the producer repays the gold from its own production.

For a gold producer, a gold loan provides two things: a means to obtain financing at better rates than in the conventional credit markets and a means to hedge price risk. On the negative side, a gold loan prohibits a producer from benefiting from a rise in gold prices. In addition, if production problems arise and the producer cannot meet the terms of loan through its own production, the company would be forced to default or to buy gold on the market to repay the loan.

Gold loans provide a means for central banks to earn a small rate of return on their gold stocks. Typically, central banks lend gold to commercial banks for short periods of time (usually three to six months) at relatively low interest rates. The commercial banks then turn around and relend the gold to producers. In essence, commercial banks utilize gold in the same way they do money: borrow at low rates and relend at higher rates.

Since producers generally sell the gold they borrow, gold loans have the effect of bringing future production onto the market today. Thus, whenever there is a flurry of gold loan activity, gold prices usually drop. Indeed, gold loan activity generally increases when producers feel there's a substantial downside risk on the price of gold.

Because gold loans only became a significant part of the gold market in the late 1980s, it's difficult to foresee how they will effect the market as they come due. Clearly, since producers will be repaying banks with their production and not selling gold onto the market, the repayments should be bullish for gold prices. On the other hand, the banks that have become active in the gold loan market may continue to lend gold on a regular basis and thus offset the supply reduction caused by repayments.

Table 5.1   Gold Supply to the Non-Communist Private Sector
                  (in tons)

	Non-Communist World Mine Production	Net Communist Sales (purchases)	Net Official Sales (purchases)	Old Gold Scrap	Total
1950	755	n/a	(288)	n/a	467
1951	733	n/a	(235)	n/a	498
1952	755	n/a	(205)	n/a	550
1953	755	67	(404)	n/a	418
1954	795	67	(595)	n/a	267
1955	835	67	(591)	n/a	311
1956	871	133	(435)	n/a	569
1957	906	231	(614)	n/a	523
1958	933	196	(605)	n/a	524
1959	1000	266	(671)	n/a	595
1960	1049	177	(262)	n/a	964
1961	1080	266	(538)	n/a	808
1962	1155	178	(329)	n/a	1004
1963	1204	489	(729)	n/a	964
1964	1249	400	(631)	n/a	1018
1965	1280	355	(196)	n/a	1439
1966	1285	(67)	40	n/a	1258
1967	1250	(5)	1404	n/a	2649
1968	1245	(29)	620	n/a	1836
1969	1252	(15)	(90)	n/a	1147
1970	1273	(3)	(236)	n/a	1034
1971	1233	54	96	n/a	1383
1972	1177	213	(151)	n/a	1239
1973	1111	275	6	n/a	1392
1974	996	220	20	n/a	1236
1975	946	149	9	n/a	1104
1976	964	412	58	n/a	1434
1977	962	401	269	n/a	1632
1978	972	410	362	n/a	1744
1979	959	199	544	n/a	1702
1980	959	90	(230)	488	1307

*n/a = not available

Table 5.1   (Continued)

	Non-Communist World Mine Production	Net Communist Sales (purchases)	Net Official Sales (purchases)	Old Gold Scrap	Total
1981	981	280	(276)	239	1224
1982	1028	203	(85)	243	1389
1983	1114	93	142	294	1643
1984	1162	205	85	291	1742
1985	1233	210	(132)	304	1615
1986	1293	402	(145)	474	2024
1987	1382	303	(72)	408	2021
1988	1538	258	(270)	324	1850

*n/a = not available

Since 1974, official sales include activities of government-controlled investment and monetary agencies in addition to central banks.

Source: Consolidated Gold Fields PLC, Gold 1989

Table 5.2 Mine Production in the Noncommunist World (in tons)

	1980	1981	1982	1983	1984	1985	1986	1987	1988
Africa									
South Africa	675.1	657.6	664.3	679.7	683.3	671.7	640.0	607.0	621.0
Zimbabwe	11.4	11.6	13.4	14.1	14.5	14.7	14.9	14.7	14.8
Zaire	3.0	3.2	4.2	6.0	10.0	8.0	8.0	12.0	12.5
Ghana	10.8	13.0	13.0	11.8	11.6	12.0	11.5	11.7	12.1
Other	8.0	12.0	15.0	15.0	15.0	17.0	18.2	25.0	27.5
Total Africa	708.3	697.4	709.9	726.6	734.4	723.4	692.6	670.4	687.9
North America									
U.S.	30.5	44.0	45.3	62.6	66.0	79.5	118.3	154.9	205.3
Canada	51.6	53.0	66.5	73.0	86.0	90.0	105.7	116.5	128.5
Total North America	82.1	97.0	111.8	135.6	152.0	169.5	224.0	271.4	333.8
Latin America									
Brazil	35.0	35.0	34.8	58.7	61.5	72.3	67.4	83.8	100.2
Colombia	17.0	17.7	15.5	17.7	21.2	26.4	27.1	32.5	33.4
Chile	6.5	12.2	18.9	19.0	18.0	18.2	18.9	20.0	22.7
Venezuela	1.0	1.5	2.0	6.0	9.5	12.0	15.0	16.0	16.0
Mexico	5.9	5.0	5.2	7.4	7.6	8.0	8.3	9.0	10.7
Peru	5.0	7.2	6.9	9.9	10.5	10.9	10.9	10.8	10.0
Bolivia	2.0	2.5	2.5	4.0	4.0	6.0	6.0	6.0	9.0
Dominican Republic	11.5	12.8	11.8	10.8	10.6	10.4	9.1	7.9	7.8
Other	4.8	6.0	6.7	6.5	7.0	9.5	13.0	15.1	16.1
Total Latin America	88.7	99.9	104.3	140.0	149.9	173.7	175.7	201.1	225.9

Table 5.2   (Continued)

	1980	1981	1982	1983	1984	1985	1986	1987	1988
Australasia									
Australia	17.0	18.4	27.0	30.6	39.1	58.5	75.1	110.7	152.0
Papua New Guinea	14.3	17.2	17.8	18.4	18.7	31.3	36.1	33.9	32.6
Other	1.0	1.1	1.2	1.8	1.8	2.8	4.0	4.5	6.2
Total Australasia	32.3	36.7	46.0	50.8	59.6	92.6	115.2	149.1	190.8
The Far East									
Philippines	22.0	24.9	31.0	33.3	34.3	36.9	38.7	39.5	42.7
Japan	6.7	5.8	5.6	5.9	7.0	9.0	14.0	13.6	14.4
Other	4.5	4.6	5.2	5.3	7.4	9.6	14.9	18.7	20.4
Total Far East	33.2	35.3	41.8	44.5	48.7	55.5	67.6	71.8	77.5
India									
India	2.6	2.6	2.2	2.2	2.0	1.7	2.1	1.6	1.8
Saudi Arabia									
Saudi Arabia	0.0	0.0	0.0	0.0	0.0	0.0	0.0	0.0	1.7

Source: Consolidated Gold Fields PLC: Gold 1989

Table 5.3 Supply of Scrap (in tons)

	1980	1981	1982	1983	1984	1985	1986	1987	1988
Middle East									
Egypt	22.0	9.0	7.0	5.5	6.0	21.5	32.3	31.2	33.8
Saudi Arabia and Yemen	6.0	3.0	8.0	20.0	9.5	19.4	99.0	72.3	23.4
Turkey	28.0	45.0	23.0	0.0	33.0	40.0	40.0	11.0	17.0
Kuwait	7.0	5.5	2.0	1.5	2.0	3.0	13.8	18.6	14.1
Iraq, Syria, and Jordan	11.0	7.7	0.0	2.3	5.0	15.0	12.5	12.5	13.0
Lebanon	3.0	0.0	0.0	0.0	0.6	3.0	13.8	18.6	14.1
Arabian Gulf States	6.6	1.5	1.8	6.4	6.9	6.6	6.9	1.4	1.2
Iran	85.0	3.0	0.0	0.0	0.0	0.0	24.0	7.0	1.0
Israel	1.0	1.0	0.0	1.0	0.7	1.0	0.7	0.5	0.5
Total Middle East	169.6	75.7	41.8	36.7	63.7	109.5	232.8	158.1	107.0
Indian Subcontinent									
India	59.0	35.0	47.5	50.8	50.0	50.0	57.5	60.0	52.0
Pakistan and Afghanistan	2.5	2.5	3.5	3.0	5.0	3.0	9.0	11.0	9.0
Bangladesh and Nepal 1.0	2.0	2.5	2.5	3.0	2.0	1.5	1.5	1.5	
Sri Lanka	0.5	0.0	0.0	0.0	0.0	0.0	1.0	0.5	0.6
Total Indian Subcontinent	63.0	39.5	53.5	56.3	58.0	55.0	69.0	73.0	63.1
North America									
U.S.	70.9	49.0	43.9	39.8	38.0	37.7	39.8	51.7	47.4
Canada	4.9	4.5	4.2	4.0	4.1	4.1	4.6	4.9	4.7
Total North America	75.8	53.5	48.1	43.8	42.1	41.8	44.4	56.6	52.1

Table 5.3   (Continued)

	1980	1981	1982	1983	1984	1985	1986	1987	1988
Far East									
S. Korea	0.0	0.5	0.8	1.8	0.1	0.0	5.4	7.0	9.0
Indonesia	70.0	10.0	5.0	30.5	5.0	5.0	39.6	17.0	6.0
Taiwan	1.0	0.0	1.0	5.0	3.0	3.0	4.0	5.0	5.0
Hong Kong	7.0	2.0	0.0	0.0	5.0	0.0	2.5	2.0	4.0
Thailand	1.0	2.0	2.0	0.0	0.0	1.5	3.5	7.0	2.0
Malaysia	2.5	2.0	2.0	2.0	2.0	1.0	2.0	2.0	2.0
Philippines	0.5	0.0	0.0	0.5	0.5	0.2	1.0	1.2	2.0
Singapore	4.0	2.0	3.0	2.5	0.6	1.5	3.0	2.0	1.0
Burma, Laos, Kampuchea	8.0	2.0	2.0	3.0	5.0	3.6	0.5	0.5	0.0
Japan	16.4	7.8	7.9	8.4	8.7	9.4	8.8	12.2	12.2
Total Far East	110.4	28.3	23.7	53.7	29.9	25.2	70.3	55.9	43.2
Europe									
Italy	18.0	7.0	10.0	10.0	13.0	15.0	8.0	8.0	6.1
Switzerland	1.9	1.7	3.0	3.5	3.5	4.5	4.0	3.8	3.5
UK, Ireland	3.0	2.3	5.0	5.0	3.5	3.0	3.5	3.7	3.5
Germany	3.5	2.5	7.5	7.0	3.9	4.0	4.0	3.5	3.0
Spain	6.8	6.8	7.0	7.5	6.0	3.5	2.3	2.0	2.5
Austria	1.0	0.5	2.0	2.2	2.2	2.2	2.3	2.4	2.3
France	0.0	0.0	2.2	3.5	3.3	2.3	2.2	2.2	2.2
Denmark	0.5	0.5	1.0	1.0	1.0	0.8	0.7	0.7	0.7
Belgium	1.4	0.9	0.9	1.5	1.4	1.2	1.3	1.0	0.6
Sweden	0.0	0.0	0.0	0.4	0.3	0.6	0.5	0.4	0.4
Yugoslavia	0.0	0.0	0.0	0.1	0.1	0.2	0.3	0.5	0.3
Portugal	0.7	0.3	0.1	0.7	0.8	0.0	0.3	0.5	0.3
Netherlands	0.1	0.1	0.1	1.9	1.3	1.1	0.2	0.3	0.3
Cyprus and Malta	0.1	0.1	0.1	0.2	0.2	0.2	0.2	0.2	0.1
Greece	0.5	0.1	0.2	0.4	0.1	0.1	0.1	0.1	0.1
Norway	0.2	0.4	0.3	0.1	0.1	0.1	0.1	0.1	0.1
Total Europe	37.7	23.2	39.4	45.0	40.7	38.8	30.0	29.4	26.0

	1980	1981	1982	1983	1984	1985	1986	1987	1988
Latin America									
Brazil	5.5	2.0	5.0	15.0	15.0	10.0	5.0	8.0	7.0
Venezuela	0.1	0.1	0.0	5.0	8.8	5.0	3.5	7.0	6.0
Argentina	5.0	6.5	16.0	23.8	17.0	5.2	5.2	4.8	4.2
Chile	0.0	0.0	0.2	1.3	2.5	1.0	1.2	2.0	2.4
Mexico	0.0	0.0	1.5	2.5	3.0	3.0	1.8	0.4	1.3
Colombia	0.0	0.0	0.0	0.0	0.0	0.3	0.3	1.0	1.0
Peru	4.0	0.0	1.0	1.3	0.6	0.3	0.3	0.2	0.1
Other	3.1	0.0	1.5	0.6	0.6	1.3	1.3	1.3	3.0
Total Latin America	17.7	8.6	25.2	49.5	47.5	26.1	18.5	24.7	25.0
Africa									
Algeria	6.2	4.8	3.0	2.5	3.8	2.0	2.8	2.5	3.0
Morocco	7.3	5.0	7.6	6.0	4.6	4.0	4.0	3.0	2.5
Tunisia	0.3	0.3	0.2	0.2	0.2	0.2	0.2	0.2	0.2
Other	0.0	0.0	0.0	0.0	0.0	1.0	1.0	1.0	1.0
Total Africa	13.8	10.1	10.8	8.7	8.6	7.2	8.0	6.7	6.7
Australasia									
Australasia	0.0	0.0	0.0	0.0	0.0	0.0	0.7	0.6	0.4
Total	488.0	238.9	242.5	293.7	290.5	303.6	473.7	405.0	323.5

Source: Consolidated Gold Fields PLC: Gold 1989

Table 5.4   Major Central Bank Gold Holdings (in tons)

	1973	**1978**	**1983**	**1987**	**1988**
U.S.	8,584	8,597	8,192	8,164	8,146
Canada	683	688	627	578	541
France	3,139	3,172	2,546	2,546	2,546
Germany	3,658	3,690	2,960	2,960	2,960
Italy	2,565	2,585	2,074	2,074	2,074
Japan	657	746	754	754	754
U.K.	653	710	591	591	591
Belgium	1,312	1,325	1,063	1,047	1,047
Netherlands	1,690	1,704	1,367	1,367	1,367
Portugal	857	688	635	624	500
Spain	444	452	454	372	339
South Africa	591	305	242	194	107
Indonesia	2	7	96	97	97
Philippines	33	47	9	87	87
Thailand	73	76	77	77	77
Australia	229	242	247	247	247
Brazil	13	50	17	87	67
Mexico	144	59	72	79	83
Saudi Arabia	96	141	143	143	143

Source: Shearson Lehman Hutton: Annual Review of the World Gold Industry, 1989.

CHAPTER 6

Gold Demand

Gold, it is often said, is a demand-driven market, meaning that changes in demand usually have more of an impact on gold prices than changes in supply. Considering that yearly gold production adds only about two percent to world gold supplies, this isn't surprising. Gold supply, in aggregate, is close to being constant. Gold demand, on the other hand, is considerably more volatile.

There are two main components to gold demand: fabrication and investment. Fabrication demand originates from the use of gold in jewelry, electronics, dentistry, coins and medals. Investment demand, on the other hand, refers to the purchase of gold, usually in bar or coin form, for purposes of anticipated price appreciation, portfolio diversification, or as a hedge against economic calamity.

Oftentimes, the distinction between fabrication and investment is unclear. For example, demand for gold to produce new coins is classified as fabrication demand. However, coin purchases are classified as investment demand. A similar lack of clarity exists in the jewelry market. Although demand for gold to produce jewelry obviously is a part of overall fabrication demand, purchases of jewelry sometimes are motivated by investment considerations. But despite these areas of overlap, the fabrication/investment approach is probably the best means to analyze gold demand, primarily because isolation of the investment component is essential to understanding price behavior.

In most years, fabrication demand makes up a larger component of overall gold demand than investment demand, a fact that surprises many investment professionals. When markets are stable, fabrication demand is usually two or three times as large as investment demand. When gold

71

prices rise, investment demand for gold normally picks up and assumes a larger proportion of total gold demand. However, even in rising markets, fabrication demand usually outweighs investment demand.

FABRICATION

The largest component of fabrication demand is jewelry, followed by coins and medals, electronics, and dentistry. In most years, demand for gold to produce jewelry accounts for about 60 percent of total fabrication demand. Demand for gold to produce coins and metals accounts for another 20 percent, with the remaining gold demand divided among electronics, dentistry, and other miscellaneous uses.

To a large extent, the fabrication markets for gold are decentralized, and particularly so in the case of jewelry. Virtually every major country in the world has a gold fabrication industry of some sort and virtually every country buys a substantial amount of fabricated gold. The major players include not only the industrialized countries, but also many developing nations such as India, Saudi Arabia, Egypt, Brazil and Mexico.

The decentralized nature of the fabrication industry makes analysis somewhat difficult. In each particular country, local economic conditions dictate demand for fabricated gold products. In any particular year, demand for fabricated gold might be booming in one country, while it slumps in another country. The key factors to consider are the local currency price of gold, economic growth, the general level of prosperity, and inflation.

JEWELRY

Despite variations from country to country, analysts frequently approach fabricated gold demand from the perspective of developed and developing nations. For the most part, gold analysts contend that gold jewelry demand in developed nations is driven by esthetic considerations—that is, people buy gold jewelry for its ornamental value. In the developing world, however, most analysts maintain that jewelry frequently is purchased as an investment.

The investment character of the gold jewelry market in developing nations appears to be borne out by the sometimes sharp year-to-year changes in demand. In 1980, for example, demand for gold from the jewelry sector dropped from 186 tons to a net liquidation of 150 tons in the developing world, as gold prices peaked and then began to weaken. As gold prices continued to fall in 1981, demand rebounded to 373 tons.

It should be noted, however, that some analysts dispute the conventional wisdom that jewelry demand in the developing world is motivated largely by investment considerations. Eugene J. Sherman, author of *Gold Investment Theory and Application*, maintains there is little difference between gold jewelry demand in developed and developing nations:

> The evidence suggests that karat jewelry demand is well defined and stable, both in the aggregate and when disaggregated into developed and less developed countries. Demand shifted upwards in 1977 becoming more inelastic. However, the increased inelasticity for aggregate karat jewelry demand originated in the less developed countries. Demand price elasticity did not appreciably change in the developed countries. The evidence suggests that karat jewelry demands are basically similar as between the developed and less developed countries, although the demand-price elasticities are different. The evidence does not support the conventional wisdom which holds that karat jewelry demands are substantially different between developed and less developed countries.

Mr. Sherman's arguments notwithstanding, most analysts maintain there are substantial differences between the quality of gold jewelry demand in the developed and developing world. The principal difference, these analysts say, is the greater inclination of gold jewelry owners in the developing world to sell their gold in response to higher gold prices or economic difficulties. In the Middle East, for example, the weak crude oil market in the late 1980s motivated a good deal of gold jewelry selling.

Moreover, in many developing nations, there is a long tradition of buying and selling jewelry of all kinds. Consequently, holders of gold jewelry in these countries are much more active in the trading markets than their counterparts in the West. Thus, even if broad statistical measures do not indicate a significant difference between gold jewelry demand in the developed and developing world, there appears to be little question that there is a stronger focus on the economic utility of gold jewelry in the developing world, analysts maintain.

Prior to the 1980s, it was generally assumed that demand for gold jewelry was positively correlated with economic growth and consumer prosperity. Very simply, as people become wealthier, they have more money available to purchase ornamental items, like gold jewelry. In the 1980s, however, that relationship broke down somewhat, primarily because jewelry manufacturers, particularly in the U.S., began to produce jewelry with lower purities and lower amounts of gold.

In the way of background, it should be understood that gold jewelry is measured in karats. A karat is a unit of fineness for gold equal to ½4th proportion of pure gold. Pure gold is described as 24 karat. In many countries, jewelry must meet strict purity levels in order for it to be called gold. For example, in Saudi Arabia, gold jewelry must be at least 18 karat. In the U.S., where 10 karat qualifies as real gold—the bulk of gold jewelry is in the 10-14 karat range.

In 1980, after gold hit its historic high, demand for gold jewelry plunged as consumers balked at the higher prices. As a result, jewelry manufacturers reduced the amount of gold in jewelry in order to make it more affordable. In some cases, manufacturers began to use hollow gold tubing and wiring in necklaces and bracelets. In other instances, they simply reduced the purity of gold. The end result was that when gold jewelry demand began to pick up again in 1982 and 1983, the amount of gold used to make the jewelry was considerably less than in the 1970s.

OFFICIAL COINS

The fabrication of gold into coins has been a fascinating part of the gold market for centuries. The first important coin was the aureus, which was issued in Rome around the time of Julius Caesar. In 1284, Venice issued the ducat, a coin that remained popular throughout the Middle Ages and the Renaissance. And in 1343, England issued its first gold coin, the florin, and followed that with the issuance of the angel, crown, and guinea.

Gold coins, of course, directly reflect the inclination on the part of people in different cultures and at different times to view gold as a store of value. Indeed, that inclination was the foundation that allowed trade to flourish between ancient Rome and the East. Wealthy Romans exchanged their gold coins for silks and spices from Eastern traders. From that beginning, the use of gold as a money became more widespread in the centuries that followed.

In recent years, there has been a resurgence in the production of gold coins by sovereign governments. Unlike in Julius Caesar's time, governments are not attempting to create a means of exchange, rather they are seeking to enlarge export earnings and to commemorate some aspect of their nation.

To a great extent, the modern interest in gold coins stemmed from the huge success of the South African Krugerrand in the late 1970s. In 1978, South Africa sold 187 tons of gold coins, the highest amount ever recorded by any country in a single year. Since then, the U.S., Canada, the U.K., Japan, China, and Australia have introduced their own gold coins.

A critical element of any gold coin is its degree of purity. In recent years, Far Eastern investors have demonstrated a preference for high purity coins, such as the 99.99-percent pure Canadian Maple Leaf and the Australian Golden Nugget coins. As a result, demand for the 91.67-percent pure American Eagle coin has been disappointing.

For the most part, individuals buy coins for the value of the gold or because they believe the coin will appreciate in value on its own. Coins that have a collector appeal are called numismatic coins. Coins that are valued principally for their gold content are called bullion coins. As would be expected, the price of numismatic coins generally reflects a premium above their gold content.

For years, small investors found it difficult to buy gold coins because most coins were one ounce in size and dealers frequently accepted orders of only more than 10 coins. However, in recent years, coin producers have begun to issue coins of ½, ¼, ⅒, and even 1⁄20 of an ounce. Moreover, dealers have begun marketing to small-sized retail customers. In a sense, gold coins have become a mass market item.

As mentioned earlier, demand for coins is classified as investment demand, while demand for gold to produce new coins is classified as fabrication demand. In recent years, demand for gold to produce new coins has been extremely volatile. After a surge in the late 1970s, demand for gold to produce Krugerrands dropped markedly in the early 1980s. In addition, gold coin production tailed off in Mexico and the United

Kingdom. As a result, the aggregate gold demand for coin production purposes dropped from 245 tons in 1980 to 108 tons in 1985.

In the following year, however, demand for gold to produce coins jumped nearly threefold to 317 tons, primarily due to the Emperor Hirohito coin issuance in Japan and the American Eagle coin issuance in the U.S. The huge jump in demand was sufficient to prop up the average price of gold in 1986 from $317.22 per ounce to $368.02 per ounce.

Since demand for gold to produce new coins is often driven by nonmarket factors, that is, the inclination of governments to issue the coins, it's very difficult to forecast over the long term. Over the short term, however, it's somewhat easier, since whenever a country decides to produce a new coin, it usually announces the fact to the world. Thus, a gold trader can at least anticipate that a sovereign government will be in the market to obtain gold and can factor it into his overall analysis.

MEDALLIONS AND IMITATION COINS

As the amount of official coin issuances has increased substantially in recent years, the production of gold medallions and decorative coins has declined. In the early 1980s, a number of Middle East oil producing states were very active in this sector of the gold market. However, with the drop in oil prices in the mid-to-late 1980s, production from the Middle East diminished.

In 1987, the medallion sector received a boost with the production of the gettono in Italy. Overall, however, this appears to be one of the most depressed sectors of the gold market.

ELECTRONICS

Gold is used in electronic equipment such as connectors, switches, and relays because of its superior corrosion-resistance and high-conductivity qualities. Due to its high cost relative to other metals, the use of gold in electronics is concentrated in high-technology defense and aerospace products, although it is also used in small amounts in a wide variety of consumer products.

The largest manufacturers of electronic products that utilize gold are the U.S. and Japan, which together account for about 70 percent of the market. In recent years, the rising industrial powers in the Far East—Taiwan, Hong Kong, and South Korea—have cut into the dominance of the U.S. and Japan, particularly in the consumer product sector.

Demand for gold from the industrial sector is partially a function of economic growth. In 1982, when the world economy was suffering through a sharp downturn, the electronics industry consumed 89 tons of gold, down from 94 tons in 1979. After the world economy began to grow again, demand for gold from the electronics industry rebounded, reaching 124 tons in 1986.

As was the case with gold jewelry, the increase in gold prices in 1980 led electronic product producers to reduce the amount of gold in their products. Technological advances allowed producers to reduce the thickness of gold plating and to substitute other metals such as palladium-nickel alloys or lead-tin solders for gold. In addition, the miniaturization of many electronic products further decreased the use of gold.

The reduction in gold use in electronic products has an ancillary effect: it makes the recovery of gold scrap from obsolete products less profitable. As more and more electronic products are produced with only marginal amounts of gold, this could become a significant factor in the gold market. At some point in the future, the market may require a significant jump in the price of gold in order to make scrap recovery profitable. For the time being, however, it would appear that the decrease in the use of gold in electronic equipment will be offset by the decline in available scrap supplies.

DENTISTRY

The use of gold in dentistry has been in a state of gradual decline since the 1970s. At its peak, about 90 tons per year of gold was used by dentists. In recent years, the figure has fallen to around 50 tons.

As in other applications, gold in dentistry has suffered from the substitution of other materials, chiefly palladium-based alloys and natural-looking, ceramic-based materials. Although the substitutes do not match gold's performance characteristics in every respect, there's little doubt that the overall trend is toward the substitutes.

In addition, the use of gold in dentistry may suffer because of the improvement in preventative dental care throughout the industrialized world.

INVESTMENT

Investment demand is considerably more volatile than demand for fabricated gold. Indeed, in the view of most analysts, investment demand is the key component in determining the movement of gold prices, although it usually constitutes less than 25 percent of total demand.

Investors purchase gold in the form of bars and coins. Bars range in size from half-ounce wafers to 400-ounce bars. The 100 ounce bar is the common physical trading unit in the professional gold market. Coins, as mentioned earlier, come in sizes of one ounce and less, and are generally the province of the retail market.

Strictly speaking, the amount of investment demand in any single year can be calculated by subtracting demand by jewelry makers and other fabricators from total supply, after adjustment is made for official government sales or purchases. If this calculation leads to a large surplus, then it can be assumed that the investment sector that year was forced to absorb a large amount of gold. In most cases, that would indicate a weak gold market. A small surplus, on the other hand, indicates that investors had to bid for limited supplies. In all likelihood, that would signify a strong market and rising prices.

Thus, to a great extent, the direction of gold prices is determined by the size of the investment surplus and the strength of investor demand. A small surplus and strong demand obviously tends to drive gold prices higher. A large surplus and weak demand tends to push prices down.

One of the most intriguing aspects of the gold market is how investor demand for gold responds to changes in price. When the price of a conventional commodity rises substantially, demand normally declines as users of the commodity cut back consumption and substitute cheaper materials. Indeed, this was precisely the response of gold jewelry makers, electronic producers, and the dentistry industry to the increase in gold prices in 1979-80.

Gold investment demand, however, tends to follow the opposite course: as prices increase, demand also increases. In the years of large price increases—1973, 1974, 1979, and 1980—investment demand for gold surged far above average yearly levels. Apparently, as a bull market in gold develops, investors of all sorts begin to buy gold, driving prices still higher. Moreover, those investors who owned gold before the bull market ensued, tend to hold onto their gold until it becomes clear that the bull market is over. In other words, they do not sell immediately in response to higher prices; they wait until after the market tops out. Conceivably investor behavior could change as more and more investors recognize their past mistakes, however, history clearly shows that investors tend to buy gold when prices are rising and sell after prices have declined a good bit.

A number of factors determine the degree of investor interest in gold: the price of gold, real interest rates, inflation, economic growth, currency values, international political tensions, the stability of the economic environment, and the rates of return on alternative investments. At any one time, one or more of these factors may be most important to investors. Just as with any commodity, the market perception of the various factors impacting price is in a state of constant change.

In the 1979-80 gold price rally, it was clear that inflation was the major force driving investor demand for gold. In 1977, the U.S. Consumer Price Index (CPI) bottomed at around five percent. Then, over the next three years, the CPI marched steadily upward before topping out in 1980 at around 14.5 percent. The inflationary surge was fueled by crude oil prices which over the same period of time rose from $11.50 per barrel to $32.50 per barrel.

At the same time that inflation was rising to levels never before seen by most investors, real interest rates (that is, interest rates minus inflation) showed negative returns, a phenomena that had been common throughout the mid-to-late 1970s. During that period in the 1970s, many investors suffered a loss in their real assets as a result of the negative real interest rates. Consequently, as inflation continued to surge in 1979-80, auguring for even poorer returns on fixed-income instruments, investors were naturally inclined to seek alternative investments. Gold, because it was viewed as the ultimate inflation hedge, was the primary beneficiary.

Other factors that contributed to investor demand for gold in 1979!80 were the weak value of the dollar, political tensions in the Mideast, and perhaps a lack of confidence in President Jimmy Carter. The gold price spiral finally ended after American hostages were released from Teheran and Ronald Reagan assumed the office of the presidency.

In 1981, when gold prices fell from over $600 to slightly under $400, many of the factors that led to the price surge in 1979-80 moved in the opposite direction. The Consumer Price Index, for example, dropped from a 12 percent annual rate at the beginning to the year to around 9 percent by year's end, despite the fact that crude oil prices continued to rise. Real rates of return on short-term interest rate instruments remained positive for the entire year, the first time that had happened since the early 1970s. And the U.S. dollar, after falling since the mid-1970s, strengthened substantially. In short, the inflationary bubble had burst, interest rates were once again attractive, and the political and economic environment had stabilized. Investors moved out of gold and into other instruments.

In the late 1980s, gold prices suffered from the perception of investors that the Federal Reserve Board would continue to maintain a tight monetary policy in order to prevent an acceleration of inflation. In addition, the relatively high degree of economic cooperation achieved between the major industrial powers in the late 1980s fostered an environment of economic stability. Consequently, most professional investors and money managers saw little reason to buy gold.

In assessing investor demand for gold, one should always compare the attractiveness of gold versus other available instruments. Essentially, investment demand for gold rises when investor interest in other instruments wanes. When real interest rates are close to negative and when the stock market is weak, money is likely to move into gold. Conversely, when other instruments show positive real returns, investor interest in gold will be minimal. In those circumstance, gold is burdened by its most salient weakness as an investment: it produces neither interest nor dividends.

Table 6.1   Popular Bullion Coins in Issue in 1989

Coin	Country of Origin	Fineness (percent)	Weight (ounces)
Krugerrand	South Africa	91.67	.1, .25, .50, 1
Sovereign	U.K.	91.67	.2354
Maple Leaf	Canada	99.99	.1, .25, .50, 1
American Eagle	U.S.	91.67	.1, .25, .50, 1
Golden Nugget	Australia	99.99	.1, .25, .50, 1
Sunshine Golden Eagle	U.S.	99.99	.1, .25, .50, 1
Britannia	U.K.	91.67	.1, .25, .50, 1
Chinese Panda	China	99.9	.05, .1, .25, .50, 1

Table 6.2   Gold Fabrication in Non-Communist Countries
(including the use of scrap) (in tons)

	1980	1981	1982	1983	1984	1985	1986	1987	1988
Far East									
Taiwan	3.3	17.7	7.4	11.8	33.4	31.6	24.8	49.8	92.9
S. Korea	2.1	7.2	9.8	8.0	10.1	10.5	17.0	35.4	78.8
Hong Kong	10.0	17.0	16.0	11.0	30.0	20.0	21.0	28.0	75.0
Indonesia	15.0	25.0	28.0	20.5	50.0	40.0	28.0	29.1	48.0
Thailand	0.0	5.0	5.1	2.1	8.4	14.0	11.0	20.5	31.2
Singapore	3.5	8.5	20.5	19.8	25.0	18.4	13.2	12.2	21.0
Malaysia	3.0	6.0	8.0	6.6	11.6	9.9	7.9	8.0	11.5
Vietnam	0.0	0.0	0.0	0.0	0.0	0.0	0.0	0.0	4.0
Philippines	1.0	2.0	2.6	3.5	1.7	1.5	1.0	1.5	2.0
Burma, Laos, Kampuchea	0.0	0.0	0.0	0.0	0.0	0.0	0.0	0.0	0.0
Japan	73.3	93.7	95.1	103.4	129.0	131.1	342.5	175.3	173.6
Total Far East	111.2	182.1	192.5	186.7	299.2	277.0	466.4	359.8	539.0
Europe									
Italy	116.9	180.9	237.2	180.3	228.6	261.6	246.9	232.8	273.7
Germany	74.8	67.1	65.6	61.4	61.2	62.3	59.5	62.5	72.1
UK, Ireland	37.4	35.4	33.1	24	25.1	30.0	29.6	37.0	37.9
Switzerland	26.9	26.1	26.1	24.3	27.2	29.2	30.0	31.3	37.2
France	23.7	22.6	25.7	24.0	22.6	23.4	26	26.7	28.8
Spain	19.3	18.3	17.1	14.6	13.8	16.7	16.7	18.1	24.1
Yugoslavia	8.2	8.0	7.9	9.6	8.5	8.5	8.5	8.7	8.5
Greece	4.7	6.2	7.0	8.0	9.2	10.6	9.1	8.3	8.4
Austria	2.6	3.6	6.7	8.0	6.6	6.7	7.9	6.5	6.5
Portugal	2.2	2.6	3.1	3.3	2.5	2.4	2.6	4.8	5.1
Netherlands	3.1	4.0	3.8	3.7	4.2	4.9	4.8	4.0	4.1
Belgium	3.5	2.6	2.6	2.3	2.2	2.3	2.0	16.4	2.2
Cyprus and Malta	0.5	0.6	0.8	1.0	1.3	1.5	1.7	1.8	2.0
Sweden	1.5	1.3	1.6	1.8	1.6	1.8	1.8	1.8	1.9

	1980	1981	1982	1983	1984	1985	1986	1987	1988
Finland	0.6	0.9	0.8	0.8	0.7	0.7	0.8	0.9	1.0
Denmark	0.4	0.4	0.8	0.7	0.8	0.8	0.9	0.9	0.9
Norway	0.8	0.5	0.6	0.6	0.6	0.7	0.8	0.8	0.9
Total Europe	327.1	381.1	440.5	368.4	416.7	464.1	449.6	463.3	515.3

North America

	1980	1981	1982	1983	1984	1985	1986	1987	1988
U.S.	150.1	149.2	145.6	172.2	181.8	159.9	223.8	236.1	203.8
Canada	60.1	31.3	38.8	45.4	44.2	71.2	60.6	55.8	46.2
Total North America	210.2	180.5	184.4	217.6	226.0	231.1	284.4	291.9	250.0

Middle East

	1980	1981	1982	1983	1984	1985	1986	1987	1988
Turkey	11.7	31.8	11.1	27.4	36.6	76.2	96.7	90.0	74.7
Saudi Arabia and Yemen	10.0	33.0	39.0	36.0	65.5	51.6	47.5	49.0	62.0
Kuwait	8.0	28.5	33.0	17.5	21.0	12.0	16.3	16.3	19.4
Egypt	17.0	33.0	37.0	38.5	52.0	30.0	27.3	29.2	33.8
Arabian Gulf States	9.6	20.7	23.0	24.1	31.5	25.9	10.8	198.7	14.9
Israel	5.8	7.6	6.5	8.9	10.2	12.4	12.0	10.5	10.7
Iraq, Syria, Jordan	6.5	37.5	31.8	18.6	19.5	15.0	11.5	11.5	10.0
Iran	0.0	0.0	0.0	3.0	0.0	0.0	0.0	0.0	2.0
Lebanon	2.0	3.0	2.0	2.0	1.0	2.0	1.0	1.0	1.0
Total Middle East	70.6	195.1	184.4	176.0	237.3	225.1	223.1	216.2	228.5

Indian Subcontinent

	1980	1981	1982	1983	1984	1985	1986	1987	1988
India	50.7	61.1	108.3	104.6	145.2	174.3	146.8	159.9	187.9
Pakistan, Afghanistan	0.0	8.5	12.5	11.0	18.0	18.0	25.0	26.0	28.0
Bangladesh, Nepal	0.0	4.0	5.5	5.5	7.0	7.0	3.0	3.0	4.5
Sri Lanka	0.0	1.0	1.0	1.0	1.0	1.5	2.0	2.0	3.0
Total Indian Subcontinent	50.7	74.6	127.3	122.1	171.2	200.8	176.8	190.9	223.4

Table 6.2   (Continued)

	1980	1981	1982	1983	1984	1985	1986	1987	1988
Africa									
Morocco	7.3	9.0	7.6	6.0	7.6	9.0	10.0	10.7	15.5
South Africa	100.7	104.8	83.2	112.5	84.9	26.2	5.5	6.5	12.4
Algeria	9.4	7.1	5.5	5.2	6.1	4.4	5.5	5.0	6.0
Libya	1.0	1.6	1.6	2.0	1.0	1.0	1.0	1.0	4.0
Tunisia	0.9	0.8	0.7	0.6	0.5	0.5	0.5	0.5	1.0
Other	0.0	3.0	2.1	3.0	2.0	2.0	3.0	3.0	4.0
Total Africa	119.3	126.3	100.7	129.3	102.1	43.1	25.5	26.7	42.9
Latin America									
Mexico	23.1	45.9	12.2	5.0	10.5	18.5	19.0	8.7	13.2
Brazil	21.5	18.4	19.5	9.0	6.1	12.6	24.1	12.0	7.5
Peru	0.1	0.6	1.1	1.7	3.1	2.4	4.4	3.1	3.1
Colombia	0.5	0.8	1.0	2.1	0.1	0.4	0.4	2.5	2.5
Venezuela	1.9	2.6	2.6	1.1	0.9	1.1	1.6	1.7	1.1
Argentina	1.1	1.8	1.8	2.3	2.1	1.1	0.8	0.9	1.1
Chile	1.3	0.5	0.2	1.3	1.0	1.0	1.2	0.5	0.5
Other	0.1	1.5	3.3	2.3	2.2	2.0	2.0	2.0	2.0
Total Latin America	49.6	72.1	41.7	24.8	26.0	39.1	53.5	31.4	31.0
Australasia									
Australasia	6.3	6.1	7.2	6.2	4.0	4.5	6.5	16.1	13.5
Total	945.0	1217.9	1278.7	1231.1	1482.5	1484.8	1685.8	1596.3	1843.6

Source: Consolidated Gold Fields PLC: Gold 1989

Table 6.3 Gold Fabrication in Developed and Developing
Countries (in tons)

	1980	1981	1982	1983	1984	1985	1986	1987	1988
Developed Countries									
Jewelry	316.9	400.1	479.3	429.2	488.9	550.6	564.5	561.1	643.7
Electronics	93.5	91.5	87.3	104.8	128.2	111.6	119.8	118.5	127.0
Dentistry	62.5	63.7	59.1	50.0	51.0	51.5	49.2	45.2	47.5
Other Industrial	57.5	57.8	54.0	49.5	52.2	49.2	51.1	51.7	53.1
Medals and Imitation Coins	18.1	12.4	5.8	22.3	15.7	3.4	4.2	6.7	7.7
Official Coins	169.7	141.5	123.6	152.2	124.3	91.0	300.9	170.3	86.1
Subtotal	718.2	767	809.1	808.0	860.3	857.3	1089.7	953.5	965.1
Developing Countries									
Jewelry	195.9	379.0	439.7	395.1	580.9	593.4	551.8	590.7	839.8
Electronics	1.8	1.4	1.6	1.7	2.3	2.9	4.2	6.1	6.9
Dentistry	1.8	1.5	1.5	0.9	1.2	1.6	1.6	3.0	2.8
Other Industrial	4.2	4.3	3.9	3.2	3.3	5.2	5.3	4.5	5.8
Medals and Imitation Coins	2.6	14.9	15.9	9.3	28.3	10.9	7.5	8.4	7.6
Official Coins	20.5	49.8	7.0	12.9	6.2	13.5	25.7	30.1	15.6
Subtotal	226.8	450.9	469.6	423.1	622.2	627.5	596.1	642.8	878.5
Total	945.0	1217.9	1278.7	1231.1	1482.5	1484.8	1685.8	1596.3	1843.6

Source: Consolidated Gold Fields: Gold 1989.

Table 6.4   Gold Fabrication in Carat Jewelry (tons)

	1980	1981	1982	1983	1984	1985	1986	1987	1988
Far East									
Taiwan	3.0	8.0	7.0	11.0	33.0	31.0	24.2	48.3	90.0
Hong Kong	10.0	17.0	16.0	11.0	30.0	10.0	21.0	28.0	75.0
South Korea	1.0	6.0	8.5	6.3	7.5	6.7	13.2	16.2	65.0
Indonesia	15.0	25.0	28.0	20.5	50.0	40.0	28.0	29.1	48.0
Thailand	0.0	5.0	5.0	2.0	8.3	14.0	11.0	20.0	31.0
Singapore	3.0	8.0	20.0	18.5	23.4	17.5	11.0	10.1	19.0
Malaysia	3.0	6.0	8.0	6.6	11.6	9.9	7.9	8.0	11.5
Vietnam	0.0	0.0	0.0	0.0	0.0	0.0	0.0	0.0	4.0
Philippines	1.0	2.0	2.6	3.5	1.7	1.5	1.0	1.5	2.0
Burma, Laos, Kampuchea	0.0	0.0	0.0	0.0	0.0	0.0	0.0	0.0	0.0
Japan	28.6	39.0	42.9	43.4	50.2	60.7	80.7	84.0	95.0
Total Far East	64.6	116.0	138.0	122.8	215.7	201.3	198.0	245.2	441.5
Europe									
Italy	107.0	171.0	228.0	172.0	220.0	253.0	238.0	222.0	262.0
Germany	32.0	30.5	32.5	33.0	33.0	34.1	35.0	39.2	45.1
Switzerland	14.7	14.8	15.8	14.9	17.8	20.4	20.3	18.6	25.3
Spain	18.0	17.1	15.8	13.4	12.6	15.7	15.6	17.0	23.0
France	13.0	14.9	18.8	17.4	16.7	17.6	19.9	20.4	22.3
UK, Ireland	9.3	11.7	12.6	11.4	12.8	14.8	15.8	17.5	21.1
Greece	4.5	5.6	6.7	7.0	9.1	10.5	9.0	8.2	8.3
Yugoslavia	5.9	5.9	6.2	6.2	5.8	6.1	6.1	6.5	6.5
Portugal	2.1	2.5	3.0	3.2	2.4	2.3	2.5	4.7	5.1
Austria	1.6	1.4	3.3	3.9	3.6	3.9	4.2	4.3	4.4
Cyprus and Malta	0.5	0.6	0.8	1.0	1.3	1.5	1.7	1.8	2.0
Belgium	2.9	2.2	2.1	2.0	1.9	1.9	1.7	1.6	1.8
Sweden	1.0	0.9	1.2	1.2	1.2	1.2	1.3	1.3	1.4
Netherlands	0.6	0.5	0.8	0.8	0.8	0.8	0.9	1.0	1.0

	1980	1981	1982	1983	1984	1985	1986	1987	1988
Finland	0.6	0.9	0.8	0.8	0.7	0.7	0.8	0.9	1.0
Denmark	0.3	0.3	0.7	0.7	0.8	0.8	0.9	0.9	0.9
Norway	0.7	0.4	0.5	0.5	0.5	0.6	0.7	0.7	0.8
Total Europe	214.7	281.2	349.6	290.3	341.0	385.9	374.4	366.6	432.0

Indian Subcontinent

	1980	1981	1982	1983	1984	1985	1986	1987	1988
India	50.0	60.4	107.5	103.8	144.5	173.4	145.9	159.2	187.0
Pakistan and Afghanistan	0.0	8.5	12.5	11.0	18.0	18.0	25.0	26.0	28.0
Bangladesh and Nepal	0.0	4.0	5.5	5.5	7.0	7.0	3.0	3.0	4.5
Sri Lanka	0.0	1.0	1.0	1.0	1.0	1.5	2.0	2.0	3.0
Total Indian Subcontinent	50.0	73.9	126.5	121.3	170.5	199.9	175.9	190.2	222.5

Middle East

	1980	1981	1982	1983	1984	1985	1986	1987	1988
Turkey	10.0	30.0	10.5	16.5	36.5	75.4	84.4	72.4	64.9
Saudi Arabia and Yemen	8.0	26.0	32.0	32.0	43.5	44.0	44.0	47.0	60.0
Egypt	17.0	33.0	37.0	38.5	52.0	30.0	27.3	29.2	33.8
Kuwait	8.0	25.5	28.0	15.5	17.0	10.5	15.7	16.0	18.7
Arabian Gulf States	9.6	20.5	23.0	23.5	29.8	24.9	10.8	8.7	13.9
Israel	5.0	6.9	6.0	8.5	9.9	12.1	11.5	10.0	10.1
Iraq, Syria, Jordan	6.0	33.5	29.0	16.3	19.0	15.0	11.5	11.5	9.0
Iran	0.0	0.0	0.0	3.0	0.0	0.0	0.0	0.0	2.0
Lebanon	2.0	3.0	3.0	2.0	1.0	2.0	1.0	1.0	1.0
Total Middle East	65.6	178.4	168.5	155.8	208.7	213.9	206.2	195.8	213.4

North America

	1980	1981	1982	1983	1984	1985	1986	1987	1988
U.S.	59.1	64.5	71.6	79.8	83.9	89.0	92.9	91.4	100.6
Canada	10.2	9.2	10.2	10.4	10.6	10.8	10.3	9.7	10.1
Total North America	69.3	73.7	81.8	90.2	94.5	99.8	103.2	104.1	110.7

Table 6.4   (Continued)

	1980	1981	1982	1983	1984	1985	1986	1987	1988
Africa									
Morocco	7.3	9.0	7.6	6.0	7.6	9.0	10.0	10.7	15.5
Algeria	9.4	7.1	5.5	5.2	6.1	4.4	5.5	5.0	6.0
Libya	1.0	1.6	1.6	2.0	1.0	1.0	1.0	1.0	4.0
South Africa	1.0	1.6	1.2	1.0	1.1	0.9	1.0	2.2	2.2
Tunisia	0.9	0.8	0.7	0.6	0.5	0.5	0.5	0.5	1.0
Other	0.0	3.0	2.1	3.0	2.0	2.0	3.0	3.0	4.0
Total Africa	19.6	23.1	18.7	17.8	18.3	17.8	21.0	22.4	32.7
Latin America									
Mexico	3.0	5.0	3.7	3.2	4.4	4.8	2.7	4.9	11.9
Brazil	19.5	17.0	18.0	8.0	5.0	11.0	22.0	9.0	5.0
Peru	0.0	0.5	1.0	1.6	3.1	2.3	4.2	2.9	3.1
Colombia	0.4	0.7	0.9	2.0	0.0	0.1	0.1	2.2	2.2
Venezuela	1.7	2.4	2.0	1.0	0.8	1.0	1.5	1.0	1.0
Argentina	1.0	1.5	1.5	2.0	2.0	1.0	0.7	0.8	1.0
Chile	0.0	0.3	0.2	1.3	1.0	0.0	0.0	0.5	0.5
Other	0.1	1.5	3.3	2.3	2.2	2.0	2.0	2.0	2.0
Total Latin America	25.7	28.9	30.6	21.4	18.5	22.2	33.2	23.3	26.7
Australasia									
Australasia	3.3	3.9	5.3	4.7	2.6	3.2	4.4	4.2	4.0
Total	512.8	779.1	919.0	824.3	1069.8	1144.0	1116.3	1151.8	1483.5

Source: Consolidated Gold Fields: Gold 1989.

Table 6.5   Gold Fabrication in Electronics (tons)

	1980	1981	1982	1983	1984	1985	1986	1987	1988
Japan	27.3	31.4	31.4	40.2	53.2	46.0	52.1	47.8	51.5
U.S.	38.3	35.7	31.9	38.8	45.7	36.6	38.3	41.4	44.0
Germany	8.3	6.2	6.0	6.7	8.2	7.8	7.9	8.4	9.4
UK, Ireland	6.6	6.2	6.2	7.1	8.4	9.0	8.8	9.2	9.2
Switzerland	3.6	2.6	3.4	3.1	3.1	3.1	3.2	3.3	3.6
S. Korea	0.2	0.2	0.2	0.3	0.8	1.4	1.5	2.5	2.9
France	3.7	3.5	3.2	3.0	2.7	2.5	2.6	2.4	2.8
Netherlands	1.2	1.9	1.8	1.9	2.4	2.5	2.5	2.0	2.0
Taiwan	0.2	0.2	0.2	0.2	0.1	0.1	0.3	1.2	1.6
Singapore	0.5	0.3	0.4	0.6	0.9	0.7	1.2	1.3	1.4
Yugoslavia	0.9	0.9	0.9	1.2	1.3	1.3	1.3	1.3	1.3
Italy	2.4	1.6	1.1	1.1	1.3	1.3	1.3	0.7	1.0
Brazil	0.6	0.4	0.5	0.4	0.4	0.5	1.0	1.0	0.8
Austria	0.1	0.2	0.2	0.3	0.4	0.2	0.4	0.6	0.8
Canada	0.6	0.8	0.6	0.7	0.6	0.6	0.6	0.6	0.6
Australia	0.1	0.1	0.2	0.3	0.5	0.3	0.4	0.4	0.4
Spain	0.3	0.3	0.3	0.3	0.3	0.3	0.3	0.3	0.3
India	0.2	0.2	0.2	0.2	0.1	0.2	0.2	0.1	0.1
Israel	0.1	0.1	0.1	0.1	0.1	0.1	0.1	0.1	0.1
Mexico	0.1	0.1	0.1	0.0	0.0	0.0	0.0	0.0	0.1
Total	95.3	92.9	88.9	106.5	130.5	114.5	124.0	124.6	133.9

Source: Consolidated Gold Fields: Gold 1989.

Table 6.6   Gold Fabrication in Dentistry (in tons)

	1980	1981	1982	1983	1984	1985	1986	1987	1988
Japan	6.4	11.6	11.3	8.5	11.5	12.0	13.5	11.9	13.0
U.S.	13.8	12.3	11.3	11.1	11.4	11.6	12.0	12.2	11.7
Germany	25.2	23.0	20.0	15.5	14.0	14.0	10.4	8.5	10.6
Italy	4.0	4.8	4.8	4.6	4.6	4.4	4.4	4.4	4.5
Switzerland	4.8	4.8	3.8	3.6	3.6	3.6	3.4	3.4	3.2
South Korea	0.6	0.6	0.6	0.6	0.9	1.3	1.2	1.5	2.0
France	2.0	1.1	1.3	1.1	1.0	0.9	0.8	0.8	0.7
Netherlands	1.0	0.9	0.8	0.7	0.7	0.9	0.8	0.7	0.7
Austria	0.5	0.5	0.6	0.6	0.6	0.6	0.6	0.5	0.6
Brazil	0.5	0.4	0.4	0.0	0.1	0.1	0.1	1.0	0.5
Yugoslavia	1.1	0.9	0.8	0.7	0.7	0.7	0.7	0.5	0.5
Sweden	0.4	0.4	0.3	0.4	0.4	0.6	0.5	0.5	0.5
UK, Ireland	0.6	0.3	0.5	0.5	0.4	0.4	0.4	0.4	0.3
Canada	0.1	0.2	0.3	0.3	0.3	0.3	0.3	0.3	0.3
Spain	0.4	0.4	0.4	0.3	0.3	0.3	0.3	0.3	0.2
South Africa	1.0	1.4	1.6	1.4	0.8	0.6	0.5	0.2	0.2
Belgium	0.2	0.2	0.2	0.2	0.2	0.2	0.2	0.2	0.2
Mexico	0.3	0.2	0.2	0.0	0.0	0.0	0.0	0.2	0.1
Israel	0.5	0.4	0.3	0.2	0.1	0.1	0.1	0.1	0.1
Australia	0.3	0.3	0.6	0.1	0.2	0.1	0.1	0.1	0.1
Venezuela	0.1	0.1	0.1	0.1	0.1	0.1	0.1	0.1	0.1
Greece	0.2	0.1	0.1	0.1	0.1	0.1	0.1	0.1	0.1
Norway	0.1	0.1	0.1	0.1	0.1	0.1	0.1	0.1	0.1
Portugal	0.1	0.1	0.1	0.1	0.1	0.1	0.1	0.1	0.0
Peru	0.1	0.1	0.1	0.1	0.0	0.0	0.1	0.1	0.0
Total	64.3	65.2	60.6	50.9	52.2	53.1	50.8	48.2	50.3

Table 6.7 Gold Fabrication in Other Industrial and Decorative Applications (in tons)

	1980	1981	1982	1983	1984	1985	1986	1987	1988
U.S.	27.9	30.1	29.1	22.7	22.6	20.9	21.1	21.0	22.1
Japan	10.4	10.5	8.9	10.9	13.7	11.9	13.8	14.6	13.5
Germany	8.1	6.6	6.1	5.7	5.8	6.2	6.0	6.2	6.7
Switzerland	2.7	2.0	1.9	1.8	1.8	2.0	2.2	2.5	2.8
France	3.3	2.7	2.2	2.3	2.1	2.2	2.3	2.4	2.7
South Korea	0.3	0.4	0.5	0.8	0.9	1.1	1.1	1.5	2.0
Italy	1.2	1.4	2.0	1.9	1.9	1.9	2.0	1.5	1.7
UK, Ireland	2.3	2.3	1.9	2.0	2.2	2.0	1.6	1.4	1.5
Brazil	0.9	0.6	0.6	0.6	0.6	1.0	1.0	1.0	1.2
India	0.5	0.5	0.6	0.6	0.6	0.7	0.7	0.6	0.8
Spain	0.3	0.4	0.5	0.5	0.5	0.4	0.5	0.5	0.6
Taiwan	0.1	0.2	0.2	0.3	0.3	0.2	0.1	0.3	0.5
Turkey	0.1	0.1	0.2	0.1	0.1	0.2	0.2	0.2	0.5
Mexico	2.1	2.1	1.4	0.4	0.6	0.5	0.5	0.4	0.4
Australia	0.1	0.1	0.1	0.1	0.1	0.5	0.4	0.4	0.4
South Africa	0.2	0.3	0.4	0.3	0.3	0.3	0.3	0.3	0.3
Colombia	0.1	0.1	0.1	0.1	0.1	0.3	0.3	0.3	0.3
Netherlands	0.1	0.4	0.3	0.3	0.3	0.3	0.3	0.3	0.2
Yugoslavia	0.3	0.3	0.0	0.3	0.3	0.3	0.3	0.2	0.2
Belgium	0.1	0.1	0.1	0.1	0.1	0.1	0.1	0.2	0.2
Argentina	0.1	0.3	0.3	0.3	0.1	0.1	0.1	0.1	0.1
Austria	0.1	0.1	0.1	0.1	0.1	0.1	0.1	0.1	0.1
Canada	0.3	0.4	0.3	0.4	0.4	0.1	0.1	0.1	0.1
Chile	0.0	0.0	0.0	0.0	0.0	1.0	1.2	0.0	0.0
Peru	0.0	0.0	0.0	0.0	0.0	0.1	0.1	0.1	0.0
Sweden	0.0	0.0	0.0	0.1	0.0	0.0	0.0	0.0	0.0
Denmark	0.1	0.1	0.1	0.0	0.0	0.0	0.0	0.0	0.0
Total	61.7	62.1	57.9	52.7	55.5	54.4	56.4	56.2	58.9

Source: Consolidated Gold Fields PLC: Gold 1989.

Table 6.8   Gold Fabrication in Medals and Imitation Coins (in tons)

	1980	1981	1982	1983	1984	1985	1986	1987	1988
Italy	1.6	1.5	1.0	0.6	0.7	0.9	1.0	4.0	4.4
Saudi Arabia and Yemen	2.0	7.0	7.0	4.0	22.0	7.6	3.5	2.0	2.0
Turkey	0.0	0.0	0.4	0.1	0.0	0.1	2.6	5.4	1.6
Switzerland	0.5	1.6	0.5	0.4	0.8	0.1	0.9	0.4	1.4
Arabian Gulf States	0.0	0.2	0.0	0.6	1.7	1.0	0.0	0.0	1.0
Iraq, Syria, Jordan	0.5	4.0	2.8	2.3	0.5	0.0	0.0	0.0	1.0
Taiwan	0.0	0.0	0.0	0.3	0.0	0.3	0.0	0.0	0.8
Kuwait	0.0	3.0	5.0	2.0	4.0	1.5	0.6	0.3	0.7
Japan	0.6	1.2	0.6	0.4	0.4	0.5	0.4	0.4	0.6
Singapore	0.0	0.0	0.0	0.0	0.1	0.1	0.8	0.7	0.5
Israel	0.2	0.2	0.1	0.1	0.1	0.1	0.3	0.3	0.4
Germany	1.2	0.8	1.0	0.5	0.2	0.2	0.2	0.2	0.3
U.S.	31.2	7.6	15.6	22.0	1.7	0.1	0.1	0.1	0.3
UK, Ireland	0.4	0.4	0.5	0.1	0.1	0.2	0.2	0.2	0.2
France	1.7	0.4	0.2	0.2	0.1	0.2	0.1	0.2	0.1
Austria	0.1	0.1	0.1	0.1	0.1	0.1	0.1	0.0	0.0
Australia	0.1	0.0	0.0	0.0	0.0	0.0	0.0	0.0	0.0
Spain	0.3	0.1	0.1	0.1	0.0	0.0	0.0	0.0	0.0
Canada	0.1	0.0	0.0	0.0	0.0	0.0	0.0	0.0	0.0
Netherlands	0.1	0.1	0.0	0.0	0.0	0.0	0.0	0.0	0.0
Sweden	0.1	0.0	0.1	0.1	0.0	0.0	0.0	0.0	0.0
Chile	0.0	0.1	0.0	0.0	0.0	0.0	0.0	0.0	0.0
Belgium	0.3	0.1	0.2	0.0	0.0	0.1	0.0	0.0	0.0
Venezuela	0.1	0.1	0.5	0.0	0.0	0.0	0.0	0.0	0.0
Greece	0.0	0.5	0.2	0.0	0.0	0.0	0.0	0.0	0.0
Mexico	0.0	0.0	0.0	0.0	0.0	0.3	0.0	0.0	0.0
Total Fabrication	41.1	29.0	35.9	33.9	32.5	13.4	10.8	14.2	15.3
Total Sales	20.7	27.3	21.7	31.6	44.0	14.3	11.7	15.1	15.3

Source: Consolidated Gold Fields: Gold 1989.

Table 6.9   Gold Fabrication in Official Coins (in tons)

	1980	1981	1982	1983	1984	1985	1986	1987	1988
Canada	48.8	20.7	27.4	33.6	36.2	66.4	42.2	42.7	71.5
U.S.	0.2	0.7	0.3	5.0	9.1	0.8	57.7	65.6	24.1
South Africa	107.1	112.2	102.3	108.7	74.1	24.4	1.7	0.6	9.7
Australia	2.4	1.7	1.0	1.0	0.6	0.4	1.2	15.4	8.7
Turkey	1.6	1.7	0.0	10.7	0.0	0.5	9.5	12.0	7.7
UK, Ireland	59.0	28.4	28.7	11.3	2.0	3.4	2.8	12.7	7.0
South Korea	0.0	0.0	0.0	0.0	0.0	0.0	0.0	13.7	6.9
Switzerland	0.6	0.3	0.7	0.5	0.1	0.0	0.0	3.1	0.9
Mexico	23.0	49.5	0.0	0.0	0.0	10.1	15.8	3.2	0.7
Austria	0.2	1.3	2.4	3.0	1.8	1.8	2.5	1.0	0.6
France	0.0	0.0	0.0	0.0	0.0	0.0	0.3	0.5	0.2
Thailand	0.0	0.0	0.1	0.1	0.1	0.0	0.0	0.5	0.2
Netherlands	0.1	0.2	0.1	0.0	0.0	0.4	0.3	0.0	0.2
Italy	0.7	0.6	0.3	0.1	0.1	0.1	0.2	0.2	0.1
Singapore	0.0	0.2	0.1	0.7	0.6	0.1	0.2	0.1	0.1
Japan	0.0	0.0	0.0	0.0	0.0	0.0	182.0	16.6	0.0
Belgium	0.0	0.0	0.0	0.0	0.0	0.0	0.0	14.4	0.0
Venezuela	0.0	0.0	0.0	0.0	0.0	0.0	0.0	1.6	0.0
Yugoslavia	0.0	0.0	0.0	1.2	0.4	0.1	0.1	0.2	0.0
Taiwan	0.0	9.3	0.0	0.0	0.0	0.0	0.2	0.0	0.0
Chile	1.3	0.1	0.0	0.0	0.0	0.0	0.0	0.0	0.0
Total Fabrication	245.0	226.9	163.4	175.9	125.1	108.5	316.7	204.1	138.6
Total Sales	190.2	191.3	130.6	165.1	130.5	104.5	326.6	200.4	101.7

Source: Consolidated Gold Fields PLC: Gold 1989.

Table 6.10   Identified Bar Hoarding Outside Europe and North
America (in tons)

	1980	1981	1982	1983	1984	1985	1986	1987	1988
Far East									
Taiwan	30.0	40.0	38.0	1.5	60.0	51.0	21.0	83.5	155.0
Hong Kong	17.0	30.0	26.0	(30.0)	40.8	29.4	(57.2)	(2.0)	24.0
South Korea	1.5	2.0	2.0	0.8	8.0	11.3	6.4	6.0	20.0
Singapore	6.0	9.0	6.0	6.5	20.8	12.0	5.0	2.0	12.0
Indonesia	(15.0)	45.0	71.0	(4.5)	13.0	9.0	14.3	(21.0)	11.0
Thailand	(2.0)	2.0	5.0	1.0	8.0	12.5	6.0	6.0	8.0
Philippines	0.0	1.0	0.5	1.0	1.0	0.7	0.0	1.0	2.0
Burma, Laos, Kampuchea	(15.0)	(4.0)	(3.0)	(1.0)	(3.0)	0.0	0.0	0.0	0.0
Malaysia	0.1	0.7	0.4	0.2	0.2	0.1	0.0	0.0	0.0
Japan	(1.7)	110.0	72.4	38.3	105.3	111.7	173.6	129.0	178.5
Total Far East	20.9	235.7	219.3	13.8	254.1	237.7	169.1	204.5	410.5
Latin America									
Brazil	4.0	3.0	8.3	17.5	10.4	12.5	18.0	41.3	35.3
Colombia	0.0	0.0	0.0	0.3	0.0	3.0	2.0	3.0	1.5
Argentina	5.0	(0.6)	0.0	0.0	0.0	0.0	0.0	0.0	0.0
Peru	(2.0)	0.0	0.0	0.0	0.0	0.0	0.0	0.0	0.0
Other	0.0	0.5	1.0	0.0	0.0	0.0	0.0	0.0	0.0
Total Latin America	7.0	2.9	9.3	17.8	10.4	15.5	20.0	44.3	36.8
Middle East									
Arabian Gulf States	0.2	3.2	8.0	2.7	7.5	5.0	2.7	1.0	5.0
Saudi Arabia and Yemen	5.0	15.0	33.0	22.0	35.0	25.0	8.0	3.5	3.0
Turkey	(15.0)	0.0	0.0	2.9	0.0	1.5	3.0	3.0	2.0
Kuwait	0.7	3.0	5.0	2.0	2.0	4.0	1.0	1.0	1.5
Jordan	0.0	1.0	1.0	0.3	1.0	1.0	(1.5)	0.0	1.2

	1980	1981	1982	1983	1984	1985	1986	1987	1988
Israel	2.0	1.5	0.0	1.2	2.0	1.0	1.4	0.8	0.4
Egypt	(5.0)	5.0	2.0	3.0	4.0	2.0	2.0	0.0	0.0
Iraq	0.0	0.0	2.0	0.0	0.0	0.0	0.0	0.0	0.0
Syria	6.0	2.0	10.0	3.0	2.0	0.0	0.0	0.0	0.0
Iran	(5.0)	0.0	0.0	0.0	0.0	0.0	0.0	0.0	0.0
Lebanon	2.0	1.0	2.0	1.0	1.0	0.0	0.0	0.0	0.0
Total Middle East	(9.1)	31.7	63.0	38.1	54.5	39.5	16.6	9.3	13.1

Indian Subcontinent

	1980	1981	1982	1983	1984	1985	1986	1987	1988
Pakistan and Afghanistan	0.0	0.0	0.0	0.0	3.0	3.0	5.0	5.0	6.0
India	(1.0)	0.0	0.0	2.0	9.0	10.0	3.0	5.0	5.0
Sri Lanka	0.0	0.0	0.0	0.0	0.0	0.0	0.0	0.0	2.0
Total Indian Subcontinent	(1.0)	0.0	0.0	0.0	2.0	13.0	8.0	10.0	13.0

Australasia

	1980	1981	1982	1983	1984	1985	1986	1987	1988
Australasia	5.0	3.5	2.1	1.5	1.2	0.5	0.1	0.1	0.1
Total	22.8	273.8	293.7	73.2	332.2	306.2	213.8	268.2	473.5

Source: Consolidated Gold Fields PLC: Gold 89.

CHAPTER 7

Price Determination of Gold Futures

Determining the causes behind gold price movements can be an inordinately complex task owing to gold's dual nature as an industrial commodity and a financial instrument. Unlike, say, crude oil or soybeans, the price of gold is not solely a function of production and usage. And, unlike stocks or bonds, the price of gold does not solely reflect its competitiveness relative to other investment vehicles. Gold, unlike most commodities, crosses both lines.

The price determination of gold is further complicated by the role of governments. Most of the gold ever produced still exists today. And a large portion of that gold is held in government vaults around the world. The decision by one single government to buy or sell a large amount of gold—a decision usually motivated by internal developments within the country—can alter gold prices significantly, overpowering the forces of commercial and investment demand.

Despite the difficulties, however, the task of analysis is not hopeless. It simply requires a sound approach to the evaluation of the myriad of factors that affect gold prices. All too often, analysts attribute gold price movements to a single factor, when in reality, the factor that's focused upon is often part of a larger market dynamic or is an indirect reflection of a more primary force. Many investors, for example, believe gold prices correlate directly with inflation. In reality, inflation plays a large role in gold prices, however, it is not necessarily more important to gold prices than real interest rates or the value of the dollar.

Before elucidating on the forces behind gold price movements, it should be pointed out that the price of gold has been fixed through most of modern history. In the U.S., for example, the price of gold was virtually constant from around 1792 to 1933, except for an official devaluation of the dollar in 1834. And in Great Britain, the first country to go on the gold standard, the price of gold was largely unchanged from 1717 until 1930.

As a result of the imposition of the gold standard, the history of free market gold prices is relatively brief. Indeed, to a considerable extent, analysts are still exploring what drives gold prices in a free market environment. Ultimately, those forces may be as mysterious as the forces that impelled ancient civilizations to bestow economic value on gold.

PHYSICAL SUPPLY AND DEMAND

In assessing gold prices, it's wise to start with physical supply and industrial demand for gold. Some investors overlook these commodity aspects of the gold market because investment demand historically has been the single most important force driving gold prices. The investors ignore the fact that industrial demand frequently plays a large role in gold prices and that the degree of industrial demand, combined with new supply, determines the quantity of gold available for investment.

To begin the analysis, then, the amount of supply over a given period of time must be determined. Such a calculation should include supply emanating from mining, the recycling of gold scrap, and government sales. In addition, trends in supply over the past few years should be assessed. How are the mining industries in the various producing countries performing? What are the governments that hold large stocks of gold doing? How are changing gold prices affecting the volume of scrap supply coming to market?

In evaluating the supply situation, keep in mind that mining activity lags gold prices by several years, but that once an uptrend or downtrend in mining activity begins, it tends to persist for several years.

This fact could be invaluable in certain market conditions, for example, in the case where prices are beginning to rise in the face of a slowdown in mining production over the last two or three years. On the other hand, be aware that supply emanating from gold scrap responds quickly to changing prices.

Finally, in regard to supply, recall that the most volatile component in supply is government sales and that the most important government in the gold market is the Soviet Union. Try to get a reading on the Soviet Union's foreign exchange needs. Assess their agricultural situation and project their demand for Western grain. If bad weather reduces crop yields, chances are the Soviets will sell an increased amount of gold to earn the currency necessary to purchase Western grain.

Unless one has extraordinary contacts, forecasting Soviet moves in the gold market is extremely difficult. Nevertheless, an analyst should try to do the best he can with available information, so he can at least anticipate general developments and not be dramatically surprised by whatever the Soviets do.

After determining supply, the next step is to evaluate fabrication demand. This can be done in a cursory fashion, by using worldwide economic growth statistics; or it can be done in a more detailed manner, by examining the fabrication markets in all the major countries in the world. Although the latter method might appear preferable, it may not be most accurate since it requires estimates for a large number of variables. If possible, both methods should be employed.

Generally, in measuring fabrication demand, one should separate demand from the jewelry industry from demand from other industrial users. Having acknowledged that, however, it should be noted that demand from both jewelry makers and other industrial fabricators is positively correlated with economic growth and the general level of prosperity, and negatively correlated with the price of gold. The primary difference between the two demand sectors is that the jewelry sector often shows tremendous variability between different countries, while the trends in the industrial sector are generally consistent from country to country.

A detailed evaluation of gold demand by jewelry makers necessitates an examination of local market conditions in Europe, the U.S., Japan, India, Turkey, Saudi Arabia, Brazil, Taiwan, Hong Kong, and Singapore. Again, principle factors affecting gold demand in each country include the local currency price of gold, economic growth, and the general level of prosperity.

Finally, close attention should be paid to gold demand for fabrication into gold coins, the most volatile demand component within the fabrication sector. Typically, a country will evidence little interest in producing gold coins and then, suddenly, it will decide to issue a coin for one reason or another. The sudden nature of this type of demand (and its sudden cessation following the coin issuance) can have a powerful effect on gold prices.

EVALUATING INVESTMENT DEMAND

The determination of aggregate supply and fabrication demand provides the basis for evaluating investment demand for gold, the single most important factor in gold price movements. As mentioned in the previous chapter, the investment demand for gold (or, more properly, the supply of gold available for investment) is equal to aggregate supply minus fabrication demand and adjustment for government sales and purchases.

The crucial determinant of gold prices at any particular time is the size of the investment "surplus" relative to investor interest in owning gold. Obviously, if the surplus is small and investor interest is high, then the ingredients of a bull market are in place. A large surplus and weak investor interest, on the other hand, augurs for a bear market.

At this point in the analysis, the question then becomes, how strong is investor interest in gold? It's important to realize, however, that this question should only be asked after examination of physical supply, fabrication demand, and government activity. Many investors, unfortunately, jump straight to this question without laying the groundwork first. In so doing, they may fail to take into account changes in supply or the fabrication markets that may alter the size of the investment surplus.

As mentioned in the previous chapter, section on investment demand, investor interest in gold is motivated by the following factors: the price of gold, real interest rates, inflation, economic growth, currency values, international political tensions, the stability of the economic environment, and rates of return on alternative investments. In terms of forecasting, the key is to isolate those factors which are most prominent at the time in question.

Price of Gold

Historical data shows a strong correlation between rising gold prices and increasing investor demand and between falling gold prices and decreasing investor demand. To a certain extent, gold investors behave like long-term traders in any market: they buy at low prices and sell at high prices. Consequently, a forecaster should monitor the response of investors as prices approach support and resistance points. If investors are buying in response to lower prices, then one can assume that prices will stabilize, at least temporarily. If investors are selling in response to higher prices, then a bull market may be entering a consolidation period.

However, gold investors, particularly in the U.S., often do not behave in accordance with conventional economic principles. As a rule, U.S. investors do not begin to buy gold until a price rally is already well underway. Similarly, U.S. investors often don't sell their gold until after prices have fallen considerably from their rally highs. As U.S. investors gain more experience with free-floating gold prices, this type of behavior may change.

The tendency of U.S. investors to jump on rallies too late and to hold their profitable gold positions too long often causes a divergence in investment and industrial demand for gold. When gold prices are rising, investment demand for gold may increase while industrial demand drops. And, as gold prices fall, industrial demand may start to pick up, while investment demand remains dormant.

When gold prices soared in 1979, for example, investor demand jumped to 389 metric tons from 155 metric tons, while industrial demand fell from 1596 metric tons to 1315 metric tons. In 1980, as prices peaked and then declined, both investor demand and industrial demand dropped substantially. As prices continued to plummet in 1981 and through the first half of 1982, investor demand dropped sharply. However, while investment demand declined during this period, industrial demand jumped dramatically from 943 metric tons in 1980 to 1222 metric tons in 1981 and to 1256 metric tons in 1982.

The same type of phenomena was evident in 1983, as gold prices rallied to $515 early in the year and remained well above 1982 levels for the bulk of the year. Predictably, industrial gold demand declined in reaction to the higher prices, falling to 1221 metric tons. However, investors in Europe and North America, perhaps sensing that another 1979-80 style of rally was underway, increased their purchases of gold from net sales of 163 metric tons in 1982 to purchases of 347 metric tons in 1983. Unfortunately, many of these investors probably lost money because gold prices fell steadily through the remainder of 1983 and 1984.

Quite clearly, gold investors are not skilled at buying low and selling high, at least at the peaks and troughs of major trends. What's also quite clear, however, is that major moves in the price of gold are associated with rises and falls in gold investment. The 1979-80 rally was driven by an increase in investment demand and the decline in prices in 1981 and 1982 was driven by a large drop in gold investment.

In a sense, the interaction between gold investment levels and gold prices is something of a chicken and egg problem. Do gold prices rise and fall because of increases or decreases in gold investment, or do rising and falling prices motivate investors to get into or out of the gold market? Which comes first: changing prices or changing investment behavior?

The answer is probably quite complex. On the one hand, investors buy and sell gold for a variety of reasons relating to their own investment objectives and their perception of the economic environment. When a number of investors buys or sells at once, prices react. Indeed, as was said earlier, investor behavior and the size of the gold "surplus" are the most important factors determining gold prices.

On the other hand, rapidly changing gold prices are a leading indicator of changes in the economy. Therefore, changing gold prices, by themselves, may alter investor perceptions of the economic environment and motivate investor action. Thus, rising gold prices, because they are perceived as a harbinger of inflation, can cause investors to buy more gold, even as industrial gold users reduce purchases in reaction to the higher prices. Similarly, falling gold prices, because they may foretell reduced inflation, could cause investors to sell gold.

Changing gold prices, therefore, contain messages about the economy that may motivate investors to buy high and sell low—the opposite of what most investors would like to do—because they feel the trend in place is likely to continue.

Inflation

Few economic statistics correlate as closely to gold prices as inflation. A brief look at table 7.1 clearly shows that the run-up in gold prices in 1979-80 was preceded by an acceleration in the Consumer Price Index. Similarly, the decline in the CPI in the early 1980s marked the beginning of an extended period of gold price weakness.

Historically, the relationship between gold and inflation is skewed because the value of gold has been fixed for most of the last 300 years. Under fixed prices, any rise in inflation reduces the purchasing power of gold, while a drop in inflation increases gold's purchasing power. This is so because under a fixed rate, the value of an ounce of gold is held at a constant price, such as $35. When inflation rises, the $35, and its one-ounce gold equivalent, loses value. In a period of deflation, the $35, and the one-ounce gold equivalent, gains in value.

Notice the distinction between the value of gold, that is, what a fixed amount of gold will purchase, and the price of gold. In a fixed rate environment, it's axiomatic that the value of gold will move inversely with inflation. That being the case, one might expect that the value of gold—that is, what a fixed amount of gold will purchase—would change substantially over time, owing to inflationary developments. For example, if inflation rises substantially, one might think the value of gold would decline. The opposite situation would prevail in a period of fixed rates and falling inflation.

In fact, historical data suggests that the value of gold tends to remain constant in a period of fixed gold prices, a thesis advanced by Ray Jastram in his 1976 book *The Golden Constant*. After examining consumer prices against gold prices in the U.S. and Great Britain from 1650 to 1930, Jastram concludes that an ounce of gold could purchase roughly the same amount of goods in 1930 as it did in 1650.

Apparently, in a fixed rate environment, consumer prices always tend to return to the fixed price of gold. Over the short-term, consumer prices may move up and down, thereby increasing or diminishing gold's value, however, over an extended period, the value of gold remains relatively constant. It is this phenomena—the historical capability of the gold standard to restrain inflation—that leads some economists to argue that gold should once again assume a pivotal role in international economic affairs.

It's important to appreciate the behavior of gold in a fixed rate environment in order to understand the interaction of gold prices and inflation in a floating rate environment. When the price of gold is fixed, consumer prices return to the price of gold, thereby preserving the purchasing power of gold over time. In a floating rate environment, however, gold prices are no longer a constant around which other prices revolve. Instead, the price of gold floats like any other commodity. Yet, even under free-floating gold prices, historical data indicates that gold retains its value, just as it does when its price is fixed. Instead of consumer prices always returning to the price of gold—the dynamic in a fixed rate environment—in a floating rate environment, gold prices adjust on their own to changes in consumer prices. As inflation rises in a floating rate environment, the price of gold rises to compensate for the higher inflation. As inflation falls, so does the price of gold. Under both the fixed rate and the floating rate systems, however, the value of gold is preserved.

Admittedly, the above conclusion regarding free-floating gold prices is based on relatively limited evidence, however, the relationship between inflation and gold prices since 1975 is so powerful that it cannot be ignored. Indeed, by examining inflation and gold prices more closely, the nature of the relationship can be more precisely defined.

In the early 1970s, just after gold prices were allowed to float, the price of gold tripled to over $150 per ounce. Concurrently, the CPI jumped from 2.5 percent to 10 percent. At first glance, the huge run-up in the price of gold seems disproportionate to the increase in the CPI. Remember, however, that gold prices had been held constant for some 30 years previously. Thus, the increase in gold prices reflected not only the inflation of the early 1970s, but also the inflationary pressures of the past 30 years, and particularly the inflationary pressures of the Vietnam War, which ultimately led to the abandonment of the gold standard.

As the CPI declined in the mid-1970s, gold prices followed suit, although the magnitude of the gold price decline was minor relative to the increase earlier in the decade. Then, starting in 1977, both the CPI and gold began to increase rapidly. The worst inflation in decades was unleashed in the U.S., and gold commenced its biggest price surge in history.

Looking more closely at the data through this period, it appears that gold prices didn't track the CPI as much as they tracked the rate of change in the CPI. When the rate of increase in the CPI accelerated, gold prices rose. When the rate of increase declined, as occurred in 1975, gold prices dropped.

Apparently, as inflation accelerates, investors become intensely interested in gold because they believe gold will retain its value better than other instruments. Typically, the intense interest causes gold prices to increase more than is necessary to counteract inflation. Indeed, during the bull market of the late 1970s, the purchasing power of gold outpaced inflation. However, as occurred in 1980, once the rate of increase in inflation begins to wane, investor interest in gold slows considerably, causing gold prices to fall despite the fact that inflation may still be rising.

It should be noted, however, that gold prices do not always rise in perfect harmony with the CPI. In early 1988, inflation began to accelerate in the U.S., a development that led the Federal Reserve (the Fed) to maintain a tight money policy. The high interest rates engendered by the Fed, and the confidence the markets had in the ability of the Fed to control inflation, caused gold prices to drop during this period, even though inflation rose in the short-term.

Economic Growth

In certain periods, there have been temporary correlations between strong economic growth and rising gold prices and weak economic growth and falling gold prices. Just as frequently, however, the correlations break down. Notice, for instance, the steep rise in economic growth in 1983 was accompanied by falling gold prices.

Generally, strong economic growth is accompanied by a rising industrial demand for gold. However, strong economic growth is not, in itself, an inducement for investors to buy gold. Rather, the relevance of economic growth levels, to gold investors, depends upon the link between growth and inflation in the current operating period.

For example, strong economic growth in 1978 was accompanied by a rapid rise in inflation. Consequently, gold prices rose as investors substantially increased their gold purchases. In 1981 and 1982, a steep decline in economic growth was accompanied by a sharp drop in inflation. Not surprisingly, investor purchases dropped and gold prices fell.

The link between inflation and economic growth broke down during the economic recovery that began in 1983. Growth levels jumped during that period; inflation, however, remained subdued. In the early stages of the recovery, investors increased their gold purchases, probably under the mistaken view that a 1970s-style inflation surge was in the offing. However, after it became clear that inflation had indeed stabilized, investor interest in gold waned, even though the economy continued to grow.

Despite their variable nature, the correlations between economic growth, inflation, and investor interest in gold should be monitored for clues of changes in market psychology. Throughout the late-1980s, world economic policymakers have been quite successful in maintaining steady levels of economic growth while keeping inflation under control, an achievement that generally has been bearish for gold prices. It's a sure bet, however, that policymakers will be unable to continue this success indefinitely.

Currency Values

Currency values of gold often have a powerful impact on gold prices. However, like most other factors in the gold market, there are no sure-fire rules about how changes in currency values affect investor behavior. Instead, there are tendencies that recur over time, but that must be analyzed in the context of the specific economic period.

As a general rule, there's an inverse relationship between the dollar and gold. A stronger dollar usually means weaker gold prices and a weaker dollar usually means stronger gold prices. The relationship has been quite pronounced in the 1980s. Indeed, some analysts maintain that changes in the value of the dollar are the primary determinant of gold prices.

To some extent, currency values relate to gold prices, largely because of their inflationary implications. A weaker dollar, obviously, portends higher U.S. inflation, while a stronger dollar suggests lower inflation. However, in some cases, changes in the value of the dollar do not correlate with changes in inflation. For example, from 1985-1987, the dollar weakened substantially, falling about 50 percent against the yen. However, while inflation rose marginally during this period, it failed to match the magnitude of the dollar fall. Consequently, gold prices strengthened somewhat, but the rally was muted.

To a considerable extent, international investors view the dollar and gold as so-called "safe-haven" investments, that is, instruments that retain value in periods of economic and political uncertainty. When the dollar is appreciating (and their native currency is weakening) many international investors will reduce gold holdings and increase dollar investments. The converse is true when the dollar is weakening.

Since gold prices and the dollar tend to move in an inverse fashion, then it follows that gold prices and major non-dollar currencies should correlate. When they do, it can provide an extra profit to international investors. For example, in a period of rising gold prices and a falling dollar, an international investor may decide to sell his depreciating dollar assets and purchase gold with his native currency. Thereupon, he profits from the rise in gold prices and from the fact he now has a larger portion of his overall assets denominated in his native currency and a lesser portion denominated in dollars. Of course, if the foreign currency strengthens to the extent that the gold price in that currency declines, then the investor may be disappointed. However, by including a long foreign currency futures position with the gold purchase, the investor can protect against that possibility.

Although the ultimate motivation of international investors in the gold market is quite similar to domestic investors, there are subtle differences. Generally, international investors are more attuned to the interconnections between gold and the currency markets. U.S. investors, in contrast, look at gold more as an inflation hedge and less as a currency-related instrument.

Real Interest Rates

Investors do not buy and sell gold in a vacuum comprised solely of the gold market and the economic environment. They compare gold versus other investment instruments, particularly interest rate securities.

Since investors view gold primarily as an inflation hedge, then it must be compared to returns on fixed income assets. If short-term government securities yield 10 percent, then gold, if it is to compete as an alternative, should also yield 10 percent over the course of the year. In fact, before buying gold, an investor should be convinced that there's a good chance that gold will appreciate to a level greater than the return on government securities in order to compensate for the increased risk of gold investment.

In evaluating interest rate instruments, investors tend to focus on real interest rates, that is, nominal interest rates minus the rate of inflation. For example, if one-year Treasury bills are yielding 10 percent and inflation is running at six percent, then the real rate of return, or the real interest rate, is four percent. In such an environment, investors can more than compensate for the rate of inflation by buying relatively risk-free government securities. Therefore, the need for an inflation hedge is minimal, all else being equal.

When real interest rates turn negative, investor interest in gold grows because investors generally will not tolerate loss in principal. If inflation is running at ten percent and one-year Treasuries return only eight percent, then an investor in Treasuries would lose two percent of his principal over the course of the year. In such an environment, one might say, inflation is eroding the value of capital. Gold, because it is viewed as a long-term store of value, becomes very popular among investors under such circumstances.

Throughout much of the mid-to-late 1970s, real interest rates were negative. Investors, obviously, were motivated to find alternative investment vehicles that would at least preserve the value of their principle. Many of them turned to gold and, as a result, gold prices soared.

In 1980, the abrupt increase in real interest rates, from around minus 8.5 percent to plus 6 percent in a matter of weeks coincided with the beginning of a long-term bear market in gold. After years in which interest rates failed to compensate for inflation, suddenly investors found they could earn a real return in excess of 5 percent. Predictably, money poured out of gold and into high-yielding interest rate vehicles.

Political and Economic Stability

Investors buy gold when they feel that the value of their money is threatened. Usually, the threat stems from inflation. However, in some cases, a threat may originate from political or economic events that lead investors to question the stability of the investment environment.

The notion that gold reacts sharply to economic and political tensions gained a great deal of credibility in the late 1970s, although many would say that the price of gold was destined to rise in any case. Nevertheless, it's difficult to ignore the fact that the sharp run-up in gold prices in late 1979 and early 1980 was preceded by the Soviet Union invading Afghanistan and the taking of U.S. hostages by Iranian militants.

In the 1980s, as the gold market turned bearish, prices reacted much less strongly to international incidents. The Falkland Islands War between Great Britain and Argentina, the downing of a Korean airliner by the Soviet Union, the U.S. invasion of Grenada, and the U.S. raid on Libya failed to elicit a sustained response in the gold market. As a result, the notion that gold always rises when international troubles break out became suspect.

During these incidents in the 1980s, it was frequently the U.S. dollar that benefitted, rather than gold. Remember, for many international investors, the dollar and gold are both viewed as safe havens. And during the early 1980s, the dollar was in the midst of a long-term bull market. Consequently, when international troubles broke out, investors were inclined to invest in dollar securities rather than buy gold.

Thus, in forecasting the likely response of gold to international events, one must keep in mind the long-term fundamentals and the attractiveness of the dollar as an alternative safe haven investment. When the dollar is weak and the gold market is strong, an increase in international tensions should bolster gold prices. Alternatively, when the gold market is weak and the dollar is strong, international troubles may elicit only a ripple in gold prices.

Table 7.1 Gold Supply and Demand in the Non-Communist World (in tons)

	1980	1981	1982	1983	1984	1985	1986	1987	1988
Mine Production	959	981	1028	1114	1162	1233	1293	1382	1538
Net Communist Sales	90	280	203	93	205	210	402	303	258
Net Official Sales (Purchases)	(230)	(276)	(85)	142	85	(132)	(145)	(72)	(270)
Scrap	488	239	243	294	291	304	474	405	324
(A) Total Supply	1307	1224	1389	1643	1742	1615	2024	2018	1850
(B) Fabrication Demand	945	1218	1279	1231	1483	1485	1686	1596	1844
(C) Net Surplus (deficit) of Supply Over Fabrication (A)–(B)	362	6	110	411	260	130	338	422	6
(D) Identified Bar Hoarding Outside Europe and North America	23	274	294	73	332	306	214	268	474
(E)[*] Net Implied Investment (Disinvestment) in Europe and North America (C)–(D)	339	(268)	(184)	338	(72)	(176)	124	154	(468)

*(E) includes the net impact of gold loan and forward sales.

Source: Consolidated Gold Fields PLC.

Figure 7.1   The Consumer Price Index vs. the Price of Gold

MONTHLY CHARTS (NEAREST FUTURES)

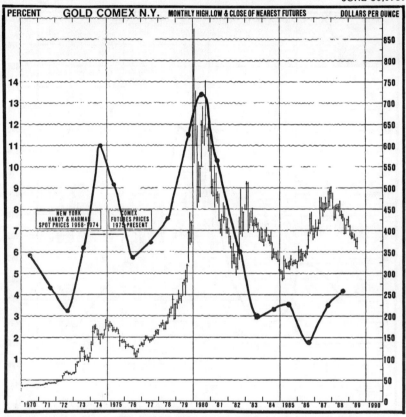

Gold Prices Courtesy of the Commodity Research Bureau.

Figure 7.2   Short-Term Interest Rates vs. the Price of Gold

MONTHLY CHARTS (NEAREST FUTURES)

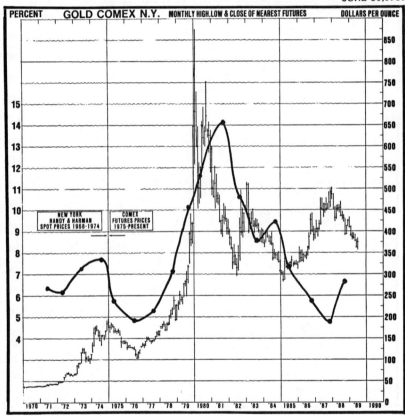

Gold Prices Courtesy of the Commodity Research Bureau.

Figure 7.3 Long Bond Yields vs. the Price of Gold

MONTHLY CHARTS (NEAREST FUTURES)

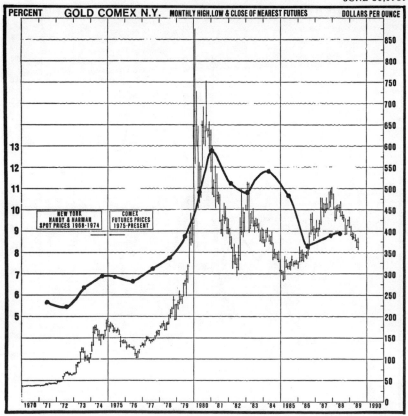

Gold Prices Courtesy of the Commodity Research Bureau.

Figure 7.4   Real Interest Rates vs. the Price of Gold

MONTHLY CHARTS (NEAREST FUTURES)

JUNE 30,1989

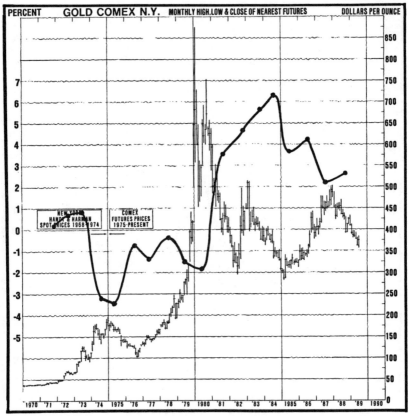

Gold Prices Courtesy of the Commodity Research Bureau.

Figure 7.5 U.S. Money Supply (M₁) vs. the Price of Gold

MONTHLY CHARTS (NEAREST FUTURES)

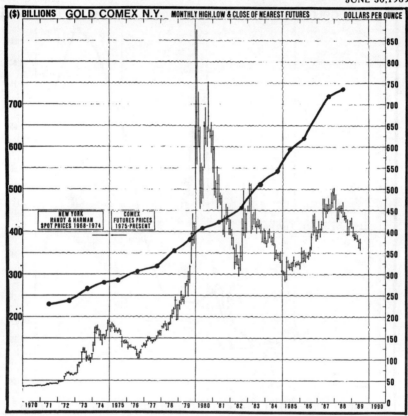

JUNE 30,1989

Gold Prices Courtesy of the Commodity Research Bureau.

Figure 7.6   U.S. Trade Deficit vs. the Price of Gold

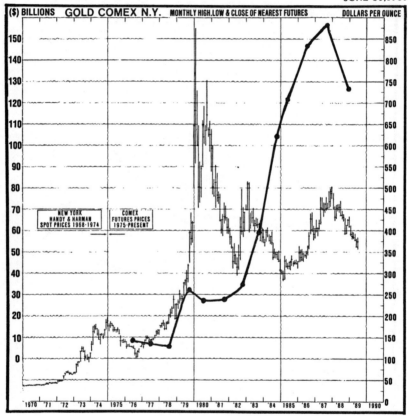

Gold Prices Courtesy of the Commodity Research Bureau.

Figure 7.7   U.S. Budget Deficit vs. the Price of Gold

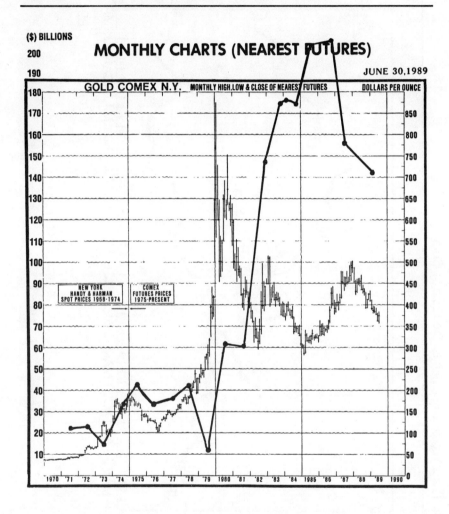

Gold Prices Courtesy of the Commodity Research Bureau.

Figure 7.8 The Trade Weighted Dollar vs. the Price of Gold

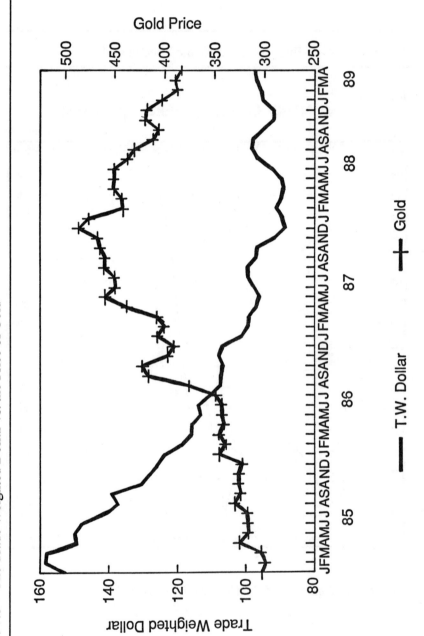

Source: World Gold Council.

Figure 7.9 Purchasing Power of Gold in 1988 Dollars

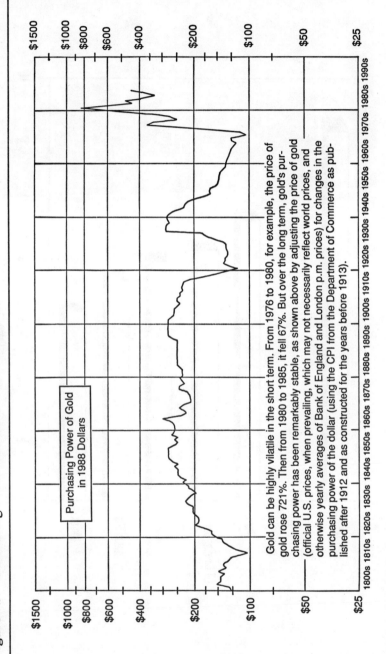

Purchasing Power of Gold
in 1988 Dollars

Gold can be highly vilatile in the short term. From 1976 to 1980, for example, the price of gold rose 721%. Then from 1980 to 1985, it fell 67%. But over the long term, gold's purchasing power has been remarkably stable, as shown above by adjusting the price of gold (official U.S. prices, when prevailing, which may not necessarily reflect world prices, and otherwise yearly averages of Bank of England and London p.m. prices) for changes in the purchasing power of the dollar (using the CPI from the Department of Commerce as published after 1912 and as constructed for the years before 1913).

Source: World Gold Council.

Figure 7.10 Gold vs. Other Financial Investments from 1968–1988

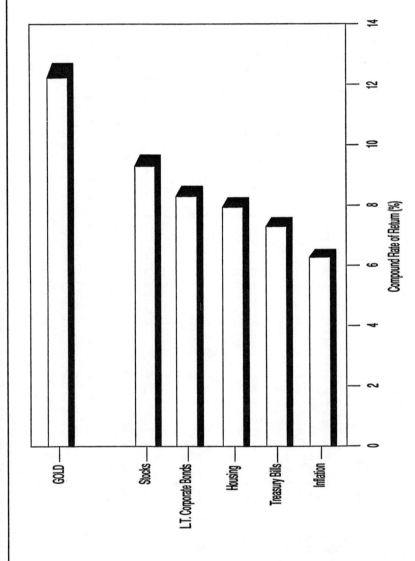

Source: World Gold Council.

CHAPTER 8

Gold Futures Spreads and Pricing Deferred Gold Contracts

Taking outright positions in gold futures is a high risk/high reward undertaking. A sudden, unexpected event such as a political assassination, an outbreak of violence in the Middle East, or a surprising economic report can ignite a fury in the gold market. Consequently, traders occasionally prefer to enter the gold futures market through so-called spread trades, strategies which often are less risky than outright positions.

In a spread, a trader hopes to profit from the increase or decrease in the price difference between two contracts. To do that, a trader will buy and sell two related futures contracts, believing that the price difference between the two contracts will either narrow or widen. If the trader thinks the price difference will narrow, he will buy the lower priced contract and sell the higher priced contract. If he thinks the difference will widen he will sell the lower priced contract and buy the higher priced contract.

A typical commodity spread might involve buying the March soybean contract at $6.25 per bushel and selling the July contract at $6.40 per bushel. If the price difference, or spread, between the two contracts narrows, the trade will be profitable. For example, if the March contract increases by ten cents and the July contract rises by seven cents, then the trade will net a three cents per bushel profit, or $150 per spread.

121

Buy 1 March soybean at $6.25   Sell 1 July soybean at $6.40
Sell at $6.35   Buy at $6.47
10 cent profit   7 cent loss

Net 3 cent per bushel profit or $150 per spread.

This strategy would also make money if prices decline, as long as the price drop leads to a narrowing of the spread. For example, if the March contract fell five cents per bushel and the July contract dropped eight cents, then the trade would again result in a three cent per bushel profit, or $150 per spread.

Many traders are more comfortable with spreads because they entail less risk than outright positions. To be sure, both legs of a spread can move against a trader, but that's rare. As a rule, since spreadable commodities are related, their prices move in the same direction. Thus, on a typical spread, the loss on one leg is offset by the gain on the other. Risk is minimized because the rate of change in the spread is almost always less than the rate of change in the prices of the two contracts.

Like so much else in the commodities industry, spreads developed in the grain markets. In the grains, the deferred contracts normally sell at a premium to the nearby contract. Thus, at the beginning of the year, the nearby March contract in soybeans might be priced at $6.50 per bushel, the May contract at $6.55, the July contract at $6.61, and the September contract at $6.65.

In the grains, as well as in a number of other commodities, the price differential between the nearby and deferred contract months reflects the cost involved in storing, insuring, and financing the commodity.

In equilibrium market conditions, a grain elevator will charge a premium for future delivery because it must bear the costs of holding the grain until the delivery date. That storage premium will be reflected in the futures price. Markets of this kind, in which the deferred contracts normally are priced at a premium to the spot price and to the nearby contract, are known as carrying charge markets.

Carrying charge markets offer enormous spread opportunities. Typically, in a bull market, the price of the nearby contract will rise faster than the deferred, causing a narrowing of the spread. That narrowing reflects the fact that the market is encouraging the commodity out of storage. In a bear market, the opposite situation usually prevails: the price of the nearby will drop faster than the price of the deferred, leading to a widening of the spread. This widening indicates the market is encouraging storage and discouraging delivery. Awareness of spreads can provide clues to price trends, as well as offering relatively low-risk trading opportunities.

Although there are exceptions, gold spreads generally behave in the opposite manner to grain spreads. When gold prices rise, the deferred contracts usually increase more than the nearby, leading to a widening of the spread. Conversely, when gold prices fall, the deferred contracts fall more than the nearby, causing spreads to narrow. The behavior of gold spreads reflects the influence of interest rates in the pricing of deferred contracts, a matter which will be discussed fully in this chapter.

There are three different kinds of spreads: calendar spreads, intercommodity spreads, and intermarket spreads.

Calendar Spreads

This is the most common type of spread in the commodity markets, although not the most popular in the gold market. A calendar spread consists of going long one month and shorting another month in the same contract.

Intercommodity Spreads

Probably the most common type of spread in the gold market. In this strategy, a trader takes advantage of the close relationship of two commodities, such as gold and silver, soybeans and soybean meal, or crude oil and heating oil. Again, the trader takes opposing positions in the two contracts in anticipation of a widening or narrowing of the price difference.

Intermarket Spreads

Another popular spread in the gold market, this strategy involves exploiting the price differential between the same commodities that are traded on two different exchanges. For example, if Comex gold rises relative to gold on the MidAmerica, a trader might sell a Comex contract and buy three MidAmerica contracts.

PRICING DEFERRED GOLD CONTRACTS

To understand gold spreads, it's necessary to understand the pricing mechanism behind deferred contracts in gold. Unlike most physical commodities, gold can be stored at very little cost, usually for only pennies a year per ounce. All else being equal, that would tend to keep prices of deferred gold contracts quite close to the price of the nearby contract.

However, since gold represents a physical store of value that pays neither dividends nor interest, then the seller of gold for future delivery must be compensated. After all, the gold holder could just as easily invest in Treasury bills where he would be assured of regular coupon payments. Since he's holding an essentially non-paying asset, the gold seller will charge an interest rate premium for future delivery. That premium will reflect the appropriate interest rate on the yield curve based on the time difference between the spot price and the delivery date, or, in the case of futures, between the nearby futures contract and the deferred contracts. In the case of the person selling gold for future delivery, the premium for one-year delivery will be roughly equal to one-year bank deposit rates; for six-month delivery, the premium will reflect six-month rates. Similarly, the price difference between spot price and a futures contract for one-year delivery should reflect one-year interest rates. In the gold trade, the price relationship between contracts of different delivery months is called contango.

When gold futures began trading on the Comex, the proper contango relationships were maintained by large commercial and investment banks and by major gold dealers. Whenever spreads between gold futures contracts moved out-of-line with interest rates, the institutions would arbitrage the differential, make a profit, and, in so doing, bring the spreads back in line with prevailing interest rates.

GOLD FUTURES ARBITRAGE

If spot gold is $400 an ounce and one-year interest rates are 12.5 percent, then the gold futures contract for delivery in one year should be $450, plus the costs for insurance and storage. (For purposes of explication, we will assume that all other carrying costs, besides financing, are zero.)

Now, if the one year futures contract diverges substantially from $450, either on the up or downside, then there is an opportunity for arbitrage.

Let's say, for instance, that the one-year futures contract goes to $460, $10 higher than its theoretical value. That would allow a gold trader to purchase spot gold at $400 an ounce and sell the one-year futures contract at $460. Assuming the trader satisfies the futures contract with physical delivery in one year, he would earn a one-year return of 15 percent, 2.5 percent higher than prevailing interest rates. In essence, the gold trader has created a fixed-income instrument through the mechanism of an overpriced gold futures contract.

Spot gold	One-year interest rates	Theoretical price of gold future for delivery in one year
$400	12.5 percent	$450

When the one-year gold contract rises to $460, the gold trader:
Buys spot gold at $400
Sells a one-year futures contract at $460
One year later, the trader:
Satisfies futures contract by delivering gold at $460. Realizes a $60 per ounce profit ($460-400), representing a 15-percent return on his investment.

If the trader does not have the cash to purchase spot gold in sufficient quantities, he could borrow money at 12.5 percent and purchase gold with the borrowed funds. That would enable him to enter into the same transaction as above, however, the results would be somewhat different. Instead of achieving a 15 percent fixed return, he would receive a 2.5 percent arbitrage profit.

Borrows $200,000 one year at 12.5-percent interest	Purchases 500 ounces of gold at $400 per ounce	Sells five futures contracts for one-year delivery
One year later:		
Pays off loan with interest: $225,000	Delivers physical gold to satisfy futures contracts at a price of $230,000	
Profit: $5000		

If, on the other hand, the one-year forward price of gold falls below the theoretical price of $450, then that would present the opposite trade. Instead of providing a fixed return superior to one-year interest rates—as was the case when the one-year futures contract was at a premium—the discount of the futures contract to theoretical contango presents an opportunity to obtain low-cost funding.

Let's say, using the same example, that the one-year futures fell to $440, $10 below the theoretical price. The trader could sell spot gold at $400 and buy a futures contract for delivery in one year at $440. Assuming the trader takes delivery of the physical gold when the futures contract expires, he would, for that year, receive a 10-percent interest rate loan, 2.5 percent below prevailing rates.

Spot gold $400	One-year interest rates 12.5 percent	Theoretical price of one-year futures $450
One-year future moves to $440. The trader:		
Sells spot gold at $400		Buys a one-year future at $440
One year later, the trader:		
		Satisfies futures contract by taking delivery of gold at $440 per ounce

In effect, the trader has received a 10-percent loan for one year, 2.5 percent better than prevailing rates.

If the trader has no need for low-cost funds, he could invest the $400 per ounce sale of gold at 12.5 percent interest and collect $50 per ounce in interest. After repurchasing the gold at $440, the trader would receive a $10 per ounce profit.

Sells 500 ounces of gold at $400 per ounce, or $200,000	Invests the $200,000 at 12.5 percent interest	Buys five futures contracts for one-year delivery at $440
One year later, the trader:		
	Collects $225,000 on investment	Takes delivery of five futures contracts at $220,000

Profit: $5000

It should be pointed out that there's another important factor that bears a strong influence on gold arbitrage: the gold lending rate set by the world's major central banks. As described in Chapter 6, central banks hold huge stockpiles of gold. Rather than let the gold gather dust, central banks will lend gold at relatively modest rates, often for only 0.5 percent to 2 percent per year. When the forward price of gold falls below the theoretical price (presenting the arbitrage opportunity of selling gold spot, investing the proceeds, and buying gold forward) most banks do not have the sufficient stocks of gold on hand to engage in the arbitrage in any meaningful way. Instead, the banks will borrow gold from a central bank, then sell it on the spot market. After repurchasing gold later in the forward market, the banks will return the gold to the central bank.

Generally, central banks only lend gold to the world's major commercial and investment banks. The lending rate varies by customer, with regular borrowers receiving a lower rate than infrequent borrowers. Some banks, in order to have continual access to low rates, make it a point to borrow gold regularly from a particular central bank. For these banks, the rate at which they can borrow gold is a critical factor in determining how low the forward price of gold must drop below the theoretical price to make arbitrage worthwhile.

In the early years of gold trading, institutional gold dealers kept gold futures prices in line with the spot price of gold and interest rates through extensive arbitrage trading. As the gold futures market matured, however, Comex floor traders gradually supplanted institutions in this function. Instead of allowing institutions to make large arbitrage profits, the traders themselves began to adjust gold futures in line with spot price and interest rate changes. As a result, price discrepancies became less pronounced and the need for arbitrage diminished. But while less arbitrage is now being done, the potential for arbitrage always overhangs the market. Indeed, it's that potential that leads Comex traders to keep prices in the proper relationship.

Generally, arbitrage opportunities are most prevalent during bull markets, when deferred contracts are being bid up. Frequently, rising gold prices coincide with rising market interest rates; thus, under those circumstances, deferred contracts rise more than the nearby. Consequently, many traders buy deferred contracts, hoping to capture a larger price move. However, overbuying of deferred contracts often drives the deferred contracts to a premium to the nearby futures and to the spot price, creating the opportunity for arbitrage.

GOLD CALENDAR SPREADS

While the previous examples applied to the spot/futures relationship, they are relevant to gold spreads between two futures contracts as well. Just as the price difference between spot gold and the one-year futures price reflects the cost of one-year financing, the difference between any two gold futures contracts reflects an interest rate factor. That interest rate factor is known as the spread yield.

For example, if the September gold contract is $420 and the December contract is $424, then the $4 difference reflects a spread yield of 3.8 percent. The formula for calculating the spread yield is:

$$\text{Spread yield} = \frac{D - N}{N} \times \frac{360}{T_d - T_n} \times 100$$

Where:
D = Price of the deferred contract
N = Price of the nearby contract
T_d = Closest delivery date for the deferred contract
T_n = Closest delivery date for the nearby contract

This formula also applies to the first set of examples in determining the implied financing rate between spot gold and a one-year futures or forward contract. In those examples, the time component part of the equation always equals one.

The time component on futures spreads is calculated on the basis of 30-day months. The time difference between the September/December spread, for example, amounts to 90 days; the April/December spread is 240 days; and so on.

If every gold spread can be reduced to a spread yield, that means that gold calendar spreads are, in effect, surrogate interest rate instruments. Accordingly, gold spreads can be used as alternatives to fixed income instruments whenever the spread yield diverges significantly from the rate on a fixed income instrument. Theoretically, a long gold spread (selling the nearby and buying the deferred in expectation that the spread will widen) could be used in place of a short Eurodollar or Treasury bill futures position. Both trades would prove profitable if interest rates rose: the gold spread would widen and the Eurodollar futures contract would decline. Similarly, shorting the gold spread (buying the nearby and selling the deferred in expectation that the spread will narrow) would be similar to buying a Treasury bill or a Eurodollar futures contract. In this case, falling interest rates would make both trades profitable.

Why is this so? Let's examine the December/June six-month gold spread. The December contract is $500, the June contract is $525. That would calculate to an annual spread yield of 10 percent:

$$\frac{525 - 500}{500} \times \frac{360}{\text{Nov. 30} - \text{May 31}} = 10 \text{ percent}$$

The June Eurodollar rate, however, may only be eight percent. (The actual price of the June Eurodollar contract would be 92. The rate is calculated by subtracting the price from 100.)

This mispricing would present the kind of arbitrage opportunity described in the previous pages. However, instead of arbitraging the difference, the high gold spread yield can be used for other purposes, namely as an interest rate instrument.

Suppose, for example, that a speculator believed interest rates were going to decline. Logically, he would go long Eurodollars, or some other interest rate instrument. However, given the high spread yield on gold futures, the speculator could conclude that gold spread yields will decline more than Eurodollar rates. Thus, he would short the gold spread; that is, buy the nearby and sell the deferred, in expectation that the price differential will narrow and the spread yield will decline.

Like all spreads, this particular spread strategy requires a smaller margin deposit and entails less risk than taking an outright position in Eurodollars. However, unless the speculator puts on a multiple of spreads in lieu of the Eurodollar position, his profit potential will be less than it would be with Eurodollars.

Let's assume that the Eurodollar rate drops a full point to seven percent. That would represent a profit of $2500 per contract. If the gold spread yield fell 200 basis points to eight percent, it would represent a profit of $500 per spread, assuming the December contract remained at $500.

Long Dec. gold at $500	Short June gold at $525	= ten percent spread yield
Dec. gold stays at $500	June gold drops to $520	= eight percent spread yield
Result: $0	$5 × 100 = $500 per spread profit	

In all likelihood, if interest rates dropped a point, gold prices would also decline, adding to the profit on the spread. That would happen because of the primary factors driving interest rates—inflationary expectations—is also a major force behind gold price changes. Thus, if the December contract fell to $450, and the spread yield dropped to eight percent, then the June contract would be $468. In that case, the gain on the short leg of the spread, $57, would offset the loss on the long leg, $50, for a net profit of $7 per ounce, or $700 per spread.

Although the gold spread trade would be less profitable than the Eurodollar position, remember that spread margins are substantially less than margins for outright positions. At the time of this writing, gold spread margins were as low as $100 per spread. Assuming a profit of $500 per spread, that would represent a 500 percent appreciation of the initial margin requirement. In contrast, the margin for one Eurodollar contract was $1000 at the time of writing. Thus, the $2500 profit on the Eurodollar contract represents much lower rate of return than that on the gold yield spread.

Of course, this strategy also works when the gold spread yield is at a discount to the comparable Eurodollar rate. In that case, a speculator who believes interest rates will rise could go long a gold spread (sell the nearby, buy the deferred in expectation that the spread will widen) in place of a short Eurodollar position.

For example, if December gold was $300 and June gold was $309, that would translate into a six-percent spread yield. The six-month Eurodollar rate might be eight percent. If interest rates increase, the spread yield will increase as well; and since the spread yield already is at a significant discount to the Eurodollar rate, chances are that it will increase more than the Eurodollar rate in a rising rate environment.

If the spread yield increases to seven percent and the price of the nearby holds at $300, the deferred June contract would move to $310.50. The profit on the spread would be $1.50 per ounce, or $150. However, if interest rates are rising, then it's quite likely that gold prices will increase as well, since gold prices generally rise in tandem with inflationary expectations. That rise in gold prices, together with the increase in the spread yield, would add to the profit on the spread.

THE TAIL

There is, however, one problem in all of this: gold prices frequently change because of factors other than interest rates. As a general rule higher interest rates and higher gold prices go together, as do lower interest rates and lower gold prices. Unfortunately, this general rule, works only part of the time. In many economic environments, it doesn't apply at all.

It would be easy, for example, to imagine an economic environment in which a combination of high interest rates and relatively low inflation encourage investment in fixed income instruments to the detriment of gold prices. That's essentially what happened in the U.S. in the early 1980s. During that period, short gold spreads benefitted from declining gold prices, but suffered because of rising interest rates. Although that period provided extensive arbitrage opportunities, it did not facilitate the use of gold spreads as surrogate interest rate instruments. Anyone who foresaw that interest rates were going to rise and decided to buy gold spreads, in expectation that the spread would widen and the spread yield would increase, would have been confounded by falling gold prices. Indeed, spread yields increased, however, the drop in gold prices minimized, or even reduced, the spread differential itself. The trader would have been much better off selling interest rate futures.

The experience of the early 1980s dramatically demonstrated that if one wishes to use gold spreads as interest rate vehicles, one must eliminate the effect of independent gold price changes on the gold spread. To do that, traders have constructed something called a tail, a device designed to prevent gold price changes from interfering with the fixed income characteristics of gold spreads.

The tail is constructed by buying or selling one leg of the spread so that when gold prices change, the price effect on the tail will be equal to and opposite to the price effect on the spread. As a result, appropriately "tailed gold spreads" will be unaffected by independent gold price moves.

To calculate the tail, one must first solve for the spread yield using the equation:

$$\text{Yield} = \frac{D-N}{N} \times \frac{360}{T_d - T_n} \times 100$$

After determining the yield, the tail can be calculated using the equation:

$$\text{Tail} = Y \times \frac{T_d - T_n}{360} \times \text{the number of contracts in one leg of the spread}$$

Very simply, a properly constructed tail enables a trader to profit from changes in the spread yield exclusively, irrespective of overall changes in the price of gold. For example, a trader that expects a 10-percent spread yield to decline would short the spread, i.e. go long the nearby and short the deferred. By using a tail, the trader would be positioned to profit if the spread yield declined, lose money if the spread yield rose, and break even if the spread yield remained the same. With the tail in place, the trader would be unaffected by the magnitude of the gold price changes; all that would matter would be the direction of the spread yield.

Suppose that the nearby contract is $400 and the one-year contract is $440, creating a 10-percent spread yield. Perhaps because of weakness in interest rates, a trader believes the spread yield will decline, so he shorts the spread. Unexpectedly, the price of gold doubles to $800 for the nearby and to $880 for the deferred, but the spread yield remains at 10 percent. The trader loses $40 per spread or $4000, even though there was no change in the spread yield.

Now, suppose the trader used a tail. To achieve round numbers, let's assume that the trader put on a 100-contract spread, a position that would have lost $400,000 in the above scenario. Utilizing the equation for the tail, the proper tail would be 10 contracts.

$$\text{Tail} = (10\%) \times \frac{360}{360} \times 100 \text{ contracts}$$

$$\text{Tail} = 10 \text{ contracts}$$

Again, using the example above where the trader shorted the spread (long the nearby, short the deferred), the tail should be added to the nearby long position. Thus, the spread would be 110 long at $400 and 100 short at $440. If the trader had gone long the spread (sold the nearby and bought the deferred), he would have shorted an extra 10 contracts in the nearby leg of the spread, making the spread 110 contracts short and 100 long.

In the example above, where the trader bought the nearby contract and sold the deferred, use of a tail would have enabled the trader to break even.

Without the tail:

Buy 100 contracts at $400   Sell 100 one-year contracts at $440
The trader enters this transaction believing the spread yield, now at 10 percent, will decline. Unexpectedly the price of gold doubles, but the spread yield remains at 10 percent.
Sell 100 contracts at $800   Buy 100 one-year contracts at $880
Profit: $4 million   Loss: $4.4 million
Result: $400,000 loss

With the tail:

Buy 110 contracts at $400   Sell 100 one-year contracts at $440
Sell 110 contracts at $800   Buy 100 one-year contracts at $880
Profit: $4.4 million   Loss: $4.4 million
Result: 0

Use of the tail protected the trader from losing (or making) money on his spread as the result of independent movements in the price of gold. Theoretically, with the tail in place, there will be no profit or loss on the spread as long as the spread yield remains unchanged. However, as shown below, if changes in the price of gold cause a change in the spread yield, then the trader is exposed to profits or losses.

Buys 110 contracts at $400   Sells 100 one-year contracts at $440
As the trader expects, the spread yield drops to eight percent. For ease of explication, we'll put the new prices at $400 and $432.
Sells 110 contracts at $400   Buys 100 contracts at $432
Profit: $0   Profit: $80,000
Result: $80,000 profit

On the other hand, the tail does not protect the trader against adverse moves in the spread yield.

Let's assume the spread yield rises to 12 percent, as the price moves to $500 and $560 respectively:

Sells 110 contracts at $500   Buys 100 contracts at $560
Profit: $1.1 million   Loss: $1.2 million
Result: $100,000 loss

Although the tail is a useful tool, it has limitations. Without a large enough spread position, it is impossible to construct a tail. In the example above, where the one-year spread yield is 10 percent, the minimum size "tailable" spread would be 10 contracts; a position that would allow for a one-contract tail. A spread position of five contracts, in the same example, theoretically would require a tail of 0.5 contracts. Conceivably, a trader could construct such a tail using a gold contract on the Mid-America Exchange. However, even when using the smaller sized MidAm contracts, in the above example, the spread position would have to be at least be five contracts.

There are also problems in precisely tailing gold spreads of sufficient size. In the example above where the one-year gold spread is 10 percent, a precise tail can be constructed for any size position that is a multiple of 10. However, any position that is not a multiple of 10 could not be tailed precisely. For example, a 25-contract spread would require a tail of 2.5 contracts, an impossibility unless one utilized the MidAm.

The variables that affect the tail are the spread yield, the duration of the spread, and the number of contracts in the spread. Change any of these variables, and the tail will have to be adjusted accordingly. In some cases—such as when the spread yield moves contrary to the trader's expectations—the trader may elect to retain the spread, but alter the tail.

Suppose, for example, that a trader sold 108 nearby contracts at $300 and bought 100 one-year contracts at $324 in anticipation that the 8-percent spread yield would rise. Unexpectedly, the spread yield drops to 6 percent as the prices move to $250 and $265 respectively. But while the trader has lost $50,000 on the trade, he may still believe the spread yield will widen. In that case, he ought to adjust the size of the tail to compensate for the lower spread yield. In this example, he should reduce the tail to six contracts by buying back two contracts on the nearby leg.

Table 8.1 Tail Adjustment for Change in Spread Yield

Spread Yield (percent)	Tail Size
4	2
5	2.5
6	3
7	3.5
8	4
9	4.5
10	5

Table 8.1 shows how tails would have to be adjusted to compensate for a change in spread yields. The table assumes a 100-contract, six-month spread position.

SPREADING AGAINST EURODOLLARS

A primary function of tailed gold spreads is to provide a mechanism to trade against Eurodollar futures. For the most part, gold spread yields and Eurodollar futures are closely correlated, although in different market conditions the yield differentials can vary a great deal. In the spring of 1987, for example, the yield differential between two-month gold spreads and the June Eurodollar contract ranged from around a 50 basis point discount to an 80 basis point premium. In contrast, in the spring of 1988, the yield differential ranged from a discount of around 80 to 150 basis points. Generally speaking, gold yields tend to run at a discount of up to 75 basis points against comparable Eurodollar futures. However, when gold prices are changing rapidly, the differentials will vary from the norm.

Although gold spread yields and Eurodollar rates are not perfectly correlated, they bear a sufficiently close relationship with one another to justify spread trading. In a particular market environment, a trader that believes the one-year gold spread yield is too low, relative to the one-year Eurodollar rate may decide to go long the gold spread (sell the nearby and buy the deferred) and short the one-year Eurodollar contract. Conversely, if it appeared that the gold spread is too high, the trader could sell the gold spread (by the nearby and sell the deferred) and buy the Eurodollar contract. Of course, the gold spreads would have to be tailed to protect against independent gold price changes.

To reduce yield curve risk in such trades, it's important that the time span between the delivery dates on the two gold contracts match, as closely as possible, to the spread period beginning on the third Wednesday of the Eurodollar futures expiration month and extending for the next three months. However, spreads can be constructed with any two contracts.

To calculate the proportion of gold spreads to Eurodollars, the following equation can be used:

$$\frac{1,000,000}{P_1 \times 100} \times \frac{90}{T_2 - T_1}$$

$1,000,000$ = The value of one Eurodollar contract

P_1 = Price of the nearby gold contract

100 = The number of ounces in the contract. For MidAm contracts, the number would be 50.

90 = 90 days

T_2 = Expiration of deferred gold contract

T_1 = Expiration of the nearby gold contract

Let's take a one-year gold spread where the nearby is priced at $500 and the deferred at $550, providing for a 10-percent spread yield. Let's further assume the one-year Eurodollar contract is priced at 88, for a 12 percent yield. The trader decides he wants to spread the one-year gold spread against the Eurodollar contract. The first step is to calculate the proportions of the spread using the equation above.

$$\frac{1,000,000}{500 \times 100} \times \frac{90}{360} = 5$$

This means that for every five gold spreads, one Eurodollar contract should be traded against it. Knowing that, the trader then solves for the tail, assuming a position size of 10 contracts. (In fact, the trader could put on any position that is a multiple of five.)

$$.1 \times \frac{360}{360} \times 10 = 1$$

The correctly tailed, long gold spread would be 11 contracts short at $500 and 10 contracts long at $550. Against that position, the trader would go long one Eurodollar contract at a price of 88.

Let's assume the that the trade works as planned: the Eurodollar contract climbs to 89, producing an 11-percent yield and the gold spread moves to $500 and $555, also producing an 11-percent yield.

Gold Spread

Sold 11 contracts at $500   Bought 10 contracts at $550
Buys 11 contracts at $500   Sells 10 contracts at $555
Profit: 0   Profit: $5000
Result: $5000 profit

Eurodollar Position

Sold Eurodollar contracts at 89
Overall result: $10,000 profit

CONVENTIONAL BULL AND BEAR SPREADS

Compared with trading tailed gold spreads against Eurodollar futures, conventional bull and bear gold spreads are much simpler. The goal in bull and bear spreads is to participate in a rise or fall in the price of gold with a minimum of risk. Unlike the trader who uses gold spreads as interest rate instruments, the trader using conventional gold spreads need not be concerned with tailing or spread yields. Mainly, he's concerned about the absolute price difference between the two contracts.

If a trader believes that the price of gold is going to rise, he may put on a bull spread by selling the nearby contract and buying an equal number of deferred contracts. As mentioned earlier, generally the price of the deferred contract will rise faster in bull markets and decline faster in bear markets than the price of the nearby. The reason is twofold.

The pricing of deferred gold futures contracts is mainly a function of interest rates. With the cash price of gold at $500 and one-year interest rates at 10 percent, the price of one-year futures contract should be $550. Obviously, if the cash price of gold rises, it will cost more to finance the gold because the gold is now worth more. Thus, if the cash price jumps $100 to $600, the deferred will move up $100, plus an incremental factor based on the increased cost of financing the higher-priced cash gold. In the example, the deferred would rise $110 to $660.

In addition to increased or decreased financing costs related to changes in the cash price of gold, prices of deferred gold contracts are also affected by changes in interest rates. In the majority of cases, rising gold prices herald rising interest rates and falling gold prices herald falling interest rates. For spreaders, that's a plus, because the normal relationship between interest rates and gold price changes benefits both bull and bear spreads. When both gold prices and interest rates are rising, the price difference between the nearby and deferred will grow ever more wider. The converse is true when gold prices and interest rates are falling. But, as was discussed in the section on tails, the relationship between gold price changes and interest rates sometimes breaks down. In those cases, the spread trader might be right about the direction of gold prices, but an adverse move in interest rates wipes out some or all of his profits.

So, while the prospective gold spread trader should be primarily concerned with the price of gold, he ought to pay at least a modicum of attention to interest rates. If it appears that interest rates will fall, it might not be a good idea to put on a bull spread. Likewise, the trader should be wary of putting on a bear spread in a period of rising rates.

BULL SPREAD

The nearby gold futures contract is at $400 and the six-month deferred contract is $420. The trader believes gold prices will rise, but does not want to take on the risk of an outright long position. Instead, he puts on a bull spread.

Sells five contracts at $400   Buys five contracts at $420

Let's assume that the nearby contract jumped to $450. With interest rates constant, the price of the six-month deferred would move to $472.50.

Buys five contracts at $450   Sells five contracts at $472.50
Loss: $25,,000   Profit: $26,250
Result: $1,250 profit

Clearly, this is a modest profit when compared to the $26,250 that could have been made by simply buying five contracts at $420. But remember, if interest rates went up, as could be expected with such a large jump in gold prices, the spread would have been more profitable. Let's assume that during the course of the price rise, the six-month rate rose from 10 percent to 11 percent. All else being equal, that would push the six-month contract up to $474.75. Recalculating the trade:

Buys five contracts at $450   Sells five contracts at $474.75
Loss: $25,000   Profit: $27,375
Result: $2,375 profit

Of course, one of the great attractions to spreads is that they require less margin commitment than outright positions. At the time of writing, Comex gold spread margins were $100 per spread, while outright position margins were $4000 per contract. Thus, in the example above, the five-contract spread would have required only a $500 margin deposit, and would have earned a return on capital of over 450 percent. In contrast, a five-contract long position on the nearby contract would have required a margin deposit of $20,000. Although the outright long position would have earned $25,000, that would represent only a 25-percent return on capital.

At the same time that spreads frequently produce higher rates of return than outright positions, they also entail considerably less risk. Using the same example as above, with the nearby at $400 and the deferred at $420, suppose the five-contract bull spread moved against the trader. That is, gold prices fell instead of rose, contrary to the traders expectations.

Sold five contracts at $400   Bought five contracts at $420
Price moves to $380   Price moves to $397
Profit: $10,000   Loss: $11,500
Net Loss: $1500

Remember, since deferred contracts tend to move more than the nearby, the example is entirely realistic in suggesting that the losses on the deferred would outweigh the gains on the nearby. Nonetheless, even with the potential for a modest loss, the bull spread trade is substantially less risky than an outright long position. Indeed, if the trader opted for a five-contract outright long position in the nearby instead of putting on bull spread, he would have lost $10,000.

Bull and bear spreads illustrate an important principle in the gold market: when price moves rapidly, the deferred contracts usually move more than the nearby.

That being the case, it would seem logical to speculate using the deferred contracts when one is confident that the market is going to move in a particular direction. Many traders use this approach, and, when they're right, they reap the benefits. However, there is a problem: the deferred contracts tend to be less liquid and have a wider bid/ask spread than the nearby. As a result, the market may have to move a substantial amount in order for the trader to benefit from the inherent tendency of the deferred to move more than the nearby. Thus, for short-term, low-profit-expectation trading, the disadvantages of the deferred contracts frequently outweigh the advantages. On the other hand, for a long-term trade in which the trader expects a substantial move, the deferred contracts often provide the greatest profit potential.

INTERMARKET SPREADS

Earlier in this chapter, we discussed how traders exploit price discrepancies between cash and futures prices. In a similar fashion, a small group of traders constantly monitor prices on the various exchanges where gold is traded. When prices move sufficiently apart, these traders are prepared to arbitrage the difference.

The Comex gold futures prices are, of course, the benchmark. The New York market has more liquidity and a larger amount of participation from commercial gold users than any other gold futures contract in the world. As a result, most of the intermarket arbitrage reflects an attempt to keep other gold futures contracts in line with the price changes at the Comex.

The major players in intermarket spreads are the same banks and brokerage firms that are active in the gold/cash market arbitrage described earlier in the chapter. In order to engage in this kind of activity, a floor presence is required so that the best possible execution can be obtained in the pit. In addition, since the arbitrage usually involves only a few ticks, large positions—requiring a great deal of capital—must be put on to make a reasonable profit.

The arbitrage works like any other kind of spread. For example, if the Chicago Board of Trade's gold contract falls to a five tick, or 50 cent, discount to the Comex contract, someone will buy the cheaper CBOT contract and sell the higher priced Comex contract. Eventually, when the contract prices converge, the spread will be unwound at a profit.

INTERCOMMODITY SPREADS

The gold/silver spread is undoubtedly the most widely known metals spread. It received a great deal of attention during the metal price surge of the late 1970s and early 1980s. In recent years, however, investor interest in the spread waned with the decreased attractiveness of metals in general.

The price ratio of gold to silver has varied considerably throughout history, from an apparent low of 6:1 in Babylon in 1800 BC to a high of 100:1 during the 1930s in the U.S. Since gold prices were allowed to float in 1973, the ratio has ranged from about a low of 18:1 to a high of about 76:1. The average ratio, during this period, has been around 35:1.

When the ratio approaches its upper levels, traders may deduce that gold is overvalued relative to silver, so they sell gold and buy silver in the belief that the ratio will narrow. Conversely, if the ratio drops to its lower levels, traders may buy gold and sell silver, in the hope that the ratio will widen.

Although spreads can be constructed using the cash market, it's much easier using futures, particularly in the case of the gold/silver spread since both gold and silver futures are traded on the Comex. Spread trades on the two commodities require lower margins and frequently lower commission costs than outright positions.

The second most widely traded metals spread is gold/platinum. In recent years, the spread has ranged from platinum at a $100 discount to a $250 premium over gold prices. Because platinum is an industrial metal, demand and price fluctuate strongly in response to economic growth.

Platinum futures contracts, which are traded on the New York Mercantile Exchange (Nymex), are 50 ounces in size. Thus, for every Comex gold contract, a trader would have buy or sell two Nymex platinum contracts. Despite being on different exchanges, the two contracts are eligible for spread margins.

CHAPTER 9

Application of Elliott Wave Theory to Gold Futures

Developed by an accountant named Ralph Nelson Elliott in the 1930s, Elliott Wave theory grew wildly popular during the 1980s due to the forecasting success of its leading modern-day practitioner, Robert Prechter. Although Prechter's reputation was tarnished somewhat by the stock market collapse in October 1987 (he predicted the market would break 3000, however, he did advise his clients to exit the market a few days prior to the 19th) the theory continues to be utilized by thousands of investors.

Underlying Elliott Wave theory is the premise that markets are driven by the vicissitudes of investor sentiment. As investors move from optimism to pessimism and back to optimism, discernible patterns, or what Elliott called waves, are formed. These waves are repeated, both in the largest and smallest possible time frames. Over the long-term, the wave patterns are unaffected by outside events and market fundamentals. Indeed, to the pure Elliott Wave theorist, outside events are the consequence of mass psychological mood shifts. The mood shifts, not the events themselves, are the key in determining the direction of the market.

Elliott Wave theory was developed from a study of the stock market, however, technicians have been applying it to the gold market for a number of years. Theorists believe that Elliott Wave may be a particularly apt technical approach to gold because psychological factors seem to play a prominent role in determining gold prices. Whether this is true or not is up to the reader to decide. In any event, the following is a brief outline of the theory, complete with examples from the gold market. Anyone desiring further information on the theory should read either *Elliott Wave Principle* by A.J. Frost and Robert Prechter or *The Major Works of R.N. Elliott,* edited by Robert Prechter.

BASIC TENETS

In its simplest form, Elliott Wave theory holds that markets advance or decline in a series of five waves, followed by a three wave correction. Figure 9.1, depicts a wave cycle in a rising market. The five waves that make up the advancing portion are often called up waves, while the three waves that make up the correction are called down waves. Within the advancing portion, the rising waves are called impulse waves and the

---

Figure 9.1 The Basic Wave Cycle

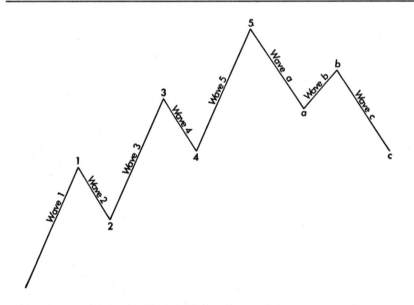

Source: Frost, A.J. and Prechter, Robert R. "Elliot Wave Principle: Key to Stock Market Profits" (Gainsville, GA: New Classics Library, Inc., 1985). Reprinted with premission.

falling waves called corrective waves. In a falling market, the wave cycle is reversed, consisting of a five-wave decline, followed by a three-wave rise. In the declining segment of a falling wave cycle, the declining waves are called impulse waves and the rising waves are called corrective waves.

According to the theory, the five-wave up/three-wave down movement reflects the basic dynamic of the market. At any one time, this basic pattern is working itself out in both the largest and smallest possible time periods. In the stock market, for example, Elliott Wave talks about a "supercycle" which involves single wave formations that take years and years to develop. On the other end of the spectrum, the theory identifies "sub-minuette" waves that take only seconds to develop.

The complete wave cycle, according to Elliott, consists of a five-wave/three-wave advance, followed by another five-wave/three-wave advance, and a final five-wave advance. This portion of the cycle produces a single up wave in the next highest wave formation. After that, the market goes through a corrective stage which consists of five-wave/three-wave decline followed by another five-wave decline. The corrective stage completes the wave cycle, while at the same time it produces a single down wave in the formation of the next highest degree. Once the wave cycle is completed, the entire process starts all over again. The complete cycle is shown in figure 9.2.

Central to Elliott Wave theory is the theorem that, at any point in time, a particular wave formation can be reduced to a single wave in the next highest formation or it can be subdivided into a number of smaller waves in the next lowest wave formation. For example, a five-wave, advancing formation typically forms a single up-wave in the next highest formation. At the same time, a single up-wave in the original formation can be divided into either a five- or three-wave advance in the next lowest formation. Thus, every wave is part of the basic 5/3 pattern itself, but, at the same time, it is part of other wave formations. The Elliott Wave analyst, therefore, must not only identify one basic formation, he must also identify how any particular wave pattern fits in with waves of higher and lower degrees.

Elliott identified nine basic wave types, from the largest to the smallest: Grand Supercycle, Supercycle, Cycle, Primary, Intermediate, Minor, Minute, Minuette, Sub-Minuette. Since each wave subdivides into the next smallest wave, it follows that the Grand Supercycle wave subdivides

---

Figure 9.2   The Complete Market Cycle

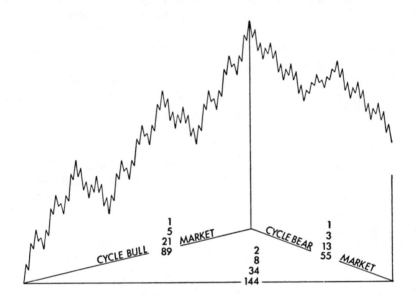

Source: "Elliot Wave Principle." Reprinted with permission.

into smaller Supercycle waves and Supercycle waves subdivide into Cycle waves, and so on down to the Sub-Minuette level.

Although Elliott maintained that markets follow a distinct wave pattern, he acknowledged that irregularities frequently occur. In impulse waves, he described several such variations: extensions, diagonal triangles, and failures. In corrective waves, he discovered other variations: zigzags, flats, triangles, and double threes and triple threes. The following is a brief description of these variations:

IMPULSE WAVES

Extensions

Impulse waves sometimes extend, creating a wave pattern that can obscure the basic five-wave up formation. Extensions can occur in waves one, three, or five. Most up-waves contain one extension, however, few waves contain more than one extension. Consequently, if the first wave extends, then it can be anticipated that waves three and five will revert to conventional form. Conversely, if waves one and three reflect normal patterns, then there's a good chance that wave five will extend.

In most cases, the impulse wave itself and its extension form five waves. Thus, when combined with the other conventional waves, the entire movement consists of nine up-waves. Frequently, it's difficult to distinguish between the conventional waves and the extensions, since

---

Figure 9.3   An Extended Fifth Wave

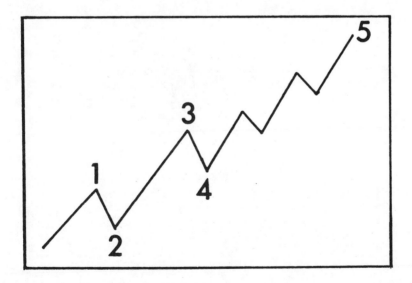

Source: "Elliot Wave Principle." Reprinted with permission.

extensions often are about the same size as conventional waves. However, that's not problematic because according to the theory, five- and nine-wave up movements possess the same technical importance.

Diagonal Triangles

Diagonal triangles occur in the fifth wave. As illustrated in figure 9.4, a diagonal triangle can be subdivided into a five-wave sequence. Moreover, each of the five waves can be further subdivided into a three-wave movement. Generally, a rising diagonal triangle is bearish and a falling diagonal triangle is bullish.

Figure 9.4   A Diagonal Triangle

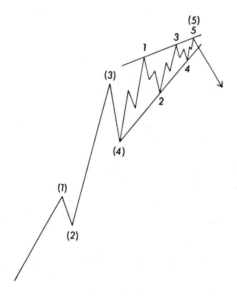

Source: "Elliot Wave Principle." Reprinted with permission.

Figure 9.5   Bull Market Failure

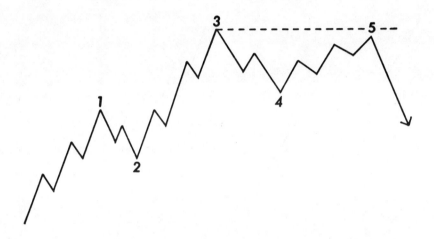

Source: "Elliot Wave Principle." Reprinted with permission.

Failure

Failures occur when the fifth wave in a five-wave up formation fails to rise above the third wave. Failures can be corroborated when the fifth wave can be broken down into five sub-waves. Obviously, a failure denotes market weakness.

CORRECTIVE WAVES

Generally speaking, corrective waves are much more difficult to track than impulse waves. Frequently, portions of a three-wave corrective sequence expand or contract, creating a very uneven formation. As a result, it's sometimes difficult for analysts to discern where a correction ends and where the next impulse sequence begins.

Figure 9.6   Zigzag Correction in a Bull Market

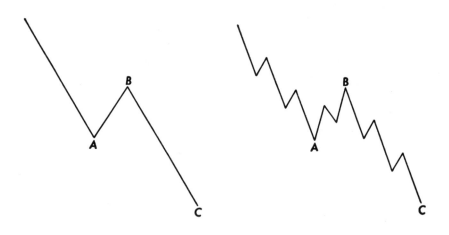

Instead of a conventional three-wave correction, in a zigzag correction each wave subdivides to form a 5-3-5 wave pattern.

Source: "Elliot Wave Principle." Reprinted with permission.

Zigzags

A zigzag is a conventional corrective wave that divides into a three-wave sequence. When broken down, the first wave of the zigzag subdivides into a five-wave sequence, the second wave into a three wave sequence, and the third wave into a five-wave sequence. However, the correction as a whole always reflects a three-wave movement; there can never be a five-wave correction. Occasionally, markets produce a double zigzag formation, consisting of two zigzag movements separated by an intervening three-wave movement.

Figure 9.7   Flat Correction in a Bull Market

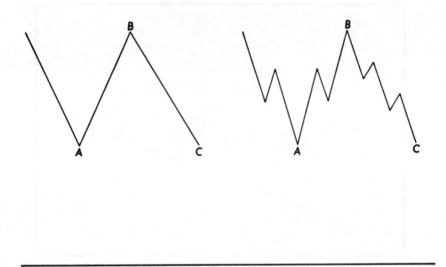

 In a flat correction each wave subdivides to form a 3-3-5 wave
pattern.

Source: "Elliot Wave Principle." Reprinted with permission.

Flats

A flat is a zigzag pattern that breaks down into a 3-3-5 wave sequence.
Generally, flats indicate weakness in the corrective movement and
strength in the broader trend. If, in a bull market, a flat-type correction
is upwardly skewed (whereby the C wave finishes higher than the A wave,
as shown in figure 9.7), then one can deduce that the market is especially
strong.

Figure 9.8   Ascending Triangle: A Corrective Bull Market
                   Formation

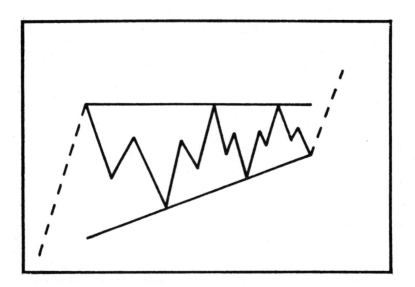

Source: "Elliot Wave Principle." Reprinted with permission.

Triangles

Triangles, as depicted in figure 9.8, usually occur prior to the final movement in the direction of the overall trend. In most cases, they break down into five waves, with each of the five waves in turn subdivided into three waves. Triangles usually move in a more or less sideways fashion and are usually characterized by low volume.

According to the theory, trendlines established by triangles tend to be highly accurate until the final wave. In the fifth wave, the trendlines frequently break down, particularly in expanding and contracting triangles. After the triangle is completed, the ensuing impulse is usually swift and relatively short, traveling a distant approximate to the widest part of the triangle.

Double Threes and Triple Threes

Some corrective waves combine elements of zigzags, flats, and triangle—creating elongated patterns that usually consist of a total of seven or eleven waves. For the most part, double and triple threes move horizontally, although they sometimes move in an angular fashion against the underlying trend. These formations usually reflect a degree of indecision or hesitation in the market. Frequently, they're followed by a strong move in the direction of the underlying trend.

RULES AND GUIDELINES

Alternation

This rule posits that wave formations rarely repeat in terms of size or complexity. If, for example, corrective wave two is short and simple, then corrective wave four almost certainly will evidence a different pattern: it may not necessarily be long and complex, however it will be different from wave two. This rule serves to keep the analyst alert to the unexpected.

Strength of Trends

Corrections are an excellent indicator of the strength of the underlying trend. Zigzags and double zigzags indicate a normal trend, while the more complicated corrective formations suggest a more powerful trend. In order of magnitude, from weakest to strongest, the bullishness of corrective formations (in a rising market) are as follows: zigzag and double zigzag; flat and irregular; double and triple threes; triangle, and running correction. In bear markets, the bearishness of corrective formations follows the same sequence.

Overlapping and Length of Waves

Elliott posited two rules regarding waves. (1) Wave four in a five-wave sequence should not overlap wave one except within diagonal triangles. (2) Wave three in a five-wave sequence can never be the shortest of the three impulse waves. Whenever it appears that a five-wave sequence

violates either of these two rules, the wave count must be retabulated in
such a way that the rules remain intact.

Wave Equality

In most five-wave sequences, two of the impulse waves will tend to be
about the same size and develop over a similar time span. This is
especially true if one of the impulse waves extends. In cases where the
two non-extending impulse waves are unequal in length and time magnitude, a ratio of 0.618 is the next most likely relationship.

Channeling

Once a wave pattern has been identified, a trend channel can be constructed by drawing a line connecting the bottoms of waves one and two
and a parallel trend line running through the top of wave one. If wave
three violates the trend line on the upside, the trend line should be
reconstructed by connecting the top of wave one with the top of wave
three and drawing a parallel line running through the bottom of wave
two. When the wave formation is completed, the final channel should
consist of a trend line connecting the bottoms of waves two and four and
a parallel line running through the top of wave three.

To create a price channel, one only needs three reference points. The
reference points are taken from the tops and bottoms of waves in an
unfolding formation. Once two bottoms have been established—i.e. the
bottoms of waves one and two—a trend line can be drawn. The upside
trend line is then drawn through a wave top—i.e. the top of wave
one—and runs parallel to the bottom trend line. As the formation unfolds
and new wave tops and bottoms are established, the price channel should
be updated.

Channeling provides a reference point that is useful in assessing how
far a wave is likely to move, determining whether a wave is completed,
and separating different waves. Although incipient trend lines often will
be violated, the nature of the violation can provide clues about the
strength of the underlying trend.

WAVE PERSONALITY

Wave personalities reflect the shifts in investor psychology that Elliott claimed are the causal agents behind price movements. As investors move from optimism to pessimism and back again, wave patterns and individual wave structures tend to be repeated. A working knowledge of the characteristics of individual waves can provide valuable clues in interpreting the structure of the larger waves.

First Waves

About 50 percent of first waves appear to be simply corrections in a down market. Market sentiment remains bearish, in these cases, and frequently wave two erases much of the wave one gains. The other 50 percent of first waves arise from a more extended basing process. Consequently, they tend to be sharper and longer, and generally retain much of their gains through the wave two correction.

Second Waves

Second waves confirm to many investors that the overall trend is down, and therefore retrace much of wave one. However, in order to confirm that a new five-wave cycle is in the making, wave two must not breach the bottom of wave one. If it does, a new analysis is in order. Generally, the bottom of wave two is characterized by a substantial decrease in trading volume.

Third Waves

Third waves frequently are the strongest wave in a formation, producing the greatest price movement and largest volume. At this stage, market psychology becomes increasingly optimistic and fundamentals become supportive of the emerging trend. Given these characteristics, it's not surprising that third waves frequently extend. To be classified as a third wave, a structure can never be the shortest wave in a formation.

Fourth Waves

Fourth waves more often than not are more complex than second wave corrections, perhaps because market psychology has become more divided at this stage. However, if the second wave was complex, expect wave four to be simple, as a result of the rule of alternation. Generally, however, the second wave is simple and the fourth wave is complex.

Fifth Waves

In the stock market, wave five is usually less dynamic than wave three, however, in commodities, wave five frequently is the strongest wave in the formation. At this stage, market psychology is extremely optimistic, a sure sign that a reversal is in order because everybody that wants to buy is already in the market. Accordingly, near the top of the market, technical signals begin to indicate an overbought situation.

Wave A

After a five-wave advancing cycle, the A wave is generally misinterpreted by most investors as a correction in a long-term bull market. An A wave can be confirmed if it breaks down into a five-wave pattern. Also, the volume in an A wave is frequently stronger than volume in waves two and four in the preceding advancing move.

Wave B

Wave B is simply a correction in the newly established downtrend. Generally, it's characterized by low volume and weak technicals. Nonetheless, a B wave may test or even exceed the market's previous high before the market turns back down.

Wave C

Wave C is usually the strongest wave in the A-B-C sequence. In most cases, Wave C will retrace all of Wave B, breaking the lows established by Wave A. As Wave C unfolds, psychology turns extremely pessimistic, a development that leaves many investors unprepared for the subsequent rise as a new advancing cycle begins.

EXAMPLES

The huge advance in the gold market in the 1970s neatly fit Elliott Wave patterns. After the two-tier price system was abolished early in the decade, gold rallied to around $70 in July 1972, completing the first wave of an Elliott cycle. Subsequently, a corrective wave brought the price down to around $60 an ounce by late November. Wave three, which stretched into mid-1973, took the price up to $125. Wave four pushed the price back down to $90 late in 1973. Finally, wave five brought the price to around $180 in April 1974, completing the five-wave structure.

At that stage, a three-wave bull market correction transpired, which was the precursor to the biggest price surge ever in the history of gold. In the A wave, the price dropped to around $125, which was followed by a B wave that reached $200 on the last day of 1974. Then, in wave C, the price dropped dramatically, falling all the way to $103.50, a move that completed the two-year, bull market correction.

The first wave of the next five-wave up cycle started modestly enough, pushing the price up to around $155 in a six-month move. The wave two correction brought the price down to $137, while wave three took the market back up to just under $190. Wave four, for its part, brought the market down a bit, to around $167. Wave five, which ultimately would top out at $850, started here, at $167.

Based on the initial four waves, Elliott Wave theory could build a strong case that wave five would bring substantially higher prices. For one thing, neither wave one nor wave three extended, and, according to the theory, one impulse wave extends in the typical structure. And, in the commodity markets, it's usually the fifth wave that extends. Moreover, the corrective waves two and four were quite weak, suggesting a very strong bullish sentiment was buttressing the market.

As might have been expected, wave five extended, bringing the market to historic highs. As figure 9.9 shows, the extension can be broken down into a five-wave pattern of its own. Together with the first four waves of the structure, wave five and its extension created a nine-wave structure, a formation that is perfectly compatible with Elliott's guidelines.

Figure 9.9   Elliott Wave Interpretation of gold prices between 1970
and 1980

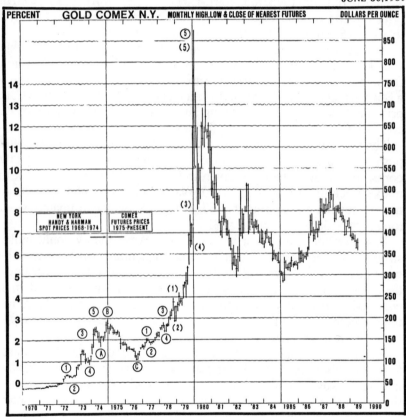

Gold Prices Courtesy of the Commodity Research Bureau.

CHAPTER 10

Market Logic Approach to Trading Gold Futures

This chapter presents a brief overview of market logic theory, followed by an application of the theory to a five-day period in the gold market. More information can be obtained from several recent books: *Markets 101* by Kevin Koy, *Steidlmayer on Markets* by J. Peter Steidlmayer and Kevin Koy, and *Mind Over Markets* by James Dalton. The market logic approach to trading, or, as its sometimes called, the Market Profile® approach, has stirred a storm of interest since its introduction in the mid-1980s. The method's novel, yet down-to-earth, approach has struck a responsive chord with veteran and neophyte traders alike. As a result of its popularity, market logic has spawned a cottage industry of data services, advisory services and a trading school.

Unlike many technical theories, the market logic approach is based on broad principles, which are drawn from and are applicable to all markets. According to market logic, futures markets are no different than the automobile market, the exotic fish market, or the stock market. Indeed, so all-encompassing and universal are the principles of market logic, proponents claim it disproves academic theories of market behavior, such as random walk and the efficient market theory.

The market logic approach starts with a simple premise: the purpose of any free market is to facilitate trade. From this premise, the theory then describes how the components of the market—price and time—interact to fulfill the market's purpose. Finally, the theory breaks down market participants by the time horizon in which they operate and describes how changes in market participation by various time-frame traders define the condition of the market and provide clues to future market direction.

PURPOSE OF THE MARKET

The implicit purpose of any market is to facilitate trade. That's true of a shoe store, an airline, or the gold market. A market is nothing more than a facility in which buyers and sellers come together for the purpose of satisfying their needs; i.e., the need of the seller to sell his product or service for a profit, and the need of the buyer to purchase that product or service at a fair price. To the extent that both buyers and sellers can accomplish their purposes in the marketplace, over a long period of time, then the market can be said to be facilitating trade. However, if either the buyer or seller is forced to pull back from the market, then trade facilitation will suffer. Importantly, the components of the marketplace act in such a way as to encourage the facilitation of trade over the long term.

An example may be illuminating. In the late 1970s, a host of events conspired to push crude oil prices to over $30 per barrel. In reaction to the higher prices, buyers took a number of steps to reduce their purchases of oil, such as conservation and fuel switching. In the vernacular of market logic, the higher prices did not facilitate trade; i.e., buyers felt the price was unfair and, as a result, they reduced their consumption. At the same time, producers recognized the higher prices as a profit opportunity, so they brought new wells on stream, thereby increasing the supply of crude oil. Eventually, the combination of decreased consumption by buyers and increased production by producers created an excess supply, which eventually forced sellers to lower prices in order to encourage consumption. In the end, prices fell to a level in which fuel switching and conservation lessened, and overall crude oil demand picked up. In other words, price moved to a level in which the market once again facilitated trade by satisfying the needs of buyers to purchase fuel at a fair price.

PRICE AND TIME

If one starts with the premise that the purpose of the market is to facilitate trade, then all market components can be defined by the manner in which they contribute to trade facilitation. In this regard, market logic differs substantially from most other market theories, which focus exclusively on price. Market logic postulates that price is only one aspect of the market, and, that to understand and forecast price movements, price must be placed in the larger context of market activity and trade facilitation.

In isolation, price has little meaning. Price is a variable, and without reference to a constant, price movements indeed are random. Thus, in order to understand its significance, price must be evaluated against a constant. That constant is time.

According to market logic theory, over time, price tends to migrate to the area that facilitates trade, which, in turn, is defined as that area where both buyers and sellers can consistently satisfy their needs. The market logic approach defines this area as value. Value can be described as follows:

Price + time = trade facilitation = volume = value

Value in any market is defined by the price or price area where the predominant portion of trade takes place. Conversely, those prices where very little volume takes place, or where price spends very little time, are prices outside of value.

Time, as the equation above demonstrates, is an essential part of the marketplace. Time defines whether a particular price is within or outside of value. Indeed, time defines all price/value relationships.

Price, as part of its role in developing value, works to promote activity by drawing the various participants into the marketplace. Price moves down to attract buyers and moves up to attract sellers. When price moves too high, as was the case with crude oil in the early 1980s, buying activity is shut off. When price moves too low, selling activity is shut off. In both these cases, price moved beyond the value area, the area where trade was facilitated. Since the purpose of the market is to facilitate trade, price eventually was drawn back to the value area.

Price then tends to stay in the area where the most volume is traded, but periodically moves up and down to draw participants into the market. Generally speaking, price will continue moving directionally higher until the last buyer has satisfied his needs and will continue directionally lower until the last seller has satisfied his needs. Thus, in rotating up and down, price fulfills its function of facilitating trade, because it attracts buyers and sellers who otherwise may have remained uncommitted if the price had stayed in the value area. At the same time, the rotational movement identifies price rejection areas (prices that are rejected by either buyers or sellers as unfair), which helps to define the parameters of the value area.

This point should be heeded by traders who use protective stops, and sometimes find the market takes out their stop and then moves in the opposite direction. Since the market's purpose is to facilitate trade, and since the market routinely rotates up and down to accomplish that end, then it stands to reason that the market will frequently take out stops that are located near the present value area. Once those stops are taken out and there's no more trading pressure, then the market will move back toward the value area. This activity reflects the market's natural disposition to facilitate trade: it does not reflect corruption on the part of pit traders or idiosyncratic market behavior.

The following theorem defines how price and time interact to fulfill the purpose of the market:

The market promotes itself through price and regulates itself through time.

Price is the mechanism by which participants are attracted into the market. Time regulates that mechanism by defining the market acceptance (or rejection) of various prices. When prices go too high or low, they spend little time there, as participants rush in to take advantage of the opportunity presented by the excess prices. Thus, time defines the excess price and, in so doing, brings an end to the price promotional move. Similarly, after prices return to a value area, time reaffirms the validity of the value area.

CAUSALITY OF PRICE MOVEMENTS

Market logic is different than most other approaches to trading in that it doesn't explicitly predict where prices will go. Instead, it seeks to define the present condition of the market, an exercise that then allows a trader to make an informed hypothesis about where prices are likely to move. For example, if higher prices are facilitating trade, then it follows that prices are likely to continue to move higher. On the other hand, if prices are not facilitating trade, and a rotational move up fails to generate much activity, then there's a good chance the market will test trade facilitation on the downside.

Thus, instead of providing predictions of where prices will go, market logic theory provides insight into whether the market is in a state of continuation or change. Very simply, to the extent that a particular activity is facilitating trade, that activity will continue. To the extent that the activity is not facilitating trade, it augurs for a change in activity.

A key to assessing market conditions is understanding the behavior of long-time-frame traders. According to the theory, long-time-frame traders cause directional price movement, while short-time-frame traders generally operate within the value area and have little effect on price direction. Short-time-frame traders generally include locals in the pits, off-exchange traders who try to scalp markets each day, and any trader who, for whatever reason, is forced to trade on that particular day. Long-time-frame traders, on the other hand, usually are off-exchange traders who are under no compulsion to trade immediately. They can afford to wait for an especially good opportunity.

By monitoring the activity of long-time-frame traders, one can develop a good reading on the condition of the market. For example, if long-time-frame buyers are aggressively buying, while long-time-frame sellers are absent from the market, prices will likely go up. However, once long-time-frame sellers begin to sell in response to higher prices, the condition of the market changes and price direction becomes more uncertain. Thus, to a great extent, the condition of the market can be defined in terms of the activity of long-time-frame traders and the degree to which their activity is facilitating trade.

BELL CURVE: THE MARKET'S ORGANIZING PRINCIPLE

In order to isolate the activity of long-time-frame traders, and, indeed, to bring to life all of the principles of market logic it's necessary to organize market data into bell curve-type structures. The bell curve is a statistical tool used to measure distribution. A perfect bell curve of test scores, for example, might have a small number of scores above 95, an equal number of scores below 65, and the rest of the scores in between, with the highest number of scores at 80.

Applied to the futures markets, a bell curve representation of a day's trading activity would look something like what you see in Figure 10.1

This, of course, only approximates the shape of a bell curve. The perfect curve would be absolutely symmetrical, with narrow extremes widening into a broad middle area. Although the markets rarely produce

---

Figure 10.1 Bell Curve

```
K
K
K
DK
DEKL
DEKLM
DEFKLM
DEFGKLM
DEFGIKLM
BDEFGIJK
BCDFGIJK
ABCDFGIJK
ABCGHIJK
ABCHI
ABCHI
ABCHI
BCH
BC
C
C
C
```

a perfect bell curve, the natural price distribution activity found in free markets consistently produces a bell-curve-type structure. In most daily trading sessions, there is little volume near the top and the bottom of the day's range, while there is a considerable amount of volume in the middle or in the middle and towards one extreme of the day's range.

The bell curve representation of the futures markets provides an excellent means to identify value and to analyze the market in terms of market logic principles. Along the vertical axis are prices; along the horizontal axis, in a less explicit fashion, is time. As depicted in the example above, each letter bracket represents a half-hour of trading. Thus the first half-hour is identified by "A," the second half hour by "B," and so on until the day's final half-hour, identified by "M."

The use of letter-designated, half-hour time brackets allows the trader to see where, during the course of the day, the market spent most of its time. That area, according to the equation Price + Time = Value, represents value for that day. Similarly, the bell-curve arrangement provides easy identification of prices outside of value, i.e. prices that existed for a short period of time.

In addition to providing a means to recognize value, the bell curve arrangement provides a framework to analyze the behavior of long-time-frame traders. According to the theory, long-time-frame activity can be isolated in three distinct areas:

Extremes

Extremes are single tick formations of at least two ticks in length that occur at the bottom and top of the day's range. In the example above, the three-tick formations in C and K are extremes.

Extremes are formed by long-time-frame traders taking advantage of prices outside of value on that particular day. Extremes on the bottom of the range are formed by long-time-frame buying. Extremes on the top of the range are formed by long-time-frame selling.

In most cases, extremes indicate the area where market rotation in one direction is overwhelmed by responsive activity in the opposite direction.

The power of any particular extreme is inversely proportional to the amount of time the market spends at the extreme. In other words, the faster the market moves away from an extreme, the more powerful is the extreme.

An extreme is only confirmed when the market fails to trade in that area during the remainder of the day. Therefore, it a single-tick formation occurs at the top or bottom of the day's range in the final half-hour period, it is not considered an extreme.

Range Extensions

In most markets, the first hour of trading is identified as the initial balance. The initial balance, in essence, represents the view of locals as to where the market will trade that day.

The top of the initial balance is the area where locals expect selling will be attracted and the bottom represents the area where they expect buying might come in. In the example on page 164, the area contained by A and B represents the initial balance.

Range extensions occur when the initial balance is broken, as was the case in periods C and D in the example. According to the market logic theory, any break in the initial balance is due to the activity of long-time-frame traders. An upward break is caused by long-time-frame buying, a downward break is caused by long-time-frame selling.

Time Price Opportunity (TPO) Count

Each individual letter in the profile represents a single TPO. To calculate the TPO count, take the price which has the most TPOs, cross it out, and count the number of TPOs above and below it, excluding single ticks. If there is more than one price which qualifies as having the most TPOs, select the price closest to the middle of the day's range. More TPOs on the bottom signifies TPO buying; more TPOs on the top signifies TPO selling.

In the example, the price with the most TPOs is ABCDEFGHIJK. Underneath that price, there are 28 TPOs, excluding the single ticks at the bottom of the range. Above that price, there are 48 TPOs. Therefore, since there are more TPOs on top, the activity is interpreted as TPO selling.

The TPO count essentially measures long-time-frame activity in the value area. As is also the case with extremes, market logic theory assumes that long-time-frame traders are sellers at the day's higher prices, and buyers at the day's lower prices.

It should be noted that TPOs are only useful in rotating markets. On trend days, the TPO reading is assumed to favor the direction of the trend, irregardless of the TPO count.

Extremes are the most powerful form of long-time-frame activity, followed by range extensions and TPO count. However, a trader should be aware that all instances of the same type of market activity are not identical: some extremes are stronger than other extremes and some range extensions are stronger than other range extensions. That being the case, in any given day, the TPO count may be more important in terms of assessing the condition of the market than an extreme or a range extension.

DETERMINING THE VALUE AREA

Value, as described earlier, is the price area where the market spends the most time and transacts the greatest amount of volume. To determine the value area on any particular day, the Market Profile® offers a somewhat arbitrary measurement: value is equal to 70 percent of the day's volume.

Since the value area, theoretically, is a reflection of transaction volume at various prices, it ought to be measured using actual volume statistics. Unfortunately, volume information is not available on an on-line basis from every exchange, so most market logic traders use a TPO or tick-based value area. In both cases, the value area is determined by identifying the high volume price—whether in terms of ticks or TPOs—and then adding prices above and below that price until 70 percent of that day's activity is accounted for.

INITIATING AND RESPONSIVE ACTIVITY

The value area provides a basis for evaluating the strength of long-time-frame activity. Each day, as a new market unfolds, long-time-frame activity is interpreted in relation to the value area of the previous day. Depending on whether long-time-frame traders are operating within or outside of the previous day's value area, long-time-frame activity is either initiating or responsive. Initiating behavior is more powerful than responsive behavior.

When long-time-frame buyers are active within or above the previous day's value area, that activity is initiating. For example, if a buying extreme occurs at a price that is within the previous day's value area, then the extreme is called initiating. Similarly, a buying range extension that occurs within the previous day's value area is initiating. On the other hand, the buying activity is deemed responsive if it takes place below the previous day's value area.

The concept behind initiating and responsive behavior is quite simple. In essence, when buyers are buying at higher prices, they are initiating. When they are buying at lower prices, they're responding.

The situation is similar with long-time-frame selling. When long-time frame selling takes place within or below the previous day's value area, the activity is initiating. When it takes place above the previous day's value area, it is responsive.

Long-time-frame trading should be interpreted in light of the market's underlying purpose of facilitating trade. In a market that's trending up, for example, it's quite likely that there will be ample evidence of long-time-frame buying, and, perhaps, a good deal of responsive selling. As long as the market is trending up, the long-time-frame buying probably will facilitate trade, or, at least, facilitate more than long-time-frame selling. When long-time-frame buying ceases, or, when it stops facilitating trade, it's a signal that the up trend may be over.

DAY STRUCTURES

In organizing markets in a bell curve arrangement, there are a handful of recurring structures. Generally, the structures reflect the modes of activity of long-time-frame traders. By recognizing the structures as they unfold, a trader can gain a great deal of insight as to how the rest of the day will progress. The most common structures are: normal, normal variation, neutral, and trend days.

Normal

In a normal day, the initial balance established during the first hour of trading holds for most of the day. The initial balance may be extended, but not by more than 20 percent. This structure is usually characterized by price rotation up and down, but a clear lack of trade facilitation on any move beyond the initial balance. Long-time-frame traders are relatively inactive.

Normal Variation

A normal variation day differs from a normal day in that it entails greater participation by long-time-frame traders. Accordingly, a normal variation day is marked by a strong range extension (in one direction only) that often is equal to the size of the initial balance. Like the normal day, the normal variation day usually resembles a bell curve.

Neutral

On a neutral day, the initial balance is extended in both directions: on the upside by long-time-frame buyers and on the downside by long-time-frame sellers. Neutral days reflect a battle between long-time-frame buyers and sellers; frequently, these occur at market turning points. Neutral days are volatile and difficult to trade.

Trend

A trend day is characterized by consistent directional price movement throughout the course of the day. Generally, trend days start off modestly, with a relatively small initial balance. Instead of attracting the opposite response, the incremental directional price movement attracts more buying or selling in the direction of the trend. Usually, the market closes near the top or bottom of the day's extreme.

Non-Trend

A non-trend day occurs when both long-time-frame buyers and sellers are absent from the marketplace. In profile form, a non-trend day is characterized by a very narrow price range and a relatively even TPO distribution. Generally, non-trend days occur when market participants lack conviction, when a trend has a stalled, or just prior to an important event such as a key economic report.

Figure 10.2 6/19/89 Comex Gold, August Contract

```
3715 E
3714 DE
3713 DE
3712 DE
3711 DE
3710 DEFH
3709 DEFGHJ
3708 DEFGHIJK
3707 DEFGHIJK
3706 DEFGHIJK
3705 DEFGHIJK
3704 CDEFGHIJK
3703 CDEFGHIJK
3702 CDEFGHI
3701 CDEFGHI
3700 CDEFGI
3699 CG
3698 CG
3697 C
3696 C
3695 C
3694 BC
3693 ZBC
3692 ZBC
3691 YZABC
3690 YZABC
3689 YZAB
3687 YZAB
3686 YZAB
3685 YZA
3684 YZA
3683 YZA
3682 A
3681 A
```

Open: 368.00
Close: 370.00
TPO center: 3703
TPO value area: 3694 to 3715
TPOs upper: 59
TPOs lower: 67
TPO total: 141

The line to the left of the price axis is the value area for the previous trading day. The line on the right is the value area for today's session.

Long-time-frame activity:
Responsive buying extreme in A.
Initiating buying range extension in B.
Initiating buying TPO.

Clearly, long-time-frame buyers were in an aggressive, initiating mode, while long-time-frame sellers were absent from the market. One could conclude that the long-time-frame buying facilitated trade, judging by the fact that the market moved sharply upward following formation of the extreme in A period and the range extension in C. In addition, note that there's more volume in the top half of the day and that the market closed in the top third of the day's range, both indications that higher values facilitated trade. Consequently, we would expect still higher values in the days to come.

Courtesy: Commodity Information Services Co.

Figure 10.3   6/20/89 Comex Gold, August Contract

3720 Y	Open: 371:30
3719 YA	Close: 369:60
3718 YA	TPO center: 3707
3717 YA	TPO value area: 3702 to 3715
3716 YA	TPOs upper: 56
3715 YZA	TPOs lower: 60
3714 YZAB	TPO total: 126
3713 YZABCE	
3712 YZABCE	
3711 YZABCE	Long-time-frame activity:
3710 YZABCDE	Initiating selling range extension in **B**.
3709 YZBCDEFG	Responsive buying TPO.
3708 YZBCDEFG	
3707 ZBCDEFGHI	The market opens higher which is not sur-
3706 BDEFGHI	prising given the fact that yesterday's buying
3705 DEFGHIJ	activity facilitated trade. However, the higher
3704 DEFGHIJ	prices stimulate selling, which eventually leads
3703 EFGHIJ	to the initiating selling range extension. The day
3702 EHIJ	ends with unchanged values, but a lower close
3701 EIJ	compared to the 19th.
3700 IJ	The lack of follow-through to the higher
3699 JK	prices at the opening calls into question our
3698 JK	expectation of higher values. However, it's sig-
3697 JK	nificant that the retreat of buyers and the ag-
3696 JK	gressiveness of sellers during the course of the
3695 JK	day did not lead to a lower value area. Indeed,
3694 JK	today's value area overlaps in the upper portion
3693 JK	of the value area on the 19th. Also, the reduced
3692 JK	number of total TPOs and the concentration of
3691 JK	TPOs in the upper half of the day's range
3690 JK	indicates that the selling did not, in and of itself,
3689 JK	facilitate trade. Therefore, we still expect higher
3688 JK	values in the near future, however, we'll remain
	alert to changes in market behavior.

Courtesy: Commodity Information Services Co.

Figure 10.4   6/21/89 Comex Gold, August Contract

```
3760 K
3759 K
3758 K
3757 K
3756 K          Open: 369.90
3755 K
3754 K          Close:375.70
3753 K
3752 K          TPO center: 3711
3751 K
3750 K          TPO value area: 3698 to 3718
3749 K
3748 K          TPOs upper: 51
3747 K
3746 K          TPOs lower: 78
3745 K
3744 K          TPO total: 172
3743 K
3742 K
3741 K
3740 K
3739 K          Long-time-frame activity:
3738 K          Initiating buying range extension in A.
3737 K
3736 K          Initiating buying TPO.
3735 K
3734 K
3733 K
3732 K
3731 K              The buyers resume their aggressive behav-
3730 K          ior of two days ago. Interestingly, they're un-
3729 K          able to push the value area significantly higher;
3728 K
3727 K          however, the fact that the value area is wider,
3726 K          the total number of TPOs is higher, and the
3725 EK         close is stronger indicates that the buying ac-
3724 EK
3723 EK         tivity facilitated trade more than the selling
3722 EK         activity of the previous day. Therefore, we con-
3721 EK         tinue to believe higher values are in the offing.
3720 EFK
3719 EFK            At the same time, however, the strong rally
3718 EFK        in K period presents an excellent selling oppor-
3717 EFJK
3716 EFGJK      tunity since the prices available in K are far
3715 EFGHJK     above the value area established in the previous
3714 EFGHJ      three days. If a trader went long during the
3713 DEFGHJ
3712 DEFGHJ     close on the 20th, K period would be an ideal
3711 CDEGHIJ    time to take profits.
3710 CDEGHIJ
3709 CDEGHIJ
3708 CDGHIJ
3707 CDHIJ
3706 BCHIJ
3705 ABCHIJ
3704 ZABCHIJ
3703 YZABCIJ
3702 YZABCIJ
3701 YZABCIJ
3700 YZABCIJ
3699 YZAI
3698 YZI
3697 Z
```

Courtesy: Commodity Information Services Co.

Figure 10.5 6/22/89 Comex Gold, August Contract

3762 ZC	Open: 375.00
3761 ZC	Close: 374.20
3760 ZC	TPO center: 3744
3759 ZC	TPO value area: 3733 to 3750
3758 ZC	TPOs upper: 70
3757 ZC	TPOs lower: 90
3756 ZC	TPO total: 169
3755 ZC	
3754 YZBC	
3753 YZBC	Long-time-frame activity:
3752 YZBC	Responsive selling range extension in B.
3751 YZBC	Initiating buying TPO.

3754 YZBC
3753 YZBC
3752 YZBC
3751 YZBC
3750 YZABCD
3749 YZABCD
3748 YZABCD
3747 YZABCD
3746 YZABCD
3745 YZABCDEF
3744 YZABCDEFK
3743 YABDEFGK
3742 YABDEFGK
3741 YBDEFGK
3740 BDEFGIK
3739 DEFGIJK
3738 EFGIJK
3737 EFGIJK
3736 EFGIJK
3735 EFGHIJK
3734 EGHIJK
3733 EGHIJK
3732 EGHIJ
3731 EHIJ
3730 HIJ
3729 HI
3728 HI

Long-time-frame activity:
Responsive selling range extension in B.
Initiating buying TPO.

The market opens in the proximity of yesterday's close, far above the value areas established the previous three days. Not surprisingly, responsive selling begins, which leads to a responsive selling range extension during B period. A rally shortly thereafter fails to break through the initial balance on the upside, so the market spends the rest of the day fulfilling the parameters of a normal variation day. Strong buying on the lower half of the day's range establishes an initiating buying TPO count.

During the course of the day, a higher value area is established, which is what we had been expecting since the 19th. However, the degree of trade facilitation is somewhat disappointing. Although the total number of TPOs is marginally higher, the value area is slightly smaller than the previous day's and the TPOs are concentrated in the bottom half of the day's range.

Quite clearly, the responsive selling evident early in the day had little follow through. Indeed, the selling pressure appears to abate near the end of the day, and, in K period, the market rallies back toward the middle of the day's range. Looking back over the past few days, long-time-frame buying provided much greater trade facilitation than long-time-frame selling. Therefore, we remain biased towards higher values.

Courtesy: Commodity Information Services Co.

Figure 10.6   6/23/89 Comex Gold, August Contract

3848 GI		
3847 GI		
3846 GI		
3845 GI		
3844 GI	3787 DE	**Open: 376.30**
3843 GI	3786 DE	
3842 GI	3785 DE	**Close: 381.80**
3841 GI	3784 DE	
3840 GI	3783 DE	**TPO center: 3817**
3839 GI	3782 DE	
3838 GI	3781 DE	**TPO value area: 3775 to 3848**
3837 GI	3780 D	
3836 GI	3779 D	**TPOs upper: 129**
3835 EGI	3778 D	
3834 EGI	3777 D	**TPOs lower: 216**
3833 EGIK	3776 D	
3832 EGHIK	3775 D	**TPO total: 370**
3831 EGHIK	3774 D	
3830 EGHIJK	3773 D	
3829 EGHIJK	3772 D	
3828 EGHIJK	3771 D	
3827 EGHIJK	3770 D	
3826 EGHIJK	3769 D	Long-time-frame activity:
3825 EGHIJK	3768 D	Initiating buying extreme in Z.
3824 EGHIJK	3767 D	Initiating buying range extension in D.
3823 EGHIJK	3766 D	Initiating buying TPO.
3822 EFGHIJK	3765 YD	
3821 EFGHIJK	3764 YD	
3820 EFGHIJK	3763 YD	
3819 EFGHIJK	3762 YD	After opening near the lower portion of
3818 EFGHIJK	3761 YD	yesterday's value area, the market begins to
3817 EFGHIJK	3760 YD	move higher, establishing an early initiating
3816 EFHIJK	3759 YD	buying extreme in Z. In C period, the market
3815 EFHIJK	3758 YD	rotates down, however, the buying extreme
3814 EFHIJK	3757 YD	remains intact. Shortly thereafter, an initiating
3813 EFHIJK	3756 YD	buying range extension is established and the
3812 EFHIJ	3755 YD	market moves substantially higher. During the
3811 EFHIJ	3754 YD	rest of the day, the market develops a new and
3810 EFHIJ	3753 YZD	higher value area.
3809 EHIJ	3752 YZD	Our long-term expectation of higher values
3808 EHIJ	3751 YZD	is fulfilled today. If we had had a long position
3807 EHIJ	3750 YZD	going into today, we would have been hand-
3806 EHIJ	3749 YZAD	somely rewarded. However, even if we had
3805 EIJ	3748 YZAD	entered today with a flat position, today's mar-
3804 EJ	3747 YZABD	ket provided a good buying opportunity early,
3803 EJ	3746 YZABD	when the downward move in C failed to erad-
3802 EJ	3745 YZABCD	icate the initiating buying extreme. That was a
3801 EJ	3744 YZABCD	signal that buyers would have the upper hand
3800 DEJ	3743 YZABC	today, thus justifying an initiating long position
3799 DEJ	3742 YZABC	in D period.
3798 DEJ	3741 YZABC	
3797 DEJ	3740 YZABC	
3796 DEJ	3739 ZABC	
3795 DEJ	3738 ZAC	
3794 DEJ	3737 ZAC	
3793 DEJ	3736 ZAC	
3792 DEJ	3735 Z	
3791 DEJ	3734 Z	
3790 DEJ	3733 Z	
3789 DE		
3788 DE		

Courtesy: Commodity Information Services Co.

CHAPTER 11

Hedging with Gold Futures

Futures markets were created to provide a means for commercial participants to defray price risk. Producers and users of commodities frequently
desire to reduce their exposure to price swings. Producers want to insure
against falling prices, while users want to protect against rising prices.
Futures contracts, by providing a mechanism to transfer price risk, can
help achieve those objectives.

The theory of hedging with futures is quite simple. Generally, futures
prices of a particular commodity move in concert with cash price of the
commodity. Therefore, if a hedger takes a futures market position that is
opposite of his cash market position, he will have created an offset to any
adverse price moves. If prices change, the hedger experiences a loss on
one side and a profit on the other. Theoretically, the profits and losses
cancel out. Therefore, once a futures market hedge is established, it's
often said that the hedger has "locked in" a price.

In practice, unfortunately, hedging is not nearly so neat. For one thing,
futures and cash prices frequently do not exhibit precise correlation. This
is less of a problem with gold than it is with other markets, such as the
mortgage-backed securities market where participants often attempt to
hedge with Treasury bond futures. However, even when the underlying
commodity and the futures instrument are the same, the movement of
basis gives rise to complications. Basis, as you recall, is the price
difference between a particular futures contract and the spot market.
Normally, gold basis behaves in a rather predictable fashion, declining
as contract expiration approaches. If a hedged position is on the wrong

175

side of the basis movement, the position will provide only a partial offset to changes in the cash price.

First, let's describe a textbook-style, theoretical hedge. Then, after demonstrating certain shortcomings in the theoretical hedge, we'll show how a hedging strategy can be refined to adapt to the real world of gold trading.

A PRODUCER HEDGE

To operate profitably, a gold mining company must be able to sell the gold it produces at a higher price than its cost of production. Consequently, a gold producer is exposed to the threat that falling gold-prices will eliminate or reduce profitability. The risk is especially acute because of the long lead-time involved in committing capital to production and bringing the newly-mined gold onto the market.

To eliminate the risk of falling gold-prices, the producer would like to establish a minimum sales price for gold. To do that, the producer will sell gold futures contracts in a volume approximate to the amount of gold it intends to sell.

For example, assume that the producer plans to produce and sell 50,000 ounces of gold over the next six months. Currently, the spot price of gold is $300 and the futures price for delivery in six months is $315. To hedge his price risk, the producer will sell 500 gold futures contracts for delivery in six months. If the price of gold falls in six months to $250 an ounce, then the profit on the short futures position will offset the losses on the physical gold sales. If the price of gold rises, the profit on the cash position will offset the loss on the short futures position. Either way, the producer has essentially locked in a price.

Spot price: $300   Six-month price: $315

The producer sells 500 gold contracts for six-month delivery to hedge an equivalent cash position.

Six months later

Spot price: $250	Futures price: $250
Sells 50,000 ounces of physical gold	Buys 500 contracts at $250
Revenue: $12.5 million, $2.5 million less than anticipated	Profit: $3.25 million

Overall revenue of cash sale and futures position: $15.75 million, or an average price of $315 an ounce.

This, of course, is an idealized hedge, however it does serve to show the basic principles involved. In reality, a number of other factors would make the hedge less neat: the difficulty in executing a 500-size position in a deferred contract; the need to offset the futures position before the price reached parity with spot; the ability to time the cash market sale to precisely coincide with the expiration of a particular delivery month; and the delivery costs associated with selling physical gold.

The example of the producer hedge is also valid for anyone having a long position in the cash market, such as a gold dealer or a central bank. In each instance, gold is held in inventory and any decline in the price of gold reduces the value of the inventory. To offset that risk, in each case, a short futures position would be utilized.

The opposite hedge could be constructed for a jewelry maker that wants to protect against the possibility of gold prices rising. In this example, the jewelry maker, who is naturally short physical gold, would go long in the futures market to create an offsetting position. This type of hedge is valid for gold fabricators of any kind or anyone who is short physical gold.

For example, suppose the spot price of gold is $400 and the one-year futures price is $440. A jewelry maker anticipates that in one year he will need to purchase 10,000 ounces of gold, however, he is afraid that prices will rise in the meantime. To hedge, he buys 100 gold contracts at a price of $440 an ounce.

Spot price: $400	One-year futures: $440

Jeweler sells 100 gold contracts for delivery in one year at $440 in an effort to protect price risk of future gold purchase.

One year later

Spot price: $450   Futures price: $450
Buys 10,000 ounces at a cost of $4.5   Buys 100 contracts at
million, $500,000 more than anticipated. $450

The profit on the futures position reduces payment for gold by $100,000 to $4.4 million, or, an average cost of $440 an ounce.

Obviously, this hedge is much less successful than the earlier one featuring the gold producer. In the first hedge, the producer was able to effectively sell his gold at $315 an ounce, $75 above the current spot price and $15 higher than the spot price at the time the futures position was constructed. In contrast, the jeweler purchased his gold at an effective price of $440, only $10 less than the current spot price and $40 more than the spot price when the futures position was put on. The hedge offset only $10 per ounce of the $50 per ounce gold price increase.

Although these hedge examples are idealized, they do take into account the fact that prices on deferred contracts in gold normally are higher than the spot price. As the deferred contracts approach expiration, the prices tend to move closer to the spot price. Thus, irrespective of what's happening to the spot price, there's a natural tendency for the deferred contracts to fall through time relative to the spot price. This tendency benefits a hedge position that is short the deferred contracts, but hurts a hedge position that is long the deferred contract. That's why the producer hedge was so much more successful than the jeweler hedge.

On closer analysis, hedges behave similarly to spreads. In a normal, carrying charge market, a spread that is long the nearby and short the deferred benefits as the spread narrows. Similarly, a gold producer or gold dealer who is long physical gold and short the deferred, benefits because of the natural tendency of futures and spot prices to converge as expiration of the futures approaches. In a very real sense, the hedge is equivalent to a spread position; the only difference is that one leg of the spread is based on a cash market position.

On the other hand, a spread that is short the nearby and long the deferred benefits when the spread widens, something that usually only happens when prices increase. This type of spread is analogous to a short cash market/long futures market hedge position. Since the natural tendency of the futures contract is to approach the value of the spot market as expiration approaches, there is virtually no chance that the hedge (or spread trade, if you will) will produce a profit if the position is held for any length of time.

In a carrying charge market (futures prices higher than spot)

Position	Result
Long cash	Profit
Short futures	
Short cash	Loss
Long futures	

In an inverted market (spot prices higher than futures)

Position	Result
Long cash	Loss
Short futures	
Short cash	Profit
Long futures	

In each of these examples, it's assumed that, as the futures contract approaches expiration, the futures and cash price will converge. However, at any point in the process, it's possible that the differential between cash and futures may widen. In all cases, this is a temporary development; at expiration, futures and cash prices will converge.

The tendency for futures and cash prices to converge over time has enormous implications for hedging. In a normal carrying charge market, hedgers who are short futures consistently profit as the basis narrows, and hedgers who are long the futures consistently lose. Thus, for anyone with a long gold position, hedging not only protects against adverse price moves, it presents an opportunity for profit. On the other hand, for anyone short physical gold, hedging with futures must be done on a selective basis since it entails the possibility of losing money.

The convergence of futures and cash prices, over time, reflects the reduction in the costs of storing and financing gold as expiration approaches. For example, with the spot price of gold at $500 and one-year Eurodollar rates at 10 percent, the one-year futures contract would be priced around $550. In six months, assuming no change in interest rates and a flat yield curve, the price of the contract would drop to $525. Three months later, the price would be $512.50. The decline reflects the fact that the financing charges associated with holding gold for future delivery decrease as delivery approaches. In other words, tying up capital in gold for one year is more expensive than tying up capital for six months, which, in turn, is more expensive than tying up capital for three months. As the cost of financing declines—reflecting the shorter holding period for gold—the price of the futures contract drops.

In effect, the predictable and orderly convergence of futures contracts to the spot price of gold provides an opportunity for a holder of gold to finance his gold inventory. The profit on a long physical/short futures position reflects the carrying cost associated with holding the physical gold. Thus, a gold producer or gold dealer can produce a profit on a physical stock of gold approximately equal to the cost of insurance, storage, and financing the non-paying asset. Moreover, the short futures position protects against gold prices falling.

On the other side of the transaction, the loss on a short physical/long futures position reflects the fact that the buyer of gold for future delivery—the effect of going long futures—must pay the storage, insurance, and financing costs associated with holding gold for the duration of the contract. Thus, a short cash/long futures hedge entails payment of what might be called an insurance premium, i.e., the cost of carrying gold. If prices do rise, the profit on the long futures position will partially offset the loss on the short cash position, perhaps justifying the payment of the insurance premium. However, if prices stay the same or decline, the cost of the insurance premium will increase the overall cost of purchasing gold.

Spot price: $300   One-year futures: $330
Hedger intends to buy 100 ounces in one year, hedges by selling one futures contract at $330.

One year later

Spot price: $300   Futures price: $300
Purchases 100 ounces of gold at a   Buys one futures contract
total price of $30,000   at a price of $300
Total outlay: $33,000
Average cost of purchasing gold: $330 an ounce.

A similar case would occur if gold prices dropped. Holding everything else the same:

One year later

Spot price: $200

Purchases 100 ounces of gold at a
total price of $20,000

Total outlay: $33,000

Futures prices $200

Buys one futures contract
at a price of $200

Average cost of purchasing gold: $330 an ounce

The short cash/long futures position results in losses in two out of three price scenarios: when prices stay the same or when prices drop. In both cases, the hedger would have been better off if he had not hedged and, instead, waited and purchased gold on the spot market. When prices rise, as in the example earlier in the chapter, the hedger receives some protection, however, he still must pay the financing and storage costs associated with holding gold, or what we referred to earlier as the insurance premium.

On the other hand, a long cash/short futures position produces a profit in two out of three price scenarios: when prices stay the same or when prices drop. In these cases, the hedger receives the financing and storage costs associated with holding gold. That income allows the hedger to receive a higher effective sales price if spot prices remain unchanged. When prices drop, the short futures position protects the hedger for the entire extent of the price decline and, in addition, provides added income from the financing and storage costs.

In both the short cash/long futures hedge and long cash/short futures hedge, the hedger locks in the price of the deferred contract. Since the deferred contract usually is priced higher than the spot price, this obviously benefits the party with a short futures position and hurts the party with a long futures position. For the hedger with a short futures position, he is locking in a profit, at least as compared with the spot price at the time of the transaction. For the hedger with a long position, he is locking in a loss when compared to the spot price. Again, however, all this assumes that the position is fully hedged and that the futures contract is offset at exactly the same price in which the spot market transaction took place.

The behavior of the two basic hedge positions obviously dictates that they be used differently in different types of markets. Although there's a school of thought that maintains that all positions should be hedged, regardless of market outlook, most hedgers integrate their hedging strategy with how they view the market.

For example, since the long cash/short futures position provides a positive payback in two out of three pricing scenarios, it ought to be used when the hedger believes prices are likely to stay the same or fall. However, if the hedger feels strongly that prices will rise, he might want to consider not hedging at all, or perhaps reducing the size of his hedge.

The short cash/long futures position should be used more sparingly since it virtually guarantees losses in two out of three pricing scenarios and has only limited effectiveness in the third scenario. If the hedger feels reasonably certain that prices will stay the same or fall, he probably should not use futures to hedge. Indeed, he should be cautious to hedge even if he thinks that prices may rise marginally. However, if accelerating inflation or some other factor makes him fear a substantial price rise, the hedger should not hesitate to put on a long futures position. Although the protection has its price, it may prevent a massive loss.

The gold market participant who is consistently short gold may want to consider option strategies to defray price risk. The simplest strategy, buying a call option, also entails a cost analogous to an insurance premium; however, in some cases, it may be preferable to buying futures contracts. On the other hand, more complicated option strategies—such as buying a call and selling a put at the same or different strike prices—reduces the cost of the option, while providing a high level of price protection. In the appendix to Chapter 11 is a list of books on options that highlight some of these strategies.

In reality, gold market participants who hedge short physical gold positions with futures frequently use strategies that are different from the examples in this chapter. Often, they will trade only when convinced that prices are beginning to rise and then will exit the market just as soon as the price rise is over. What they're doing is really a mixture of hedging and speculation. If carried out by a skilled trader, such a strategy can be far more successful than a mechanically hedged position.

FORWARD MARKET HEDGING

It should be noted that many major gold producers prefer to hedge using forwards rather than futures. Although particular aspects of hedging in the two markets differ, the strategies and pricing behaviors are alike.

Nonetheless, the forward market has several advantages over the futures market: better liquidity, more flexible delivery standards, and less burdensome margin requirements.

The forward market expanded rapidly in the early 1980s in response to the hedging needs of the plethora of new producers that came into the industry at that time. By the late 1980s, forward gold contracts were offered by about a dozen major financial institutions. Many of these same institutions also began to offer over-the-counter gold options and gold loans, providing the gold industry with an array of instruments to hedge price risk.

The forward market, which is probably the most popular means to hedge gold price risk, is relatively liquid out to two years, but can be used as far out as five years. The futures market, in contrast, is liquid to about a year. Generally, the bid/ask spread in the gold futures market widens the further out the delivery month, particularly for large orders. Nonetheless, pricing of deferred futures contracts is usually competitive to or slightly superior to pricing on the forward market.

Many gold producers are able to achieve a more favorable margin situation with forward market participants than they can on a futures exchange. In the futures market, producers must maintain a margin deposit that is approximately equal to the extreme limits of daily volatility. If the price moves against the producer's position by a certain amount, more money must be deposited in the account. In contrast, in the forward market, many banks require little or no up-front margin. If the position moves against the producer, the forward contract may require that margin be deposited, however, even then, the bank margin requirements are usually more favorable than in the futures market.

In recent years, many gold producers have begun to combine forwards and futures with options. One of the most popular strategies involves buying a call option in conjunction with a forward contract. In effect, the forward contract provides the producer with a floor price for his gold, while the call option allows the producer to benefit if the price of gold rises. Another popular strategy involves selling a call at a strike price well above the market price and using the proceeds to buy a put. This hedge provides the producer with a floor price (created by the put) at very little cost because of the income generated by selling the call.

Appendix

**Gold Futures Contract Specifications
and Delivery Rules**

Commodity Exchange, Inc.
Four World Trade Center
New York, New York   10048
(212) 938-2900

Trading Hours: 9:00 A.M. to 2:30 P.M., New York time.

Trading Symbol: GC

Trading Unit and Grade: 100 troy ounces (5 percent more or less) of refined gold, assaying not less than 995 fineness, cast either in one bar or in three one-kilogram bars and bearing a serial number and identifying stamp of a refiner approved and listed by Comex.

Trading Months: The current calendar month, the next two calendar months; any February, April, June, August, October, and December falling within a 23-month period beginning with the current month.

Delivery: Notice of deliveries and trading deadlines are given according to the following schedules:

First notice day is the last business day of the month prior to a maturing delivery month, for example, March 29 in the case of April 1985 delivery.

Last notice day is the second last business day of the maturing delivery month, for example, April 29 in the case of April 1985 delivery.

Last trading day is the third last business day of the maturing delivery month, for example, April 26 in the case of April 1985 delivery.

Price Multiples: Ten cents per troy ounce, equivalent to $10 per contract.

The Commodity Exchange
New York, New York
Gold Rules

13.01 Tenderable Gold

In fulfillment of every contract of gold, the seller must deliver 100 troy ounces (5 percent more or less) of refined gold, assaying not less than 995 fineness, cast either in one bar or in three one-kilogram bars by an approved refiner. The weight, fineness, bar number and identifying stamp of the refiner must be clearly incised on each bar by the approved refiner. (Amended 03/14/85)

13.02 Approved Refiners; Licensed Depositories; Licensed Weighmasters; Approved Deliverers; Approved Assayers.

(a) The Board of Trade Group, upon the recommendation of the Committee on Precious Metals, shall designate as approved refiners those gold refiners whose gold bars shall be accepted as tenderable gold in connection with deliveries of gold in fulfillment of an Exchange contract for gold. Additional approved refiners may be designated in the same manner from time to time. In addition, the Board of Trade Group may at any time terminate the designation of a gold refiner as an approved refiner, and from and after the date of such termination, gold produced by such refiners may not be placed in a licensed depository for delivery in fulfillment of an Exchange contract for gold. Neither the addition nor deletion of a gold refiner as an approved refiner shall be deemed to affect the amount of money to be paid or the grade or quality of gold to be delivered in fulfillment of an Exchange contract for gold, and shall be binding upon all contracts entered into before as well as after the adoption of any such change, anything in these Rules to the contrary notwithstanding.

(b) The Board of Trade Group, upon the recommendation of the Committee on Precious Metals, shall license facilities located in the Borough of Manhattan, City of New York, in which gold may be stored for delivery on Exchange contracts ("Licensed Depositories"). Licensed depositories may be added to or eliminated from time to time, and the Committee on Precious Metals shall notify members of such changes and of the time when such changes shall become effective. The addition to or elimination of the names of licensed depositories shall not be deemed to affect the amount of money to be paid or the grade or quality of gold to be delivered on Exchange contracts, and shall be binding upon all such contracts entered into before as well as after the effective date of any such change, anything in these By-Laws to the contrary notwithstanding.

(c) Each licensed depository for gold shall also be designated as a licensed weighmaster for gold. Other weighmasters may be licensed and/or designated by the Board Trade Group wither upon application to said group or upon the Board Trade Group's own motion.

(d) The Board Trade Group shall designate as approved deliverers of gold, firms which are authorized to deliver gold to licensed depositories. Authorized deliverers may be added to or eliminated from time to time by the Board Trade Group, which shall notify members of such changes and of the time when such changes become effective.

(e) The Board Trade Group shall designate as approved assayers firms whose assay certificates shall be accepted in connection with deliveries of gold in fulfillment of an Exchange contract for gold.

(f) There shall be on file in the Office of the Secretary current lists setting forth (i) the names of approved refiners: (ii) the names and locations of licensed depositories; (iii) the names of licensed weighmasters; (iv) the names of approved assayers; and (v) the names of approved deliverers. (Rule 13.02 Amended 03/14/85).

13.03 Weight Certificates and Assay Certificates for Gold

(a) Every warehouse receipt issued by a licensed depository for a lot of gold tendered for delivery upon an Exchange contract shall be accompanied by a weight certificate issued by an Exchange licensed weighmaster certifying the weight of each bar of gold in the lot and setting forth the serial number and the name of the approved refiner of each bar.

(b) Every assay certificate issued by an approved asssayer shall certify that each bar of gold in the lot assays not less than 995 fineness and weight of each bar and the name of the approved refiner which produced each bar.

(c) The weighmaster's certificate issued by an Exchange licensed weighmaster shall show the weight of each bar of gold in the lot measured to 1/100 of a troy ounce (two decimal points). In accomplishing such measurement, each bar shall be weighed to the nearest 1/1000 of a troy ounce (three decimal points); weights of 4/1000 of a troy ounce or less shall be rounded down to the nearest 1/100 of a troy ounce and weights of 5/1000 of a troy ounce or more shall be rounded up to the nearest 1/100 of a troy ounce and weights of 5/1000 of a troy ounce or more shall be rounded up to the nearest 1/100 of a troy ounce.

(d) Depository receipts and weighmaster certificates for bars of gold placed in store directly from an approved refiner by an approved deliverer prior to the commencement of trading may be presented by the approved deliverer to the Exchange for registration in accordance with Rule 13.05. (Rule 13.03 Amended 03/14/85).

13.04 Packaging of Tenderable Gold

Every bar of gold tendered for delivery upon an Exchange contract may be packaged in a manner satisfactory to the Exchange. (Rule 13.04 Amended 03/14/85).

13.05 Storage of Gold

(a) Gold, to be eligible for delivery upon an Exchange contract, after being packaged as required by these By-Laws, shall be delivered to a licensed depository by an approved deliverer as follows:

(i) directly from an approved refiner for the account of such approved refiner or a clearing member;

(ii) directly from an approved assayer for the account of a clearing member; provided, that such gold is accompanied by an assay certificate of such approved assayer; or

(iii) directly from another licensed depository for the account of a clearing member; provided, that such gold was placed in such other licensed depository pursuant to paragraphs (i) or (ii) of this Rule 13.05(a).

The licensed depository receiving such gold shall issue a negotiable warehouse receipt in such form as may be approved by the Exchange,, to which shall be attached the weight certificate of a licensed weighmaster for each bar in the lot and, if required, the assay certificate of an approved assayer, and shall then deliver the same to the clearing member for whose account such gold has been placed in storage. Each holder of a warehouse receipt, weight certificate and assay certificate shall be deemed to agree that the Exchange may cause the gold represented by such warehouse receipt to be weighed, examined and otherwise tested for the purpose of ascertaining that such gold meets the requirements of an Exchange contract for gold, and that neither the Exchange nor its governors, officers, employees or agents shall be under any liability or obligation to any holder of a warehouse receipt, to any person who is entitled to receive a warehouse receipt, or to any other person because gold described in a warehouse receipt is different (in quantity or quality or both) from the description contained on such warehouse receipt.

(b) Warehouse receipts for gold shall be in negotiable form. Each warehouse receipt (i) shall be lettered or numbered consecutively by the licensed depository issuing it and no two warehouse receipts issued by an licensed depository shall bear the same letter or number (if letters are used, they must not exceed three (3) characters, and if used in combination with numbers, they must precede the numbers. The numbers must not exceed seven (7) digits); (ii) shall be issued for only one lot of gold; (iii) shall identify the accompanying weight certificate and, if required, assay certificate; (iv) shall specify the name of the approved refiner, serial number, weight and fineness of each bar in the lot: and (v) shall describe the package in which each bar is contained. The Committee on Precious Metals may adopt regulations from time to time specifying the form and content of warehouse receipts for gold, but such regulation shall not render warehouse receipts issued prior thereto ineligible in connection with delivery on a gold contract. (Rule 1305 Amended 03/14/85).

13.06 Gold Deposit Annual Audit Procedures

Every depository licensed by the Exchange for the storage of gold shall:

(a) have an annual audit conducted by independent certified public accountants selected by it (and satisfactory to the Exchange) on a date to be selected by such accountants without prior notice to such depository, which audit shall consist of the following:

(i) observation of and participation in accounting for all gold receipts issued by the depository since the date of the inauguration of trading in gold futures contracts on Commodity Exchange, Inc., or the date of the last audit performed in accordance with this rule whichever is later;

(ii) observation of and participation in the counting of all bars of gold on hand and reconciling such counts with the depository's records of gold stored;

(iii) for selected lots of gold observation of and participation in determining serial numbers and weight imprinted on each bar therein reconciles with the receipt therefore;

(iv) confirmation by direct communication with holders of receipts (to the extent considered necessary by such accountants) that the depository's records with respect to their gold in storage are correct;

(v) confirmation by direct communication with former holders of receipts who have withdrawn their gold from the depository (to the extent considered necessary by such accountants) that the depository's records of such withdrawals are correct;

(vi) study and evaluation of the depository's internal controls relating to the accountability for and the custody of all gold placed in the depository;

(vii) not drilling any bars of gold or employing any alternative procedures for the purpose of verifying the true content of the bars counted, nor physically weighing any bars of gold to determine that the weights imprinted thereon are accurate;

(b) notify the Exchange not later than January 15 in each year of the name of such independent Certified Public Accountants and at the same time deliver to the Exchange, a signed copy of an agreement from such accountants in the form appended hereto provided however, that if a depository appoints new independent Certified Public Accountants in any year prior to the time the audit described in (a) above is conducted, such depository shall, within 15 days after such appointment, notify the Exchange of the name of the new independent Certified Public Accountants and deliver to the Exchange, a copy of the agreement in the form appended hereto, signed by such new accountants.

(c) furnish to the Exchange within 5 days after receipt thereof by the depository, a signed copy of any other audit, examination, or report with respect to its gold vault made by its independent Certified Public Accountants, any government agency or department having jurisdiction over such depository, or by its own internal auditing staff;

(d) notify the Exchange immediately upon discovery by it of any shortage, error, or other discrepancy with respect to gold stored thereat, or with respect to receipts for gold issued by it. (Rule 13.06 Amended 03/14/85).

13.07 Form of Gold Contract

All contracts for the future delivery of gold shall be in the following form:

COMMODITY EXCHANGE, INC.
GOLD CONTRACT

New York, NY (date)

A.B. has this day (sold or bought) and agreed to (deliver to or receive from) C.D. 100 troy ounces (5 percent more or less) of bar gold, assaying not less than 995 fineness, at the price of per ounce in accordance with the provisions, By-Laws and Rules of Commodity Exchange, Inc., deliverable from licensed depository in the Borough of Manhattan, City of New York, between the first and last delivery days of ___, inclusive, the delivery within such time to be at seller's option, upon notice to buyer as provided by the By-Laws and Rules of Commodity Exchange, Inc.

Either party may call for a margin, as the variations of the market for like deliveries may warrant, which margin shall be kept good.

This contract is made in view of, and in all respects subject to the By-Laws and Rules of Commodity Exchange, Inc.

For and in consideration of one dollar to the undersigned, in hand paid, receipt whereof is hereby acknowledged, the undersigned accepts this contract with all its obligations and conditions.

Verbal contracts (which shall always be presumed to have been made in the approved form) shall have the same standing, force and effect as written ones, if notice in writing of such contracts shall have been given by one of the parties thereto to the other party during the day on which such contract is made (Rule 13.07 Amended 03/14.85).

13.08 Delivery Months for Trading in Gold

Trading in gold shall be conducted for delivery in every calendar month, the immediately following two calendar months and such additional calendar months as the Board from time to time may specify by resolution. (Rule 13.08 Amended 03/14/85).

13.09 Price Multiples for Gold

Prices for gold on future delivery contracts shall be in multiples of ten cents (10 cents) per ounce. Contracts made on any other basis are prohibited. (Rule 13.09 Amended 03/14/85).

13.10 Price Fluctuation Limitation for Gold

There shall be no limitation on price fluctuations on gold futures contracts. (Rule 13.10 Amended 5/22/87).

13.11 Delivery Notice for Gold

(a) The following definitions shall be applicable to the delivery of gold. "Date of Presentation" shall mean a day notice(s) of intention to deliver are presented to the Clearing Association or its designee. "Date of Issuance" shall mean a day on which invoices are issued by the Clearing Association or its designee and shall be the business day prior to the day of delivery of the gold specified in the notice of intention to deliver. "Notice Price" shall be the settlement price of the current month on the date of presentation.

(b) Except as provided in (c), notices of intention to deliver gold must be presented to the Clearing Association or its designee, not later than one hour after the close of the market on the day preceding the date of issuance. Such notices will be allocated by the Clearing Association on the date of issuance in accordance with its rules.

(c) On the last day for the presentation of notices of intention to deliver in the current month, notices against contracts remaining open on said day shall be presented to the Clearing Association or its designee not later than 12:30 PM on said day.

(d) The notice of intention to deliver gold shall be presented by the member making delivery to the Clearing Association or its designee in a computer-readable form by the Association or its designee. Said notice shall indicate the approved gold refiner, the receipt number of the warrant, the weight and fineness thereof and the licensed depository in which the same is stored and shall be accompanied by a Notice Summary in the following form:

New York, (date)

Commodity Exchange, Inc.
Notice of Intention to Deliver
Gold

Clearing Member ID   Clearing Member Name

House Customer (H/C)

Total Number of Notices   Issuance Date

To CLEARING ASSOCIATION, INC.

Take notice that on (date) for each delivery notice record attached, we shall deliver to the clearing member to which you allocate this notice 100 troy ounces (5 percent more or less) of bar gold assaying not less than 995 fineness of the brand or marking and from the licensed warehouse or vault indicated on each record in accordance with the terms of our contract sale to said clearing member at the delivery notice price established by the Clearing Association.

Signature

(e) All notices of intention to deliver shall be presented to the Clearing Association or its designee in accordance with such rules as the Association may adopt.

(f) On the date of issuance, the clearing member to which the notice of intention to deliver has been allocated shall receive from the Clearing Association, or its designee, an invoice for the gold specifying the refiner, the warrant number, the weight and fineness, and the licensed depository in which the gold is stored, the price, and the name of the member making delivery.

(g) A member to whom delivery notice is allocated shall be obligated to accept delivery in accordance with the By-Laws & Rules of the Exchange and may not transfer this obligation.

(h) In the event that the automated delivery system is not operational, the Exchange will notify all clearing members of this occurrence and advise them of the substitute procedure to be followed.

(i) In the event that the office of a member to whom a notice of intention to deliver has been allocated shall be closed, good delivery of the invoice shall be effected by handing it to the Secretary of the Exchange, who shall endorse thereon the data and the time of its receipt and post notice thereof on the bulletin of the Exchange.

(j) The Secretary shall, at the close of business of the Exchange on the date of presentation, post the notice price upon the bulletin board of the Exchange. Gold shall be paid for at the notice price and on the basis set forth in Rule 13.12. The deliverer shall also at the time of delivery, render a statement to the receiver covering the difference between the notice price and the settlement price of the business day previous to delivery, as determined by the Clearing Association, said difference to be calculated on the basis of 100 troy ounces, the resulting amount to be paid promptly by the receiver in case said settlement price is in excess of the notice price, otherwise to be paid by the deliverer.

(k) No notices of intention to deliver shall be presented, no invoices shall be issued, and no transmittal of delivery documents shall be made on a Saturday or any other day designated as a holiday by the By-Laws, by the Exchange, or by the Board, except as provided in paragraphs (1) and (m) of this Rule 13.11.

(l) When the last date of issuance is declared a holiday too late to permit the presentation and allocation of notices of intention to deliver such notice may be given in the usual manner on the holiday.

(m) When the last delivery day is declared a holiday too late to permit a notice of invention to deliver to be presented and allocated requiring delivery on the business day preceding the last delivery day, then the delivery shall be completed on the holiday.

(n) Members having contracts open in the current month must keep their offices open for the purpose of receiving the notices or of completing such deliveries. (Rule 13.11 Amended 03/14/85)

13.12 Delivery of Gold

(a) Gold may be delivered in fulfillment of an Exchange contract for gold only from a licensed depository. A negotiable warehouse receipt issued by and signed on behalf of a licensed depository, endorsed as provided in this Rule 13.12, and accompanied by a weight certificate and, if required, an assay certificate and invoice, shall be good delivery in fulfillment of an Exchange contract for gold and shall be deemed a liquidation of the contract in respect of which such delivery is made.

(b) All gold must be delivered to the receiver with handling and storage charges paid up to and including the business day following the day of delivery, and the buyer may require the seller to furnish satisfactory proof of payment thereof. Any storage charges prepaid by the seller for a period extending beyond the business day following the delivery day (but not in excess of thirty days) shall be refunded by the buyer to the seller on a pro rata basis for the unexpired term, and an adjustment made upon the invoice.

(c) A warehouse receipt must be endorsed by each party whose endorsement is necessary to pass title thereto and, in addition, must be endorsed and dated by every Exchange member who transfers it in connection with an Exchange transaction.

(d) A member to whom delivery is made in fulfillment of an exchange contract for gold shall not be required to accept the same if the gold delivered weighs more than 5 percent above or below 100 troy ounces or is otherwise not in accordance with these Rules.

(e) The member to whom delivery is made shall at once make payment to the member making delivery by a certified check drawn upon a bank in the City of New York. Payment shall be made upon the basis of the weight as certified in the weight certificate for the lot and the fineness of such gold up to 9999 fine as stamped on the bars.

(f) The invoice distributed by the Clearing Association or its designee shall be accepted by the delivering member as a legal demand for the gold. Before 2:00 PM on the day of delivery, the delivering member shall tender to the member allocated the delivery notice the warehouse receipt and weight certificate as herein above provided.

(g) By the tender of a warehouse receipt for gold, duly endorsed for transfer, the endorser shall be deemed to warrant that the gold described therein weights 100 troy ounces (5 percent more or less) and is not less than 995 fine. Such warranty shall remain in effect through successive endorsements of the warehouse receipt in connection with deliveries of gold in fulfillment of an Exchange contract for gold, and shall be for the benefit of each member of the Exchange who shall have taken delivery of the gold in fulfillment of an Exchange contract for gold and for the benefit of the immediate principal of such member.

(h) Each delivery of gold in fulfillment of an Exchange contract and the delivery of any invoices required in connection therewith, shall be made at the location of the party taking delivery except where the member taking delivery does not have an office for the purpose of accepting deliveries in fulfillment of Exchange contracts located on or south of

Canal Street, in the Borough of Manhattan, City of New York and the member making delivery does have an office for the purpose of accepting deliveries in fulfillment of Exchange contracts located on or south of Canal Street, in the Borough of Manhattan, City of New York. In that case, delivery shall be made at the offices of the Exchange. Any delivery pursuant to the previous sentence shall be made and accepted between the hours of 12:00 noon and 2:00 PM on the day of delivery. The Exchange shall designate an office at the offices of the Exchange at which such deliveries shall take place but the Exchange shall not be liable or responsible for any failure to make or take delivery at such office or for any other act or omission such can or may occur in connection therewith.

In the event that such Exchange member or principal shall claim a breach of such warranty, the lot shall be immediately submitted for sampling, assaying and/or weighing to an assayer designated by the Exchange. The expense of sampling, assaying and/or weighing shall, in the first instance, be borne by the claimant. If a deficiency in quality and/or quantity shall be determined by such assayer, the claimant shall have the right to recover the difference in the market value and expenses incurred in connection with the sampling, assaying, and/or weighing, and any cost of replacement of the gold. The claimant may, at his option, proceed directly against the original endorser of the warehouse receipt upon an Exchange delivery without seeking recovery from his immediate deliverer on the Exchange contract, and if the claim is satisfied by the original endorser of the warehouse receipt, intervening endorsers will be thereby discharged from liability to the claimant. If the claimant seeks recovery from his immediate deliverer, and his claim is satisfied by such endorser, the party thus satisfying the claim will have a similar option to claim recovery directly from the original endorser of the warehouse receipt or from his immediately preceding endorser. Such claims as are in dispute between members of the Exchange, shall in each case be submitted to arbitration under the rules of the Exchange.

The liability of an endorser of a warehouse receipt, as provided herein, shall not be deemed to limit the rights of such endorser against any person or party for whose account the endorser acted in making delivery on an Exchange contract. If it shall be determined in such arbitration proceeding that any endorser of a warehouse receipt, or the person or party for whom such endorser acted was aware of the breach of warranty, or was involved in a plan or arrangement with the original endorser (or his principal) to place such inferior gold in licensed depositories for use in deliveries upon Exchange contracts, such endorsers shall not be entitled to recover from any prior endorser for the breach of warranty. (Rule 13.12 Amended 03/14/85)

COMMODITY EXCHANGE, INC.

OFFICIAL LIST OF APPROVED REFINERS AND BRANDS

Producer	Refined At	Computer Code	Brand Names
Argor, S.A.	Chiasso, Switzerland	ARGO	ARGOR S.A. CHIASSO-SAA
ASARCO Inc.	Amarillo, Texas	ASAT	ASARCO GOLD-AMARILLO, TEXAS
Casa da Moeda do Brasil	Rio de Janeiro, Brazil	CASA	CASA DA MOEDA DO BRASIL-CMB
Compagnia des Metaux Precious	Ivry, France	CMPP	COMPAGNIE DES METAUX PRECIEUX PARIS (may also contain letters CMP).
From the same producer: SDBS; SOCIETE DE BANQUE SUISSE.			
Comptoir Lyon-Alemand Louyot	Noisy Le Sec, France	CLAL	COMPUTER LYON ALEMAND, LOUYOT-PARIS (w/Affineur Fondeur within octagon)
Degussa A.G.	Hanau-Wolfgagn, W. Germany	DEGU	DEGUSSA FEINGOLD (w/1/2 sum & 1/4 moon within diamond)
Degussa Canada Limited	Burmington, Ontario	DECA	DEGUSSA CANADA LTD, (w/1/2 sun & 1/4 moon within a diamond)
H. Drijfhout & Zoon's Edelmetaalbedrijven BV	Amsterdam, Netherlands	HDZA	H. DRIJFHOUT & ZOON-AMSTERDAM-MELTERS (within octagon)
Engelhard Corp.	Carteret, N.J.	ENNE	ENGELHARD (may also be ENGELHARD NEW JERSEY-U.S.A. or ENGELHARD U.S.A.).

Same producer and refinery: BAKE; BAKER (within circle stop triangle)

Producer	Refined At	Computer Code	Brand Names
Same producer: Cinderford, England; ENCI; ENGELHARD, LONDON			
Same producer: Thomastown, Australia; ENTH; ENGELHARD AUSTRALIA			
Same producer: Aurora, Ontario; ENAU; ENGELHARD (w/circle connected to 1/2 moon to left of name; may also be ENGLEHARD INDUSTRIES OF CANADA LTD.			
Handy & Harman	Attleboro, Mass.	HAND	HH HANDY & HARMAN
W.C. Heraeus, G.m.b.H.	Hanau, W. Germany	HERA	HERAEUS FEINGOLD (w/Harseus Edelmetalle GmbH-Hanau encircling 3 roses)
Homestake Mining Co.	Lead, South Dakota	HMCO	HOMESTAKE MINING COMPANY (w/HMC all within circle)
Johnson Matthey, Inc.	Winslow, New Jersey	MBUS	MATTHEY BISHOP U.S.A. (within an oval)
Johnson Matthey Ltd.	Brampton, Ontario	JMMC	JOHNSON MATTHEY & MALLORY-CANADA (within an oval)
Same producer and refinery: JMCA; JM (w/crossed hammers)			
Same producer and refinery: JMJM; JOHNSON MATTHEY-JM (w/crossed hammers and assay stamp: J.M. LTD.-CANADA-ASSAY OFFICE)			
Johnson Matthey Ltd.	Kogarah, Australia	MGPS	MATTHEY GARRETT PTY.-SYDNEY REFINERS (without an oval)
Same producer and refinery: JMLA(JOHNSON MATTHEY LIMITED AUSTRALIA)			
Johnson Matthey Chemicals Ltd.	Royston, England	JMLO	JOHNSON MATTHEY LONDON (within an oval)
Johnson Matthey & Pauwels S.A.	Brussels, Belgium	JMPA	JOHNSON MATTHEY & PAUWELS (within an oval)

Producer	Refined At	Computer Code	Brand Names
Johnson Matthey Refining, Inc.	Salt Lake City, Utah	JMRI	JOHNSON MATTNEY-JM (w/crossed hammers and assay stamp: J.M.R.I.-U.S.A.-ASSAY OFFICE)
Metallurgie Hoboken Overpelt S.A.	Hoboken, Belgium	MHOV	METALLURGIE HOBOKEN OVERPELT
Metalli Preziosi S.p.A.	Milan, Italy	MPSP	METALLI PREZIOSI S.p.A. MILANO - AFFINAZIONE (w/MP within a circle)

LICENSED DEPOSITORIES AND WEIGHMASTERS FOR GOLD

Depository	Computer Code
CHASE MANHATTAN BANK One Chase Manhattan Plaza New York, N.Y. 10081 212-552-1850	1001
CITIBANK 399 Park Ave. New York, N.Y. 10043 212-559-7776	2001
IRON MOUNTAIN DEPOSIT CORP. 26 Broadway New York, N.Y. 10004 212-912-8530	3001
REPUBLIC NATIONAL BANK OF NEW YORK 450 Fifth Ave. New York, NY 10018, 212-930-6439	5001

Depository	Computer Code
SWISS BANK CORP. 4 World Trade Center New York, NY 10048 212-574-3644	6001

Additional Licensed Weighmasters for Gold

International Testing Laboratories, Inc.
578-582 Market St.
Newark, N.J. 07105
201-589-4772

Ledoux & Company
359 Alfred Ave.
Teaneck, N.J. 07666
201-837-7160

Lucius Pitkin, Inc.
50 Hudson St.
New York, N.Y. 10013
212-233-2737

Approved Assayers For Gold

Ledoux & co.
359 Alfred Ave.
Teaneck, NJ 07666
212-947-0953
201-837-7160

Lucius Pitkin, Inc.
50 Hudson St.
New York, N.Y.
212-233-2737

APPROVED DELIVERERS

Amored Transport Of New York
275 West St.
New York, N.Y. 10013
212-431-1990

Brinks, Inc.
66 Murray St.
New York, N.Y. 10007
212-577-0600

Brooks Armored Car Service, Inc.
13 East 35th St.
Wilmington, DE 19899
302-762-5444
215-727-7711

Federal Armored Express, Inc.
P.O. Box 333
Baltimore, MD 21203
301-285-7000

Purlator Armored Express, Inc.
222-17 Northern Blvd.
Bayside, N.Y. 11361
718-224-0800

Wells Fargo Armored Service Corp.
350 West St.
New York, N.Y. 10014
212-924-7023

Chicago Board of Trade
LaSalle at Jackson
Chicago, Illinois 60604
(312) 435-3558

Kilo Gold Futures

Trading Unit: One kilogram (32.15 troy ounces)

Deliverable Grade: One bar of refined gold (995 fineness) weighing exactly one kilogram (32.15 troy ounces) and bearing brands and markings approved by the CBOT

Price Quotation: In dollars and cents per troy ounce

Delivery Method: By vault receipt issued by a CBOT-approved vault in Chicago or in New York.

Tick Size: 10 cents per troy ounce ($3.22 per contract)

Daily Price Limit: $50 per troy ounce ($1607.50 per contract) above or below the previous day's settlement price.

Contract Months: Current month and the next two calendar months and February, April, June, August, October, and December.

Trading Hours: 7:20 A.M. to 1:40 P.M., Chicago time

Last Trading Day: No trades in Kilo gold futures deliverable in the current month shall be made during the last three business days of that month.

Ticker Symbol: KI

Gold Rules

A. One Kilo Gold

Trading Conditions

1501.00 Authority

Whenever it shall be permitted by the U.S. Government trading in Gold may be conducted under such terms and conditions as the Board may prescribe by regulation. Trading in Gold shall be supervised as directed by the Board.

1502.01 Application of Regulations

Transactions in Gold futures shall be subject to the general rules of the Association as far as applicable to trading in Gold.

1504.01 Unit of Trading

The unit of trading shall be 1 (one) gross kilogram of gold. Bids and offers may be accepted in lots of 1 (one) gross kilogram or multiples thereof.

1505.01 Months Traded In

Trading in Gold may be conducted in the current month and any subsequent months.

1506.01 Price Basis

All prices of gold shall be basis in store in approved vaults in Chicago, Illinois or New York, New York in multiples of ten cents per fine troy ounce. Contracts shall not be made on any other price basis.

1507.01 Hours in Trading

The hours of trading for future delivery in Gold shall be from 7:20 a.m. to 1:40 p.m. On the last day of trading in an expiring future, the closing time with respect to such future shall be 1:40 p.m., subject to the otherwise applicable provisions of the second paragraph of Rule 1007.00

1508.01 Trading Limits

(See 1008.01)

1508.01A Trading Limits

(See 1008.01A)

1509.01 Last Trading Day

No trades in Gold futures deliverable in the current month shall be made during the last three business days of that month and any contracts remaining open must be settled by delivery or as provided in Regulation 1509.02 after trading in such contracts has ceased; and if not previously delivered, delivery must be made no later than the last business day of the month. Tender shall be one business day prior to delivery.

As is the case with other contracts, delivery notices and supporting data processing (Delivery) cards must be made delivered to the Clearing House by 4:00 p.m. on position day except that, on the last notice day of the delivery month, delivery notices and supporting date processing cards may be delivered to the Clearing House until 2:00 p.m. on the intention day.

1509.02 Trading in the Last Three Days of the Delivery Month

After trading contracts for future delivery in the current delivery month has ceased in accordance with Regulation 1509.01 of this chapter, outstanding contract for such delivery may be liquidated by means of bona fide exchange of such current futures for the actual cash commodity. Such exchange must, in any event, be made no later than the last business day of the delivery month.

1510.01 Margin Requirements

Margin requirements shall be determined by the Board by regulation. (See 431.03)

1511.01—Disputes

All disputes between interested parties may be settled by arbitration as provided in the Rules and Regulations.

1512.01—Position Limits and Reportable Positions

(See 425.01)

Delivery Procedures

1536.01 Standards

The contract grade for delivery on futures contracts made under these Regulations shall be 1 (one) bar of refined gold cast in a gross weight of 1 kilogram minimum, (for the purpose of this contract a kilogram is a weight equal to 32.150 troy ounces), assaying not less than 995 fineness and bearing brands and markings officially approved by the Exchange.

Settlement shall be the basis of the fine troy ounces of gold delivered.

1540.01 Brands and Markings of Gold

Brands and markings deliverable in satisfaction of futures contracts shall be listed with the Board of Trade upon approval by the Board that the requirements adopted by the Board have been met. The Board may require such sureties as it deems necessary. The Secretary's Office shall keep on file the brands and markings of gold bars which are deliverable. The addition of brands and markings shall be binding upon all contracts outstanding as well as those entered into after approval.

1540.02 Withdrawal of Approval of Gold Brands and Markings

If at anytime a brand and marking fails to meet the requirements adopted by the Board or the metallurgical assay of any gold bars bearing a brand and marking on the official list depreciates below 995 fineness, the Board may exclude said brand and marking from the official list unless deliveries of bars bearing said brand and marking are accompanied by certificates of analysis of an official assayer showing a gold fineness of not less than 995, and such additional bond as the Board may deem necessary. Notice of such action shall be given promptly in writing to each regular vault and shall be posted upon the bulletin board of the Association and the official list shall indicate the limitation upon deliveries of said brand and marking.

1540.03 Approved Brands

(See Appendix 15A)

1540.04 Assaying

The Board of Trade at its sole discretion shall have the authority at any time to have assayed any Gold bars covered by vault receipts delivered against futures contracts. Cost to be borne by the Board of Trade.

1541.01 Delivery Points

Gold located at regular vaults at points approved by the Board of Directors (Regulation 1581.01) may be delivered in satisfaction of futures contracts.

1542.01 Deliveries by Vault Receipts

Deliveries on Gold futures contract shall be made by the delivery of depository vault receipts issued by vaults which have been approved and designated by the Board as regular vaults for the storage of Gold. Gold bars must be good delivery bars as defined by Board regulations and shipped under bond directly to the regular vault from an approved vault; or must be bars purchased from an approved source and shipped directly from that source under bond to the regular vault. Gold bars entering a regular vault for delivery must be weighted at the vault by a weigher approved by the Association.

The gross weight of the bars shall be recorded by the approved weigher on the vault receipt (Regulation 1544.01) to the nearest one thousand (0.001) of a troy ounce.

The vault receipt issued by Chicago vaults shall evidence that storage charges have been paid up to and including the end of the Calendar quarter. A clearing member delivering a New York vault receipt must also tender an attachment stating that storage charges have been paid up to and including the end of the calendar quarter. Prepaid Storage Charges shall be charged to the buyer by the seller from the date of delivery to the expiration of the storage charge period. In order to effect a valid delivery, each vault receipt must be endorsed by the clearing member making delivery. If the owner removes gold from a vault, any prepaid storage charges shall be refunded by the vault to the owner from the date of removal of the gold to the expiration of the storage charge period.

By the tender of a vault receipt for gold duly endorsed by delivery on an Exchange contract, the endorser shall be deemed to warrant, to his transferee and each subsequent transferee of the receipt for delivery on Exchange contracts, and their respective immediate principals, the genuineness and worth of such receipt, the rightfulness and effectiveness of the transfer thereof, and the quantity and quality of the gold shown on the receipt.

In the event that such Exchange member or principal shall claim a breach of such warranty, and such claim relates to the quantity or quality of the gold, the lot shall be immediately submitted for sampling and assaying to any assayer approved by the Exchange; the gold must be shipped under bond, and at the owner's expense, to the assayer. The expense of sampling and assaying shall in the first instance, be borne by the claimant. If a deficiency in quantity or quality shall be determined by the assayer, the claimant shall have the right to recover the difference in the market value and expenses incurred in connection with the sampling and assaying and any cost of replacement of gold. The claimant may, at his option, proceed directly against the original endorser of the warehouse or vault receipt upon Exchange delivery, or against any endorser prior to claimant without seeking recovery from his immediate deliverer on the Exchange contract and if the claim is satisfied by the original endorser of the warehouse or vault receipt, or any other endorser, all the endorsers will be thereby discharged from liability to the claimant. If the claimant seeks recovery from any endorser and his claim is satisfied by such endorser, the party thus satisfying the claim will have a similar option to claim recovery directly from any endorser prior to him. such claims as are in dispute between members of the Exchange may in each case be submitted to arbitration under the Rules of the Exchange.

The liability of an endorser of a vault receipt as provided herein shall not be deemed to limit the rights of such endorser against any person or party for whose account the endorser acted in making delivery on an Exchange contract. If it shall be determined in such arbitration proceeding that any endorser of a vault receipt or the person or party for whom such endorser acted was aware of the breach of warranty or was involved in a plan or agreement with the original endorser (or his principal) to place such inferior gold in licensed store for use in deliveries upon Exchange contracts, such endorsers shall not be entitled to recover from any prior endorser for the breach of warranty.

1543.01 Issuance of Vault Receipts

Vault receipts, in order to be eligible for delivery, must be issued by a regular vault according to the following procedures and with the following documentation retained by the regular vault:

(1) For all vault receipts

(a) Receipts shall be issued in numerical order.

(b) Copies shall be kept of any canceled or voided receipts

(c) A record shall be kept of the bar number and the corresponding receipt number.

(2) For gold delivered into the vault directly from a refiner or an approved source.

(a) Copy of the bar listing which depicts the date of smelting, serial numbers, brand marking and troy ounces.

(b) Copy of the bonded carrier receipt for the transport of the gold from the refiner of the approved source directly into the regular vault.

(3) For gold converted from a receipt issued by another exchange:

(a) A copy of such other exchange's receipt which has been canceled.

Regular vaults shall also notify the Board of Trade each day that there is a change in the number of its outstanding vault receipts.

1543.02 Deposit of Gold with Vaults

Gold in bars must be ordered into a regular vault by a clearing member of the Association who shall furnish the vault with the following written notice:

1. Request to receive gold.
2. Brands and markings.
3. Number of bars.
4. Identification (serial number) of each bar.
5. Weight of each bar.
6. Source
7. Clearing member
8. Carrier
9. Date of arrival

Shipment must be prepaid unless otherwise arranged with the regular vault.

1544.01 Receipt Format

The following form of vault receipt shall be used:

_____

(Name of Issuer)

_____

(Address)
Bearer Receipt No. _____
Chicago, Ill _____ 19 ____
RECEIVED from _____ and stored at the above address in the safety deposit vaults of the undersigned, as a Bailee, subject to the provisions of Article 7 of the _____ Uniform Commercial Code and the terms and conditions stated hereon, a gold bar SAID TO CONTAIN the amount shown hereon of gold of the fineness indicated.

Said bar is deliverable only at said vaults to the BEARER of this receipt upon surrender hereof and upon payment of storage charges and other proper charges and expenses relating to said bar, for which charges and expenses the undersigned claims a lien.

Payment of handling charges for deposit of said bar and of storage charges to the end of the current calendar quarter is hereby acknowledged. Storage charges for each subsequent calendar quarter are to be paid to the undersigned, in advance, at or before the expiration of the preceding calendar quarter.

Bar identification markings of bar covered by this receipt as shown hereon, have been recorded by the undersigned on the basis of markings appearing on said bar. THE UNDERSIGNED HAS NOT ASCERTAINED, AND IS NOT RESPONSIBLE FOR THE AUTHENTICITY OR CORRECTNESS OF MARKINGS ON, OR THE CONTENT, WEIGHT OR FINENESS OF SAID BAR.

_____

(Issuer)

By _____

(Authorized Signature)

Gross Weight as determined by a weigher approved by the Board of Trade of the City of Chicago _____ troy ounces.

_____

Approved weigher of the Board of Trade of the City of Chicago

Bar Identification Markings

	Gross Weight			
Serial Number	Troy Ounces	Kilograms	Mark of Brand	Fineness

Totals

STORAGE AND HANDLING CHARGES: Storage charges of _____ per calendar day per contract, minimum _____ per contract plus _____ handling charge per contract for each deposit and withdrawal.

Endorsements

Date _____ By _____

Date _____ By _____

1546.01 Date of Delivery

Where gold is sold for delivery in specified month, delivery of such gold may be made by the Seller upon such day of the specified month as the

Seller may select. If not previously delivered, delivery must be made upon the last business day of the month.

1547.01 Delivery Notices

(See 1047.01)

1548.01 Method of Delivery

(See 1048.01)

1549.00 Time of Delivery, Payment, Form of Delivery Notice

(See 1049.00)

1549.02 Buyers' Report of Eligibility to Receive Delivery

(See 1049.02)

1549.03 Sellers' Invoice to Buyers

In addition to the requirements of 1049.03, the seller shall mail a copy of the invoice to the vault or faults who issued the vault receipts being delivered. The seller will thereby notify the vault of the transfer of ownership of the indicated vault receipts from the seller to the buyer. The seller will be responsible for the payment of storage charges unless the vault has been notified thereby.

1549.04 Payment

Payment is to be made by a check drawn on and certified by a Chicago bank or by a Cashier's check by a Chicago bank.

1550.00 Duties of Members

(See 1050.00)

1551.01 Office Deliveries Prohibited

(See 1051.01)

1554.00 Failure to Accept Delivery

(See 1054.00)

1556.01 Storage and Transfer Fees

Storage charges, transfer fees and in-and-out charges shall be set by each depository vault and the schedule of such charges shall be posted with the Association, which shall be notified at least 60 days in advance of any changes in the rate schedule. Except as otherwise provided, all charges for storage, etc., shall remain the responsibility of the Seller until payment is made.

Regularity of Vaults

1580.01 Duties of Vault Operators

If shall be the duty of the operators of all regular vaults.

(a) to accept gold for delivery on Chicago Board of Trade contracts provided such gold is ordered into the vault by a clearing member of the association, and all space in such vaults allotted for such purposes is not already filled or contracted for.

(b) to ascertain that gold bars are weighed by a weigher approved by the association.

(c) to notify the Board of Trade of any change in the condition of their vaults.

(d) to release to the bearer of a receipt the bar covered by said receipt upon presentation of the receipt and payment of all storage and other charges no later than three business days following compliance with these provisions.

(e) to keep gold in storage in balance with gold represented by its outstanding vault receipts.

1581.01 Conditions of Regularity

Companies operating depository vaults as owners or lessees (herein called "operators") who desire to have such depository vaults made regular for delivery of gold under the rules and regulations shall make application for a Declaration of Regularity on a Form prescribed by the Board. Application for renewal of regularity must be made prior to May 1 in each year for the year beginning July 1 and shall be on the same form. If the Board approves such application it shall cause the Declaration of Regularity to be posted on the bulletin board and thereafter the vault receipts for gold stored in such vaults shall be deliverable in satisfaction of futures contracts under the Rules and Regulations. The following shall constitute the requirements and conditions for regularity:

(1) The Board shall cause the vault making application to be inspected.

(2) The operator of such vault must be a Bank (either federal or state charter), or an entity owned and controlled by any such bank with capital (Capital, surplus and undivided earnings) in excess of $250,000,000 or be a depository corporation with first loss insurance of $250,000,000 issued by an insurer satisfactory to the Chicago Board of Trade. The Board may also require whatever sureties it deems necessary.

(3) Such vault shall be provided with standard equipment and appliances for the convenient and safe storage of gold, the weighing of gold, and provide for proper security.

(4) The operator of such vault shall furnish to the Registrar all needed information to enable him to keep correct record and account of all gold received and delivered by them daily and of that remaining in store at the close of each week.

(5) The operator of such vault shall accord every facility to any duly authorized committee for the examination of its books or records for the purpose of ascertaining the stocks of gold. The Board shall have the authority to employ experts to determine the quantity and quality of gold in said vault.

(6) No vault shall be deemed suitable to be declared regular it its location, accessibility, tariffs, or other qualifications shall depart from uniformity to the extent that its receipts as tendered in satisfaction of futures contracts will unduly depress the values of futures contracts or impair the efficacy of futures trading in this market, or if the operator of such vault engages in unethical or inequitable practices, or if the operator fails to comply with any laws, Federal or State, or Rules or Regulations promulgated under those laws.

(7) The operator shall make such reports. keep such records, and permit such vault visitation as the Board of Trade may prescribe, and shall comply with all applicable Rules and Regulations.

(8) Depository vaults must be in the City of Chicago, Illinois, or in New York, New York.

1584.01 Revocation of Regularity

Any regular vault may be declared by the Board to be irregular at any time if it does not comply with the conditions above set forth, or fails to carry out its prescribed duties. If the designation of a vault as regular shall be revoked by the Board, the Board shall announce such revocation on the Bulletin board and also the period of time, if any, during which the receipts issued by such vault shall thereafter be deliverable in satisfaction of futures contracts in Gold under the Rules and Regulations.

1585.01 Application for Declaration of Regularity

All applications by operators of vaults for a Declaration of Regularity under Regulation 1581.01 shall be on the following form:

Application for a Declaration of Regularity for the storage of gold upon contracts for future delivery under the charter, rules, and regulations of the Board of Trade of the City of Chicago.

Board of Trade of the City of Chicago
141 West Jackson Blvd.
Chicago, Illinois 60604
Gentlemen:

_____ (hereinafter called Vault), located at
_____ and licensed
_____ and incorporated under the laws of
_____ having allocated storage capacity of
_____ troy ounces (hereinafter called Regular

Capacity) for the storage of gold for delivery in satisfaction of futures contracts on the Board of Trade of the City of Chicago (hereinafter called Exchange) does hereby make application to the Exchange for Declaration of Regularity to handle, receive and store gold (hereinafter called gold) for a period beginning _____ and ending midnight June 30, 19___.

Conditions of Regularity

Such Declaration of Regularity, if granted, shall be cancelable by the Exchange whenever the following conditions shall not be observed.

1. The vault must:

(1) give such bonds to the Exchange as may be reasonably required by the Board of Directors thereof.

(2) notify the Exchange promptly of any material change in ownership or condition of its premises.

(3) make such reports, keep such records, and permit such inspections as the Exchange may reasonably prescribe.

(4) comply with all applicable Rules and Regulations of the Exchange and comply with all requirements of the Exchange permitted or required by such Rules and Regulations.

2. The Vault must be:

(1) In the City of Chicago, Illinois or in New York, New York.

(2) properly safeguarded and equipped to weigh and to provide safe and convenient storage of gold.

Agreements of Vault

The vault expressly agrees:

(1) in the event of revocation or expiration of regularity to bear the expense of the transfer of gold under bond to another regular vault satisfactory to the holders of its vault receipts.

(2) neither to withdraw as regular vault nor withdraw any Regular Capacity during the life of this Declaration of Regularity except after sixty (60) days notice to the Exchange or having obtained the consent of the Exchange.

(3) to notify the Exchange at least sixty (60) days in advance of any changes in its maximum storage and handling charges as shown in the attached schedule.

Submitted herewith is a specimen of the Vault's proposed vault receipt.

_____

_____ By _____

Date   Title

This application is recommended by the Warehouse, Weighing and Custodian Committee of the Board of Trade of the City of Chicago.

_____

_____ By _____

Date   Committee Chairman

This application is approved and a Declaration of Regularity is hereby granted.

Board of Trade of the City of Chicago

By

_____

Chairman of the Board

_____

Date

By

Secretary

1586.01 Regular Vault

(See Appendix 15B)

Chicago Board of Trade

100-Ounce Gold Futures

Trading Unit: 100 troy ounces

Deliverable Grade: Refined gold in the form of one 100-ounce bar or three one-kilo bars assaying not less than 995 fineness. the total pack cannot vary from a 100 troy ounce weight by more than 5 percent.

Price Quotation: In dollars and cents per troy ounce

Delivery Method: By vault receipt issued by a CBOT-approved vault in Chicago or in New York.

Tick Size: 10 cents per ounce or $10 per contract.

Daily Price Limit: $50 per troy ounce or $5000 per contract.

Contract Months: Current month and the next two calendar months and February, April, June, August, October and December

Trading Hours: 7:20 A.M. to 1:40 P.M., Chicago time. Evening trading hours are from 5:00 P.M. to 8:30 PM (Central Standard Time) or from 6:00 P.M. to 9:00 P.M. (Central Standard Time), Sunday through Thursday.

Last Trading Day: No trades in 100-ounce gold futures deliverable in the current month shall be made during the last three business days of that month.

Ticker Symbol: GH

Gold Rules

B. 100 Ounce Gold
Trading Conditions

1501.00 Authority

Whenever it shall be permitted by the U.S. Government trading in Gold may be conducted under such terms and conditions as the Board may prescribe by regulation. Trading in Gold shall be supervised as directed by the Board.

1502.01 Application of Regulations

Transactions in Gold futures shall be subject to the general rules of the Association as far as applicable to trading in Gold.

For the purposes of this chapter, the trading day begins with the commencement of trading in each evening session and ends with the close of trading in the next afternoon session.

1504.01 Unit of Trading

The unit of trading shall be 100 fine troy ounces of gold. Bids and offers may be accepted in lots of 100 fine troy ounces or multiples thereof.

1505.01 Months Traded In

Trading in Gold may be conducted in the current month and any subsequent months.

1506.01 Price Basis

All prices of gold shall be basis in store in approved vaults in Chicago, Illinois or New York, in multiples of ten cents per fine troy ounce. Contracts shall not be made on any other price basis.

1507.01 Hours in Trading

The evening hours of trading for future delivery in gold shall be determined by the Board. The daytime hours of trading for future delivery in gold shall be from 7:20 a.m. to 1:40 p.m. On the last day of trading in an expiring future, the closing time with respect to such future shall be 1:40 p.m. subject to the otherwise applicable provisions of the second paragraph of Rule 1007.00.

1508.01 Trading Limits

(See 1008.01)

1508.01A Trading Limits

(See 1008.01A)

1509.01 Last Trading Day

No trades in Gold futures deliverable in the current month shall be made during the last three business days of that month and any contracts remaining open must be settled by delivery or as provided in Regulation 1509.02 after trading in such contracts has ceased; and if not previously delivered, delivery must be made no later than the last business day of the month. Tender shall be one business day prior to delivery.

As is the case with other contracts, delivery notices and supporting data processing (Delivery) cards must be made delivered to the Clearing House by 4:00 p.m. on position day except that, on the last notice day of the delivery month, delivery notices and supporting date processing cards may be delivered to the Clearing House until 2:00 p.m. on the intention day.

1509.02 Trading in the Last Three Days of the Delivery Month

After trading contracts for future delivery in the current delivery month has ceased in accordance with Regulation 1509.01 of this chapter, outstanding contract for such delivery may be liquidated by means of bona fide exchange of such current futures for the actual cash commodity. Such exchange must, in any event, be made no later than the last business day of the delivery month.

1510.01 Margin Requirements

Margin requirements shall be determined by the Board by regulation. (See 431.03)

1511.01 Disputes

All disputes between interested parties may be settled by arbitration as provided in the Rules and Regulations.

1512.01 Position Limits and Reportable Positions

(See Regulation 425.01)

Delivery Procedures

1536.01 Standards

Each futures contract made under these regulations shall be for 100 fine troy ounces of gold, although variation in the quantity of the delivery unit not in excess of five percent of 100 fine troy ounces shall be permitted. Delivery shall be by no more than three cast bars of refined gold, no less than 995 fine and bearing brands and markings officially approved by the Exchange; and no bar which contains less than 31 fine troy ounces of gold may be delivered in fulfillment of a contract.

Settlement shall be the basis of the fine ounces of gold delivered. Refined gold of fineness above 999.9 shall be considered to be 999.9 pure for the purpose of calculating the fine gold content.

1540.01 Brands and Markings of Gold

Brands and markings deliverable in satisfaction of futures contracts shall be listed with the Board of Trade upon approval by the Board that the requirements adopted by the Board have been met. The Board may require such sureties as it deems necessary. The Secretary's Office shall keep on file the brands and markings of gold bars which are deliverable. The addition of brands and markings shall be binding upon all contracts outstanding as well as those entered into after approval.

1540.02 Withdrawal of Approval of Gold Brands and Markings

If at anytime a brand and marking fails to meet the requirements adopted by the Board or the metallurgical assay of any gold bars bearing a brand and marking on the official list depreciates below 995 fineness, the Board may exclude said brand and marking from the official list unless deliveries of bars bearing said brand and marking are accompanied by certificates of analysis of an official assayer showing a gold fineness of not less than 995, and such additional bond as the Board may deem necessary. Notice of such action shall be given promptly in writing to each regular vault and shall be posted upon the bulletin board of the Association and the official list shall indicate the limitation upon deliveries of said brand and marking.

1540.03 Approved Brands

(See Appendix 15A)

1540.04 Assaying

The Board of Trade at its sole discretion shall have the authority at any time to have assayed any Gold bars covered by vault receipts delivered against futures contracts. Cost to be borne by the Board of Trade.

1541.01 Delivery Points

Gold located at regular vaults at points approved by the Board of Directors (Regulation 1581.01) may be delivered in satisfaction of futures contracts.

1542.01 Deliveries by Vault Receipts

Deliveries on Gold futures contract shall be made by the delivery of depository vault receipts issued by vaults which have been approved and designated by the Board as regular vaults for the storage of Gold. Gold bars must be good delivery bars as defined by Board regulations and shipped under bond directly to the regular vault from an approved vault; or must be bars purchased from an approved source and shipped directly from that source under bond to the regular vault. Gold bars entering a regular vault for delivery must be weighted at the vault by a weigher approved by the Association.

The gross weight of the bars shall be recorded by the approved weigher on the vault receipt (Regulation 1544.01) to the nearest one thousand (0.001) of a troy ounce.

The vault receipt issued by Chicago vaults shall evidence that storage charges have been paid up to and including the end of the Calendar quarter. A clearing member delivering a New York vault receipt must also tender an attachment stating that storage charges have been paid up to and including the end of the calendar quarter. Prepaid Storage Charges shall be charged to the buyer by the seller from the date of delivery to the expiration of the storage charge period. In order to effect a valid delivery, each vault receipt must be endorsed by the clearing member making delivery. If the owner removes gold from a vault, any prepaid storage charges shall be refunded by the vault to the owner from the date of removal of the gold to the expiration of the storage charge period.

By the tender of a vault receipt for gold duly endorsed by delivery on an Exchange contract, the endorser shall be deemed to warrant, to his transferee and each subsequent transferee of the receipt for delivery on Exchange contracts, and their respective immediate principals, the genuineness and worth of such receipt, the rightfulness and effectiveness of the transfer thereof, and the quantity and quality of the gold shown on the receipt.

In the event that such Exchange member or principal shall claim a breach of such warranty, and such claim relates to the quantity or quality of the gold, the lot shall be immediately submitted for sampling and assaying to any assayer approved by the Exchange; the gold must be shipped under bond, and at the owner's expense, to the assayer. The expense of sampling and assaying shall in the first instance, be borne by the claimant. If a deficiency in quantity or quality shall be determined by the assayer, the claimant shall have the right to recover the difference in the market value and expenses incurred in connection with the sampling and assaying and any cost of replacement of gold. The claimant may, at his option, proceed directly against the original endorser of the warehouse or vault receipt upon Exchange delivery, or against any endorser prior to claimant without seeking recovery from his immediate deliverer on the Exchange contract and if the claim is satisfied by the original endorser of the warehouse or vault receipt, or any other endorser, all the endorsers will be thereby discharged from liability to the claimant. If the claimant seeks recovery from any endorser and his claim is satisfied by such endorser, the party thus satisfying the claim will have a similar option to claim recovery directly from any endorser prior to him. such claims as are in dispute between members of the Exchange may in each case be submitted to arbitration under the Rules of the Exchange.

The liability of an endorser of a vault receipt as provided herein shall not be deemed to limit the rights of such endorser against any person or party for whose account the endorser acted in making delivery on an Exchange contract. If it shall be determined in such arbitration proceeding that any endorser of a vault receipt or the person or party for whom such endorser acted was aware of the breach of warranty or was involved in a plan or agreement with the original endorser (or his principal) to place such inferior gold in licensed store for use in deliveries upon Exchange contracts, such endorsers shall not be entitled to recover from any prior endorser for the breach of warranty.

1543.01 Issuance of Vault Receipts

Vault receipts, in order to be eligible for delivery, must be issued by a regular vault according to the following procedures and with the following documentation retained by the regular vault:

(1) For all vault receipts

(a) Receipts shall be issued in numerical order.

(b) Copies shall be kept of any canceled or voided receipts

(c) A record shall be kept of the bar number and the corresponding receipt number.

(2) For gold delivered into the vault directly from a refiner or an approved source.

(a) Copy of the bar listing which depicts the date of smelting, serial numbers, brand marking and troy ounces.

(b) Copy of the bonded carrier receipt for the transport of the gold from the refiner of the approved source directly into the regular vault.

(3) For gold converted from a receipt issued by another exchange:

(a) A copy of such other exchange's receipt which has been canceled.

Regular vaults shall also notify the Board of Trade each day that there is a change in the number of its outstanding vault receipts.

1543.02 Deposit of Gold with Vaults

Gold in bars must bc ordered into a regular vault by a clearing member of the Association who shall furnish the vault with the following written notice:

1. Request to receive gold.

2. Brands and markings.

3. Number of bars.

4. Identification (serial number) of each bar.

5. Weight of each bar.

6. Source.

7. Clearing member.

8. Carrier.

9. Date of arrival.

Shipment must be prepaid unless otherwise arranged with the regular vault.

1544.01 Receipt Format

The following form of vault receipt shall be used:

_____
(Name of Issuer)

_____
(Address)
Bearer Receipt No._____
Chicago, Ill _____ 19____
RECEIVED from _____
and stored at the above address in the safety deposit vaults of the undersigned, as a Bailee, subject to the provisions of Article 7 of the _____ Uniform Commercial Code and the terms and conditions stated hereon, a gold bar SAID TO CONTAIN the amount shown hereon of gold of the fineness indicated.

Said bar is deliverable only at said vaults to the BEARER of this receipt upon surrender hereof and upon payment of storage charges and other proper charges and expenses relating to said bar, for which charges and expenses the undersigned claims a lien.

Payment of handling charges for deposit of said bar and of storage charges to the end of the current calendar quarter is hereby acknowledged. Storage charges for each subsequent calendar quarter are to be paid to the undersigned, in advance, at or before the expiration of the preceding calendar quarter.

Bar identification markings of bar covered by this receipt as shown hereon, have been recorded by the undersigned on the basis of markings appearing on said bar. THE UNDERSIGNED HAS NOT ASCERTAINED, AND IS NOT RESPONSIBLE FOR THE AUTHENTICITY OR CORRECTNESS OF MARKINGS ON, OR THE CONTENT, WEIGHT OR FINENESS OF SAID BAR.

_____
(Issuer)
By _____
(Authorized Signature)
Gross Weight as determined by a weigher approved by the Board of Trade of the City of Chicago _____ troy ounces.
_____ Approved weigher of the Board of Trade of the City of Chicago
Bar Identification Markings

Serial Number	Gross Weight Troy Ounces	Kilograms	Mark of Brand	Fineness
Totals				

STORAGE AND HANDLING CHARGES: Storage charges of _____ per calendar day per contract, minimum _____ per contract plus _____ handling charge per contract for each deposit and withdrawal.
Endorsements
Date _____ By _____
Date _____ By _____

1546.01 Date of Delivery

Where gold is sold for delivery in specified month, delivery of such gold may be made by the Seller upon such day of the specified month as the Seller may select. If not previously delivered, delivery must be made upon the last business day of the month.

1547.01 Delivery Notices

(See 1047.01)

1548.01 Method of Delivery

(See 1048.01)

1549.00 Time of Delivery, Payment, Form of Delivery Notice

(See 1049.00)

1549.02 Buyers' Report of Eligibility to Receive Delivery

(See 1049.02)

1549.03 Sellers' Invoice to Buyers

In addition to the requirements of 1049.03, the seller shall mail a copy of the invoice to the vault or faults who issued the vault receipts being delivered. The seller will thereby notify the vault of the transfer of ownership of the indicated vault receipts from the seller to the buyer. The seller will be responsible for the payment of storage charges unless the vault has been notified thereby.

1549.04 Payment

Payment is to be made by a check drawn on and certified by a Chicago bank or by a Cashier's check by a Chicago bank.

1550.00 Duties of Members

(See 1050.00)

1551.01 Office Deliveries Prohibited

(See 1051.01)

1554.00 Failure to Accept Delivery

(See 1054.00)

1556.01 Storage and Transfer Fees

Storage charges, transfer fees and in-and-out charges shall be set by each depository vault and the schedule of such charges shall be posted with the Association, which shall be notified at least 60 days in advance of any changes in the rate schedule. Except as otherwise provided, all charges for storage, etc., shall remain the responsibility of the Seller until payment is made.

Regularity of Vaults

1580.01 Duties of Vault Operators

If shall be the duty of the operators of all regular vaults.

(a) to accept gold for delivery on Chicago Board of Trade contracts provided such gold is ordered into the vault by a clearing member of the association, and all space in such vaults allotted for such purposes is not already filled or contracted for.

(b) to ascertain that gold bars are weighed by a weigher approved by the association.

(c) to notify the Board of Trade of any change in the condition of their vaults.

(d) to release to the bearer of a receipt the bar covered by said receipt upon presentation of the receipt and payment of all storage and other charges no later than three business days following compliance with these provisions.

(e) to keep gold in storage in balance with gold represented by its outstanding vault receipts.

1581.01 Conditions of Regularity

Companies operating depository vaults as owners or lessees (herein called "operators") who desire to have such depository vaults made regular for delivery of gold under the rules and regulations shall make application for a Declaration of Regularity on a Form prescribed by the Board. Application for renewal of regularity must be made prior to May 1 in each year for the year beginning July 1 and shall be on the same form. If the Board approves such application it shall cause the Declaration of Regularity to be posted on the bulletin board and thereafter the vault receipts for gold stored in such vaults shall be deliverable in satisfaction of futures contracts under the Rules and Regulations. The following shall constitute the requirements and conditions for regularity:

(1) The Board shall cause the vault making application to be inspected.

(2) The operator of such vault must be a Bank (either federal or state charter), or an entity owned and controlled by any such bank with capital (Capital, surplus and undivided earnings) in excess of $250,000,000 or be a depository corporation with first loss insurance of $250,000,000 issued by an insurer satisfactory to the Chicago Board of Trade. The Board may also require whatever sureties it deems necessary.

(3) Such vault shall be provided with standard equipment and appliances for the convenient and safe storage of gold, the weighing of gold, and provide for proper security.

(4) The operator of such vault shall furnish to the Registrar all needed information to enable him to keep correct record and account of all gold received and delivered by them daily and of that remaining in store at the close of each week.

(5) The operator of such vault shall accord every facility to any duly authorized committee for the examination of its books or records for the purpose of ascertaining the stocks of gold. The Board shall have the authority to employ experts to determine the quantity and quality of gold in said vault.

(6) No vault shall be deemed suitable to be declared regular it its location, accessibility, tariffs, or other qualifications shall depart from uniformity to the extent that its receipts as tendered in satisfaction of futures contracts will unduly depress the values of futures contracts or impair the efficacy of futures trading in this market, or if the operator of such vault engages in unethical or inequitable practices, or if the operator fails to comply with any laws, Federal or State, or Rules or Regulations promulgated under those laws.

(7) The operator shall make such reports. keep such records, and permit such vault visitation as the Board of Trade may prescribe, and shall comply with all applicable Rules and Regulations.

(8) Depository vaults must be in the City of Chicago, Illinois, or in New York, New York.

1584.01 Revocation of Regularity

Any regular vault may be declared by the Board to be irregular at any time if it does not comply with the conditions above set forth, or fails to carry out its prescribed duties. If the designation of a vault as regular shall be revoked by the Board, the Board shall announce such revocation on the Bulletin board and also the period of time, if any, during which the receipts issued by such vault shall thereafter be deliverable in satisfaction of futures contracts in Gold under the Rules and Regulations.

1585.01 Application for Declaration of Regularity

All applications by operators of vaults for a Declaration of Regularity under Regulation 1581.01 shall be on the following form:

Application for a Declaration of Regularity for the storage of gold upon contracts for future delivery under the charter, rules, and regulations of the Board of Trade of the City of Chicago.
Board of Trade of the City of Chicago
141 West Jackson Blvd.
Chicago, Illinois 60604
Gentlemen:
_____ (hereinafter called Vault), located at
_____ and licensed
_____ and incorporated under the laws of
_____ having allocated storage capacity of

_____ troy ounces (hereinafter called Regular Capacity) for the storage of gold for delivery in satisfaction of futures contracts on the Board of Trade of the City of Chicago (hereinafter called Exchange) does hereby make application to the Exchange for Declaration of Regularity to handle, receive and store gold (hereinafter called gold) for a period beginning _____ and ending midnight June 30, 19___.

Conditions of Regularity

Such Declaration of Regularity, if granted, shall be cancelable by the Exchange whenever the following conditions shall not be observed.

1. The vault must:

(1) give such bonds to the Exchange as may be reasonably required by the Board of Directors thereof.

(2) notify the Exchange promptly of any material change in ownership or condition of its premises.

(3) make such reports, keep such records, and permit such inspections as the Exchange may reasonably prescribe.

(4) comply with all applicable Rules and Regulations of the Exchange and comply with all requirements of the Exchange permitted or required by such Rules and Regulations.

2. The Vault must be:

(1) In the City of Chicago, Illinois or in New York, New York.

(2) properly safeguarded and equipped to weigh and to provide safe and convenient storage of gold.

Agreements of Vault

The vault expressly agrees:

(1) in the event of revocation or expiration of regularity to bear the expense of the transfer of gold under bond to another regular vault satisfactory to the holders of its vault receipts.

(2) neither to withdraw as regular vault nor withdraw any Regular Capacity during the life of this Declaration of Regularity except after sixty (60) days notice to the Exchange or having obtained the consent of the Exchange.

(3) to notify the Exchange at least sixty (60) days in advance of any changes in its maximum storage and handling charges as shown in the attached schedule.

Submitted herewith is a specimen of the Vault's proposed vault receipt.

—————————————————— By ——————————————————
Date   Title

This application is recommended by the Warehouse, Weighing and Custodian Committee of the Board of Trade of the City of Chicago.

—————————————————— By ——————————————————
Date   Committee Chairman

This application is approved and a Declaration of Regularity is hereby granted.

Board of Trade of the City of Chicago
By
——————————————————
Chairman of the Board

——————————————————
Date
By
Secretary

1586.01 Regular Vault

(See Appendix 15B)

Brands Approved for Delivery Against Gold Contracts

Brand   **Argor S.A.**

Refiner   Argor S.A.
           Via C. Cattaneo
           Chiasso, Switzerland

Parent   Union Bank of Switzerland
           Bahnhofstrasse 45
           8021 Surich, Switzerland

Brand   **ASARCO**

Refiner   ASARCO Inc.
           Amarillo, Texas

Parent   ASARCO Inc.
                120 Broadway
                New York, NY 10005

Brand   Baker
Refiner   Engelhard Industries Division
                429 Delancy St.
                Newark, NJ 07105
Parent   Englehard Minerals and Chemicals Corp.
                299 Park AVe.
                New York, NY 10017

Brand   Canadian Copper Refiners Ltd.
Refiner   Canadian Copper Refineres Ltd.
                Montreal East
                Quebec, Canada
Parent   Noranda
                PO Box 45
                Commerce Court West
                Toronto, Ontario
                Canada, M5L 1B6

Brand   Casa Da Moeda Do Brasil - CMB
Refiner   Casa Da Moeda Do Brasil - CMB
                Rua Rene Bitencourt, no 371
                Distrito Industrial de Santa Cruz
                CEP
Parent   Casa Da Moeda Do Brasil - CMB
                Rua Rene Bitencourt, no 371
                Distrito Industrial de Santa Cruz
                CEP: 23.500 - Rio de Janeiro - RJ/Brasil

Brand   Compagnie des Metaux Precieus (CMP)
Refiner   Compagnie des Metaux Precieus S.A.
                75, Boulevard P.V. Couturier
                942000 IVRY-France
Parent   Swiss Bank Corp.
                Paradeplatz

8001 Zurich, Switzerland

Brand   **Comptoir Lyon-Alemand Louyot**

Refiner   Comptoir Lyon-Alemand Louyot
             41 Rue de Paris
             93130 NOISY LE SEC
             France

Parent   Comptoir Lyon-Alemand Louyot
             13 Rue de Montmorency
             75139 Paris Cedex 03 France

Brand   **Credit Suisse**

Refiner   Valcambi
             6828 Balerna, Switzerland

Parent   Swiss Credit Bank
             8021 Zurich, Switzerland

Brand   **Degussa**

Refiner   Degussa
             Metallwerk Wolfgang
             6450 Hanau
             Stadtteil Wolfgang

Parent   Degussa
             6000 Frankfurt
             Weissfauenstrasse 9
             Federal Republic of Germany

Brand   **Degussa Canada Ltd.**

Refiner   Degussa Canada Ltd.
             4621 Mainway Drive
             Burlington, Ontario
             L7R 3Y8, Canada

Parent   Degussa AG of Frankfurt
             Federal Republic of Germany

Brand   **DRW**

Refiner   United States Metal Refining Co.
             Carteret, NJ

Parent   AMAX Inc.

200 Park Ave.
New York, NY 10017

Brand   **Engelhard and Engelhard with Trade Mark**
Refiner   Engelhard Industries of Canada Ltd.
               512 King St. East
               Toronto, Ontario M5A 1M2 Canada
Parent   Engelhard Industries of Canada Ltd.
               512 King St. East
               Toronto, Ontario M5A 1M2 Canada

               Engelhard (logo)
Brand   **Engelhard E (frank)**
Refiner   Engelhard Industries Division
               429 Delancy St.
               Newark, NJ 07974
Parent   Engelhard Minerals and Chemicals Corp.
               299 Park Ave.
               New York, NY 10017

Brand   **Engelhard - London**
Refiner   Engelhard Industries Ltd.
               Cox Lane Chessington
               Surrey, England
Parent   Engelhard Industries Ltd.

Brand   **St. Nicholas House**
               St. Nicholas Rd.
               Sutton Surrey, England

Brand   **HH Handy & Harman**
Refiner   Handy & Harman
               Frank Mossberg Drive
               Attleboro, Mass. 02703
Parent   Handy & Harman
               850 Third Ave.
               New York, NY 10022

Brand   **Johnson Matthey London**

Refiner   Johnson Matthey Chemicals Ltd.
             Orchard Rd.
             Royston Hertfordshire SG8 5HE
             England
Parent   Johnson Matthey Chemicals Ltd.
             Stockingswater Lane
             Brimsdown Enfield
             Middlesex EN 37PW England

Brand   **Johnson Matthey Canada**
Refiner   Johnson Matthey Ltd.
             130 Glidden Rd.
             Brampton, Ontario L6W 3M8
Parent   Johnson Matthey 7 Co., Ltd.
             15 King St.
             London EC2 England

Brand   **Johnson Matthey Inc., Salt Lake City, Utah**
Refiner   Johnson Matthey Inc.
             4601 West 21000 South
             Salt Lake City, Untah 84120-1221
Parent   Precious Metals Division of Johnson Matthey PLC

Brand   **Matthey Bishop**
Refiner   Matthey Bishop, Inc.
             Piney Hollow Rd.
             Winslow, NJ
Parent   Matthey Bishop, Inc.
             Malvern, PA 19355

Brand   **Metallurgie Hoboken Overpelt**
Refiner   Metallurgie Hoboken Overpelt
             Hoboken, Belgium
Parent   Metallurgie Hoboken Overpelt S.A.
             Adolf Greinerstraat 14
             B-2710 Hoboken, Belgium

Brand   **Metaux Precieus S.A. Neuchatel**
Refiner   Metaux Precieux S.A.

Avenue due Vignoble 2
CH - 2000 Neuchatel, Switzerland

Parent   Swiss Bank Corp.
Paradeplatz 8001 Zurich, Switzerland

Brand   Mitsubishi

Refiner   Osaka Refinery of Mitsubishi
Metal Corp.
Kita-ku Osaka, Japan

Parent   Mitsubishi Metal Corp.
#5-2 Ohte-machi 1-Chome
Chiyoda-ku Tokyo Japan

Brand   Norddeutsche Affinerie (N.A.)

Refiner   Norddeutsche Affinerie
Hovestrase 50
2000 Hamburg 28 West Germany

Parent   Norddeutsche Affinerie
Alsterterrase 2
Postfach 67 2000 Hamburg 36
West Germany

Brand   The Royal Canadian Mint

Refiner   The Royal Canadian Mint
Parent   The Royal Canadian Mint
320 Sussex Drive
Ottawa, Ontario
Canada K1A 0G8

Brand   Sheffield Smelting Co. Ltd.

Refiners   Sheffield Smelting Co. Ltd. (1)
Cox Lane Chessington
Surrey, England
Engelhard Industries Division (2)
Engelhard Minerals & Chemicals Corp.
430 Mountain Ave.
Murray Hill, NJ 07974
Engelhard Industries of Canada (3)

Parent	512 King St. East
	Toronto 248 Canada
	Engelhard Industries Ltd.
	St. Nicholas House
	St. Nicholas Road
	Sutton Surrey SM1 1EH England

Brand **Societe de Banque Suisse (SBS)**

Refiner Metaux Precieux S.A.
CH-2000
Neuchatel 9 Switzerland
(also Le Locle Switzerland)

Parent Swiss Bank Corp.
Paradeplatz
8001 Zurich, Switzerland

Brand **Tanaka**

Refiner Hiratsuka Works No. 2
Tanaka Kikinzoku Kogyo K.IK. 2-14
Nagatoro Hiratsuka Kanagawa
Prefecture 254 Japan

Parent Tanaka Kikinzoku Kogyo K.IK.
6-6 Nihonbashi Kayabacho 2-Chome
Chuo-ku Tokyo 103 Japan

Brand **Valcambi**

Refiner Valcambi, S.A.
1628 Balerna, Switzerland

Parent Swiss Credit Bank
Paradeplatz
8000 Zurich, Switzerland

Note: Brands are approved on both the one kilo and 100 ounce gold contract, except for ASARCO and DRW which are approved only on the 100 ounce gold contract.

Vaults Approved for Gold Storage

The following is a listing of vaults approved for the storage of gold for the period July 1, 1989, through June 30, 1990.

Continental Illinois National Bank and Trust Co. of Chicago Chicago, IL	1,000,000
Harris Trust and Savings Bank Chicago, IL	745,000
Citibank, N.A. New York, NY	30,000,000

Official Assayers

Ledoux & Co.
359 Alfred Ave.
Teaneck, NJ 07666
(201) 837-7160

International Testing Laboratories
580 Market St.
Newark, NJ 07105
(201) 589-4772

Approved Sources and Vaults

Asarco Inc.
P.O. Box 4500
Amarillo, Texas 79105

Bank of Nova Scotia
44 Kind St., West
Toronto, Ontario, Canada

Brink's France Ltd.
64/66 Rue de Khefir
94, LaSenia, France

Canadian Imperial Bank of Commerce
Commerce Court West
Toronto, Ontario, Canada

Chase Manhattan Bank
1 Chase Manhattan Plaza
New York, New York 10015

Citibank, N.A.
Madison Avenue & 65th St.
New York, New York 10022

Citibank, N.A.
399 Park Ave.
New York, New York 10022

Citibank, N.A.
2 Broadway
New York, New York 10004

Citibank, N.A.
55 Wall St.
New York, New York 10004

Compagnie des Metaux Precieus
75, Boulevard P.V. Couturier
94200 Ivry
France

Engelhard Industries Division
of Engelhard Minerals & Chemicals Corp.
429 Delancy St.
Newark, NJ 07974

Engelhard Industries Ltd.
Cox Lane
Chessington, Surrey
England

Engelhard Industries of Canada Ltd.
521 King St. East
Toronto, Ontario M5A 1M2, Canada

Handy & Harman
525 Nuber Avenue
Mount Vernon, NY 10550

Harris Bank and Trust Co.
111 West Monroe St.
Chicago, IL 60690

Iron Mountain Depository Corp.
26 Broadway
New York, NY 10004

Johnson Matthey Bankers Ltd.
73-84, Hatton Garden
London ECI, England

Johnson Matthey Chemicals Ltd.
Orchard Rd.
Royston Hertfordshire, England

Johnson Matthey Ltd.
130 Glidden Rd.
Brampton, Ontario L6W 3M8
Canada

Matthey Bishop, Inc.
Piney Hollow Rd.
Winslow, N.J.

Matthey Bishop, Inc.
Malvern, Pennsylvania 91355

Metallurgie Hoboken-Overpelt
Adolf Greinerstraat 14
B-2710 Hoboken, Belgium
Mocatta & Goldsmid Ltd. (Vault)

Park House
16 Finsbury Circus
London, EC2M 7DA
England

N.M. Rothschild & Sons Ltd.
New Court
St. Swithin's Lane
London EC4P 4DU
England

Republic National Bank of New York
115 Broadway
New York, NY 10018

Samuel Montagu & Co. Ltd.
114 Old Broad St.
London, EC2P 2HY
England

Sharps Pixley & Co. Ltd.
34 Line St.
London, EC3M 7LX
England

Swiss Bank Corp.
120 Broadway
New York, NY 10018

Swiss Bank Corp.
Paradeplatz
800 Zurich, Switzerland

Swiss Credit Bank
Paradeplatz 8
8001 Zurich, Switzerland

Credit Suisse
100 Wall St.
New York, NY 10005

Union Bank of Switzerland
Bahnofstrasse 45
8021 Zurich, Switzerland

United States Metals Refining Co.
Carteret, NJ

Zurich Bonded Warehouse Co., Ltd.
Kloten Airport
Zurich, Switzerland

The MidAmerica Commodity Exchange
LaSalle at Jackson
Chicago, Illinois 60604

Trading unit: 33.2 fine troy ounces

Delivery months: All months

Trading hours: 7:20 A.M. to 1:40 P.M. Chicago time

Minimum fluctuation: 10 cents per fine troy ounce or $3.32 per contract

Delivery grade: A single bar within 10 percent (plus or minus) the contract weight is deliverable, assaying not less than 995.0 fineness and bearing one of the brands and markings officially listed by the Exchange.

Delivery: Deliveries on gold futures shall be made by delivery of negotiable vault receipts issued by an Exchange-approved depository, or negotiable warehouse depository receipts issued by the Exchange upon deposit of such negotiable vault receipts.

Ticker Symbol: XK

Gold Rules

1501: Commodity Specifications

Each futures contract shall be for 33.2 fine troy ounces of gold not less than 0.995 fine contained in one bar.

1503: Futures Call

A. Trading Months: Trading in gold for future delivery may be conducted in the current month and any subsequent months.

B. Size of Trading Unit: The size of the trading unit shall be 33.2 fine troy ounces of gold.

C. Price Increments: Minimum price fluctuations shall be in multiples of $0.10 (10 cents) per fine troy ounce.

D. Position Limits: The limit on the maximum net long or short position which any person may hold or control in all gold futures contracts traded on the Exchange is 50,000 troy ounces in any one month or 100,000 troy ounces in all months combined; provided, that in no event may such person hold or control such a net long or short position which, when combined with a respective net long or short position in all gold futures contracts traded on the Chicago Board of Trade, would exceed the applicable position limits for such Chicago Board of Trade contracts. In determining whether any person has exceeded the limits established under this rule, all positions in accounts for which such person by power of attorney or otherwise directly or indirectly controls trading shall be included with the positions held by such person; such limits upon positions shall apply to positions held by two or more persons acting pursuant to an expressed or implied agreement or understanding, the same as if the positions were held by a single person. Position limits shall not apply to positions which are bona fide hedging; intra- or inter-market spreads vis-a-vis another gold contract traded on the Exchange or another board of trade prior to the first notice day in the nearby leg (except where the exemption is granted per rule 419); or changing positions, insofar as the changer is evenly spread between two markets.

This rule shall not be construed to exempt the changer from applicable limits on the changed market.

Amended, effective October 25, 1988.

E. Termination of Trading: Futures trading shall terminate on the business day immediately preceding the last two business days of the contract month.

F. Contract Modification: Specifications shall be fixed as of the first day of trading of a contract except that all deliveries must conform to government regulations in force at the time of delivery. If the U.S. government, an agency, or duly constituted body thereof issues an order, ruling, directive, or law inconsistent with the trading pursuant to these rules, such order, ruling, directive, or law shall be construed to take precedence and become part of these rules and all open and new contracts shall be subject to such governmental orders.

G. Hours of Trading: The hours of trading in gold for futures delivery shall be from 7:20 AM to 1:40 PM.

1503: Delivery

Delivery of gold shall be effected as follows:

A. Delivery Days: Delivery may be made on any Exchange business day of the contract month.

B. Seller's Duties: to effectuate delivery, the clearing member representing the seller, at the time of filing with the clearing house a notice of intention to deliver, shall have on hand in his office on forms prescribed by the Exchange, a delivery notice; a negotiable warehouse receipt certificate and invoice; and all other documents that may be required by the Exchange. The negotiable warehouse receipt shall contain the name and location of the storing depository, the date of issuance, the identification number of the gold bars, and the name of the refiner, assayer, or other Exchange approved certifying authority.

By the tender of a negotiable warehouse receipt for gold duly endorsed for the delivery pursuant to an Exchange contract, the endorser is deemed to guarantee to his transferee and each subsequent transferee of the receipt for delivery on Exchange contract, and their respective immediate principals, the quantity and quality of the gold as shown on the receipt.

C. Buyer's Duties: A buyer receiving a notice of intention to deliver shall present at the office of the seller such notice of intention to deliver prior to 5:00 PM on the day of delivery, whereupon delivery and payment shall take place.

D. Payment: Payment shall be made on the basis of the number of fine troy ounces of gold contained and delivered. The fine gold content of a bar for good delivery is calculated to 0.001 of an ounce troy by multiplying the gross weight by the assay, but in no case by more than 0.9999. The fourth decimal place in the product of the multiplication is ignored unless it is a nine, in such case the third decimal place is increased by 0.001.

Payment is to be made by a check drawn on and certified by a Chicago bank or be a cashier's check issued by a Chicago bank.

E. Notices of Intention to Deliver: A notice of intention to deliver must be tendered to the clearing house by 12:00 noon two days prior to the day of delivery except on the last notice day of the contract month when such notices shall be tendered by 11:00 AM on the day prior to delivery; provided that a clearing member representing a long taking delivery on the Commodity Exchange, Inc. and making delivery on MidAmerica shall tender notice of intention to delivery one hour before the opening of the market one day prior to delivery, such tender to be dated the previous business day. The clearing house shall, before the opening of the market on the day prior to delivery (by the close of market on last notice day), pass such notice of intention to deliver to the buyer obligated by the oldest contract to take delivery. The notice of intention to deliver shall include the identity of the issuer of the receipt, the receipt number and registration number, the gross ounces of the bars and fineness thereof, the licensed depository in which said bars are stored, the name of the Exchange approved refiner, and the net fine troy ounces covered by each receipt. If the manager of the clearing house shall so require, the seller shall also tender keypunch cards including the foregoing information, in a form prescribed by the clearing house. At the close of trading on the day of issuance of a notice of intention to deliver, the holder of such outstanding notice shall be deemed the holder of a delivery notice and shall obligate the holder to take delivery. Such holder of a delivery notice shall, not later than 5:00 PM, two days after the date of tender, present the delivery notice at the office of the seller by whom it was issued together with a certified or cashier's check for the amount due per rule 1503.D, and, thereupon the warehouse receipts and other necessary documents shall be delivered by the seller to the buyer.

F. Notice Prior for Gold: At the close of business on the day of tender the clearing house shall post the notice price for gold. Gold shall be paid for at the notice price on the basis set forth in rule 1503.D.

1504: Par Delivery

A. Par Delivery: Each futures contract shall be for 33.2 fine troy ounces of gold no less than 0.995 fine contained in no more than one bar.

In accordance with the accepted practices of the trade, each bar for good delivery must be of good appearance, easy to handle, and convenient to stack. the sides and bottom should be reasonable smooth and free from cavities and bubbles. The edges should be rounded and not sharp. Each bar, if not marked with the fineness and stamp of an approved refiner, assayer, or other certifying authority must be accompanied by a certificate issued by an approved refiner, assayer, or other certifying authority, stating the serial number of the bars, the weight, and the fineness.

B. Delivery points: Par delivery shall be made at the seller's option from Exchange approved depositories located in New York, New York.

C. Quantity: Variations in the quantity of the delivery unit not in excess of ten percent of 33.2 fine troy ounces shall be permitted.

1505: Product Certification and Shipment

To be eligible for delivery on the Exchange, all gold must be certified as to fineness and weight by an Exchange approved refiner, assayer, or other Exchange approved certifying authority and must be shipped directly from the Exchange approved refiner, assayer, or certifying authority via Exchange approved carriers to Exchange approved depositories.

All gold, if not continuously in the custody of an Exchange approved depository or carrier, must be recertified as to fineness and weight to be eligible for delivery.

1506: Cost of Inspection, Weighing, Storage, and Delivery

All charges associated with the delivery of gold and all costs associated with inspections, weighing, and Exchange documentations, through the day of delivery, shall be paid by the delivering party. The delivering party shall pay storage charges through the business day following the day of delivery. The receivers shall pay all charges including storage charges incurred after the day of delivery.

A holder of an Exchange approved warehouse receipt for gold may request recertification at his expense at any time while the unit represented by such receipt is in the Exchange approved depository. such recertification shall be made by an Exchange approved certifying authority or assayer, selected by such holder.

Revised effective August 15, 1984.

1507: Refiners, Depositories, Weighmasters, Assayers, and Deliverers

Exchange approved refiners, depositories, weighmasters, assayers, and deliverers may be listed with the Exchange upon approval by the Board. The Secretary's office shall maintain and make available such lists. The addition of refiners and depositories shall be binding upon all contracts outstanding as well as those entered into after approval.

1508: Deposit of Gold in Vaults

Gold shall be placed into a regular vault accompanied by the following information:

A. Refiner,

B. Serial number of each piece and

C. Weight of each piece.

After the gold has been placed in a vault, negotiable warehouse or vault receipts shall be issued to its owners with the following information:

A. Refiner and

B. Serial number of each piece.

Receipts shall be lettered or numbered consecutively by each ware-house or vault. No two receipts shall bear the same letter or number. No receipt shall be issued for more or less than one contract unit.

1509: Form of Delivery Notice

Notices shall be in a form prescribed by the clearing house of the Exchange.

1510: Form of vault or warehouse receipt

Receipts shall be in a form prescribed by the clearing house of the Exchange.

Tokyo Commodity Exchange for Industry
10-8 Nihonbashi-Horidome 1-chome,
Chuo-Ku,
Tokyo 103
Tel: (03) 661-9191
Fax: (03) 661 7568

Standard Grade: Gold bar with a purity of 99.99 percent

Contract Size: 1 kilogram

Price Multiples: One yen per one gram

Trading Hours: 9:10 AM to 11:30 AM; 1:10 PM to 3:45 PM, Tokyo time

Contract Months: Current or next odd numbered month, and all even months.

Last Day of Trading in Current Month: The third business day preceding the delivery day.

Delivery Day: Delivery shall be made by the end of the contract month. When the day falls on a holiday or half day-holiday, it shall be moved up one day ahead.

Method of Trading: When quantities of buying and selling in the process of the auction have been finally reached even at a certain price, the Exchange's staff shall decide the price as the formal single price by clapping wooden clappers.

Price Fluctuation Limits: Daily quotations on the transactions are not allowed beyond the prices provided by the board of the Exchange, based upon the following range above or below the previous day's closing prices. However, no limit is applicable to the current month from the first business day in the precious metals market and on and after the 15th of the contract month (When the day falls on a holiday, it shall be moved up one day ahead).

Less than Y1600	Y80
Y1600 to Y2100	Y110
Y2100 to Y2600	Y140
Y2600 and greater	Y170

Deliverable Brands: Deliverable grades of a commodity shall be designated by the board of the Exchange.

Place of Delivery: In principle, at the designated warehouses authorized by the Exchange.

Delivery Method: As a rule, delivery is made based on an alienable
warehouse warrant.

Allowable Weight for Delivery: The maximum and minimum allowable weight for delivery of a commodity shall be provided by the
Exchange.

Settlement of Differences: The Exchange revalues all members' outstanding contracts every trading day, using that day's closing price, and
profits or losses arising from this repricing process are paid out or
collected in cash to ensure sound transactions among members.

Assurance of Execution of Contracts: The Exchange requires members
to deposit not only the prescribed membership trust money and guarantee
money for transactions but also the special security money and so forth
with the Exchange to ensure the execution of the contracts among
members.

Safeguard for Customer's Claim: The Exchange requires ring members to deposit security money for commission business with the Exchange for the benefit of their customers.

Delivery

Article 36—Delivery Points

Delivery points on the market of precious metals shall be such designated
warehouses selected and appointed by the Chairman of the Exchange
after deliberation of the Board of Directors from among licensed warehouses in Tokyo-to and Kanagawa-ken.

Article 37—Day and Time for Delivery

As for the day and time for delivery, delivery shall be made by 0:45 PM
on the last day of every month (the 24th in the case of December);
provided, however, that the relevant day shall be moved up in order when
it falls on a holiday or half-holiday.

Article 38—Delivery Price

Delivery prices shall be the settlement prices for current month delivery
on the closing session day.

Article 39—Payment for Delivery

Payment for delivery, in case of standard commodities shall be the sum determined by multiplying the delivery price by the quantity delivered, and, in the case of commodities other than the standard commodities, shall be the sum determined by multiplying the delivery price to be adjusted with addition or subtraction made according to the designated schedule of the Exchange for differences in the grades of the commodities to be delivered by the quantity delivered.

Article 40—Warehouse Receipt for the Delivered Commodity

Delivery shall be made against such Warehouse Receipts issued by warehouses designated in advance by the Chairman of the Exchange in accordance with the provisions of Article 36; provided, however, that if the receiver's agreement has been obtained, delivery may be effected against such Delivery Order issued by a warehouse designated by the Chairman of the Exchange according to the provisions of Article 36, with clear statement that the commodity is in store and shall be delivered only against the Delivery Order (provided that the Delivery Order is delivered within 3 months from its date of issuance).

Article 41—Storage Fee until Completion of Delivery

The storage fee and insurance premium shall be for the account of the deliverer, such fee and premium shall be paid up to the term including the date on which the Warehouse Receipt of the Delivery Order is delivered to the receiver by the Exchange.

Article 42—Loss of or Damage to Commodity after Delivery

In the event that the object commodity is lost or damaged in whole or in part by reasons not attributable to the parties concerned with the delivery after the deliverer's submission of the warehouse receipt to the Exchange for delivery and before the Exchange's delivery of the same to the receiver, the loss shall be for the account of the deliverer.

In the case of the preceding paragraph, the deliverer shall, without delay, give the Exchange notice in writing to such effect and shall furnish a warehouse receipt of substitute commodity within five business days counting from the business day following the date of the said notice in order to complete the delivery.

If the deliverer finds it impossible to furnish the whole or a part of the substitute notwithstanding the provisions of the preceding paragraph, he may refuse delivery of such portion after approval by the Board of Directors.

In such case, the Exchange shall regard that the delivery has been completed, and out of the payment submitted to the Exchange by the receiver, shall return the amount corresponding to such portion not delivered to the receiver against the loss or damage.

In case of the preceding paragraph or the second paragraph of this section, the receiver shall not be allowed to refuse such delivery.

Article 43—Premature Delivery

A Member holding purchase and sale commitment for current month delivery may make delivery of the whole or a part of such commitments prior to the delivery day (hereinafter referred to as "Premature Delivery").

Article 44

Necessary matters concerning delivery, except the provisions of this Chapter, shall be provided in the Detailed Rules of Delivery.

Hong Kong Futures Exchange
Room 911, 9/F
New World Tower
16-18 Queen's Road
Central Hong Kong
Tel: (5) 251-0058   Fax: (5) 810-5089
Telex: HKFE HX

Standard grade: Refined gold of not less than 99.5 percent fineness.

Contract Size: 100 troy ounces

Tenderable grades: Bars of 100 oz., 50 oz., and 1 kilogram

Delivery point: Hong Kong

Price quotation: U.S. dollars

Minimum Price Fluctuation: 10 cents per oz.

Value of One Tick: $10

Trading Hours: 9:00 AM to Noon; 2:30 PM to 5:30 PM, Hong Kong time

Delivery Months: Even months, spot month, and following two months

Daily Price Limits: $40, however no limit is imposed on the spot month.

Last Trading Day: Trading in the current delivery month shall cease on the completion of the morning session on the last business day of the month.

At the time of publication, the Hong Kong Futures Exchange was petitioning the government for permission to alter the specifications and delivery rules of its gold contract. Further information can be obtained by contacting the exchange at the number listed above.

Singapore International Monetary Exchange Ltd.
1 Raffles Place, # 07-00
OUB Centre
Singapore 0104
Tel: 535-7382   Fax: 535:7282
Telex: RS 38000 SINMEX

Contract Size: 100 fine troy ounces of gold
Ticker Symbol: GD
Contract Months: February, March, April, June, August, September, October, and December.
Minimum Price Fluctuation: U.S.$0.10 per oz.
Value of One Tick: U.S.$10.00
Daily Price Limit: 250 Ticks (U.S.$25 per troy oz.)
Trading hours: 9:30 AM to 3:15 PM, Singapore time
Last Trading Day: Trading terminates on the business day preceding the fifth last business day of the delivery month.
Delivery Day: The first to the last business day of the contract month.
Delivery: Physical Delivery
At the time of publication, the SIMEX was revising the specifications and delivery rules of its gold contract. Further information can be obtained by contracting the exchange at the telephone number listed above.

Bolsa Mercantil & de FuturosPraca Antonio Prado, 48Sao Paulo, SP 01010 Brazil
Tel: (5511) 239-5511   Fax: (5511) 35241
Telex: (5511) 26928

Contract Size: 250 grams
Minimum Price Fluctuation: 0.10 Cruzado/gram
Trading Hours: 10:00 AM to 4:30 PM, Sao Paulo time
Delivery: Even months

Sources of Information on Gold

Over the years, dozens of books on gold have been published. Some of the more useful ones include:

Green, Timothy, *The New World of Gold Today,* Walker, 1973. The best book available on how the gold markets actually function. Must reading for the gold enthusiast.

Jastram, Roy, *The Golden Constant, The English and American Experience, 1560-1976,* Ronald Press 1977. This book examines the purchasing power of gold over the past 400 years, and, in so doing, suggests how to utilize gold to profit from monetary and inflationary developments.

Moffitt, Michael, *The World's Money,* Simon & Schuster, Inc. 1983. A lively and in-depth account of the breakdown of the Bretton Woods system and the abolishment of the gold standard.

Nichols, Jeffrey, *The Complete Book of Gold Investing,* Dow Jones Irwin 1987. A highly readable guide to gold investing, exploring the futures, options, and coin markets. Excellent primer for the retail investor.

Sarnoff, Paul, *Trading in Gold,* Woodhead Faulkner, 1989. A guide to gold trading that should be useful to both retail and professional traders. Examines some of the more recent innovations in the gold market.

Publications

Gold. Published annually by Consolidated Gold Fields PLC, 31 Charles II Street, St. James's Square, London SW1Y 4AG. The pre-eminent authority on worldwide gold supply and demand.

Annual Review of the World Gold Industry. Shearson Lehman Hutton,
London Metals Research Unit. Similar to *Gold.* The Shearson report
provides a great deal of information on production developments in
various countries.

Sherman, Eugene, *Gold Investment Theory and Application,* New York
Institute of Finance, Prentice Hall, 1986. A rigorous examination of
gold price determination and the role of gold in an investment portfolio. Academic in style.

Index